WHY ARE ALL THE GOOD TEACHERS CRAZY?

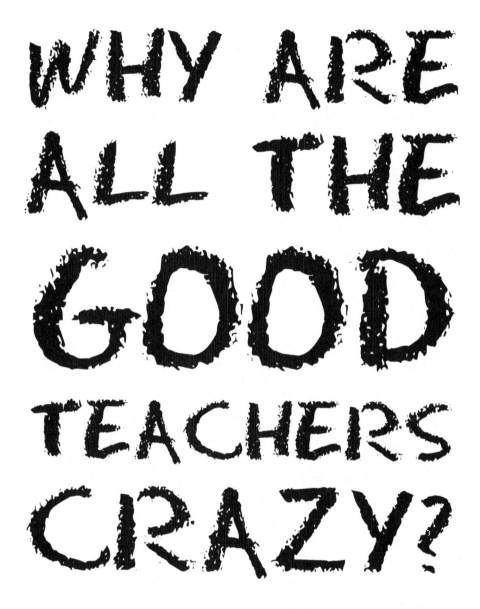

AUTHOR: FRANK STEPNOWSKI

Outskirts Press, Inc.
Denver, Colorado

Why Are All the Good Teachers Crazy?
All Rights Reserved.
Copyright © 2009 Frank Stepnowski
v3.0

Outskirts Press, Inc.
http://www.outskirtspress.com

ISBN: 978-1-4327-4829-6

Outskirts Press and the "OP" logo are trademarks belonging to Outskirts Press, Inc.

PRINTED IN THE UNITED STATES OF AMERICA

Table of Contents

Cantos*

A canto is a subdivision of an epic poem. Not that I think my life is epic poetic, but my students can never remember this word, so maybe this will help!

"To those who'd ground me, take a message back from me..."

- The Wicked Witch
Defying Gravity

A Dedication in ABAB rhyme scheme

Only one person really believed that I would write a novel or two
At long last that person's in luck
Thanks, mom – this book is dedicated to you,
even the parts that suck.

Foreword

Rather than trot out the tired old tradition of having someone famous write my foreword, I though it would be sporting to allow one of the young lions that will, ultimately, eat me and take over the pride, to get his first crack in the writing world. I give you my dark apprentice, Mr. Ed Trautz! (PS, if you don't like his foreword, don't judge the book by it, he can't carry my jock in the writing department but he makes me laugh and I love him like a brother.) -Step

I can pretty much tell you what kind of person you are by they way you'll react to this book. If you learn something, laugh, and perhaps tell a friend, then you're a smart one. If you jump to your feet, rip off your shirt, and throw your arms to the air screaming, "I have found the voice of the revolution! Death to the infidels!" then you are the sort of rare, freakishly brilliant mind I'd enjoy meeting. If you are disgusted, appalled, offended, and might just write a letter of complaint, then you are a worthless piece of excrement that does not deserve the ability to read (In fact, you probably don't understand the symbols on this paper. Who are we kidding; you can't WRITE a LETTER, you'll probably bang a stick against the ground and express your displeasure in a rudimentary series of grunts and facial gestures.).

Was that a bit bold for a foreword?

Well then, I'd say we're getting off to a good start for this opus by my mentor, my brother in arms (though mine are pipe cleaners and his are the size of my legs), and my friend, Frank Stepnowski, or as the students know him: Step. When I read Step's book, I told him that I could sum up my reaction in a sentence: I needed that. And any teacher you know needs this epic you're holding; one that will inspire a lot of things – harder work, a sense of pride in the job, jaw dropping... Since this is a book on teaching through the epic experiences of Step, I'm going to divide the foreword into the teaching profession, Step, and then an analysis of the relation between the two; it'd be great organizational outline for an essay, so hopefully it will work on a foreword.

———— ((●)) ————

I, like Step, am a teacher of English in a slightly urban high school and, like him, I love my kids. Yes, MY kids. Deal with them ten hours a day at daycare (read: school), teach them to tie a tie, explain to them accountability, show them how to restrain themselves and how to question the world around them, e-mail them back and forth with advice when they get knocked up, and then go home to plan the next day. Sounds like I am daddy, and they are MY kids.

The scariest part of teaching is NOT: when two students get pulled out of your class and arrested the first week of school for decapitating a homeless man as part of a gang initiation (true story), when the fight you're breaking up turns two or ten students against you (again, true,) when the parent wants your supervisor's phone number, when they ask the question to which you do not know the answer, when the principal wants to have a word with you, or when the adolescent girl tells the whole school she wants to bone you. (1)

The absolute, shriveled dick fear in teaching is, as Hunter S. Thompson wrote best, "how long can we maintain?" (If you have never read <u>Fear and Loathing in Las Vegas</u>, read it immediately after you finish this book.)

Yes, we all know, teachers have the sweetest job ever because we're out by 3 P.M., and we get summers off, blah blah blah and just keep talking until one of the kids we didn't "reach" shanks you for your wallet. But when you wake up with bloodshot eyes every morning, inhale enough coffee to keep up a village of Europeans for a week, and go into a room where it's you and a group of kids who, at best, make you want to slam their heads into the ground until their faces are unrecognizable and the blood ruins your socks, it's not difficult to lose focus, hate the job, or just plain allow your edge to dull. That face part? I use that threat regularly in class. I realized it worked when the father of a girl in one of my threatened classes told the superintendent that I was teaching my students to be productive adults, and that he should, "hire 500 Mr. Trautzes".

This goes to show that kids HEAR *words* and UNDERSTAND *motives.* My kids are my motives. Same goes for Step.

⸺ ◆ ⸺

The sad fact is this: while there are many honorable men and women who take part in our career every day, striving to the best of their abilities, there are also those stereotypical watch-the-clock

---

1   Author's note: Trautz swears this happens all the time, but other than one confused dwarf Polynesian male with an eating disorder, I've never seen ANYbody offer to "bone" him. Just thought you should know. (2)

2   Author's note to my own note: I'm kidding. The skinny bastard is the subject of many a schoolgirl fantasy. I'm just jealous, and older, and jealous.

motherfuckers you can wholeheartedly bash *along with me* for their "schedules" and "work ethic."

You (SHOULD) get into this job to be a positive force in the formation of the future (let's all hold hands and sing, now... *I believe the children are the future...*) great intentions, a heart for the work, a mind-boggling devotion to creating, revising, starting over, editing, and teaching lesson after lesson. Somewhere along the way a lot of teachers just can't maintain. Maybe it's the insults, the vulgarity, the student apathy, the parent apathy, the know-nothing administration, the hours, the lowered expectations, the ether...whatever. But they fail to find their ways back, and these leeches suck off more salary and waste more students' time than I care to speak about at this time, as there are witnesses.

Does it happen to all of us? Do we all hit that wall from time to time? About as surely as a student will ask me today why those lead paint chips taste funny.

And THAT is why teachers need this book.

We all need, and I'm not just talking teachers here, something to remind us that what we do in life is important. Step's book is that something. And Step, I'm fortunate and grateful to say, has been that person for me for years.

That, ladies and gentlemen, was a fantastic transition into the second section of this foreword – the man himself, Frank Stepnowski. Mr. Stepnowski is the stereotypical big scary guy with a pussycat demeanor, and if you buy that I've got cheap land for sale in Antarctica.

The truth is, Step is the perennial father figure. Not just to his family, which I must take a moment to say is an amazing example of how families CAN and SHOULD work. Step has an incredible, incredible family, and this is a result of the same breed of fervor and dedication that makes great teachers. His students see it, and they respond wholeheartedly.

Like I said, students have this amazing intuitive power to separate the ones who genuinely care from the ones who can't do and thus teach. His students respect him, love him, learn from him, and forge lifelong relationships with him. As for teachers — same story. We all look up to Step, (those of us that can handle his honesty, that is,) and routinely come to kiss the ring. If you thought that was innuendo, dead wrong. If you don't know what innuendo is, you're missing a lot of good times.

Step is a living, breathing, motivating force (and the force is strong in him.) Imagine the wise old sage on top of the mountain, but instead of a decrepit octogenarian who was given the mountaintop, there's one massive dude who fought and won "King of the Mountain." Teachers go to him when they need a kick in the ass, a big laugh, or a nudge in the right direction. He selflessly shares EVERY idea, lesson, and tactic he comes up with, and it is NEVER less than stellar. That is not hyperbole, although the man really has a well-earned mythical reputation that has come from saying what he means, doing what he knows is necessary, even if it's unpopular or unpleasant, and backing up words with action.

When I started my teaching career at our shared edifice of edification, Step approached me. What did he see in this young upstart? Well, as they introduced the new staff to the forced polite handclaps of the disgruntled vets, I demanded with a wave of my hand that the veteran staff applaud LOUDER. That bit of hubris seemed to get Step's attention - a little cockiness goes a long way; and I'm glad it did, as I was shown the ropes by a cross between Mickey and Thunderlips. (That was an *allusion* to Rocky III. If you don't know what allusion is, Step will teach you. That's what he does.)

Step simply does not take shit. That comes from a mix of beating Philly punks' heads in, beating Philly students' ears in, and, well, knowing he's right. One of my "Step lines" came recently as he told a group of teachers why he'd love for a parent to come in and question his teaching methods. He would listen very attentively to the parent's explanation of how to teach, and would then calmly explain to the parent how to raise a child. I'd back Step against the village on that one. (Did you catch that **allusion** to Hillary Clinton? Great! You're learning already!)

One of the life lessons I teach my students is to align yourself with those whose air you don't feel you have a right to share. Basically, I explain to them that you don't get better at anything by hanging with the losers who make you feel good about yourself. This is one of the major reasons that I love Step. If I'm on my "A" game today, he could call up his "B" game and slam me against the wall. But I learn. Oh, the things I learn. And while one might mistake our association as competition, I don't see it as such. There will never be competition between two people whose ultimate goal is the improvement of their students; furthermore, I love the man, as both a teacher and a friend.

A student wrote to me early in my teaching career (Yes! If you're good at this job, and do it for the kids, they will love you and reach out to you in ways that will make you choke back tears! You should SEE the stuff Step gets!) and told me to always remember that *this job isn't about me.* I will never forget those words, and Step embodies them. He is absolutely dedicated to our craft, and makes me, and I'll bet he will make you, want to improve with every day. This book is a collection of the stories that Step tells often, usually resulting in uproarious laughter and high fives.

xiv

Do not take the confidence as excessive, the vulgarity as unnecessary, or the methods as inappropriate. Quit your bitching, and realize that this job isn't as easy as you think. Then read on, knowing that these are the words of a man who does not make it look easy; he makes it look honorable.

Now if you'll excuse me, I have to get back to covering an essay in red pen.

- Ed Trautz

A Few Words from Your Humble Author

"Now I've done things I regret, and it's time to reverse the roles
I just want to make good on, all the promises I have made...

I Will be Heard
- Hatebreed (I Will Be Heard)

Before you ask, all of the stories in this book are...huh? What's that?

Excuse me, my legal counsel has reminded me that this is a fictional novel based on actual events, and that if any lawyer wishes to contact me about something, *please know that I made that particular story up entirely.*

While we're at it, let's get the language "issue" out of the way right now.

There are **A LOT** of potentially offensive words in this book; however, most of them occurred in actual conversations that took place in the classrooms, hallways, gymnasiums, and offices of very real schools. If you don't think that's possible, come out from under your rock and seek out a teacher. Ask them if what's going on inside schools is really that bad. (Hopefully, they'll be holding the hardback version of this book so they can slap some sense into you.) The same goes for the tsunami of inappropriate behavior, violence, sexuality, political incorrectness, etc. Once again, if you don't believe me...

I, however, will not throw anybody under the bus but myself, as I take full responsibility for any of the "bad" words (oxymoron,) "extreme" methods or "inappropriate" actions that I may have used when I was trying my best to *"teach the un-teachable in an atmosphere where learning is virtually impossible." (1)*

Pay attention, this is the important part: Do you know whyyyyyy I was able to engage in all of the shenanigans this book and still keep a job and earn the respect of my students, peers, and bosses? My students know why.

Because I loved them.
That's it,
although any real teacher could've probably told you that.
Many will disagree with me I'm sure.
Fuck 'em.
I didn't write this book for them.
Who DID I write this book for?
Funny you should ask...

"You should write a book!" That's what everybody always says, right? When you're telling stories, and people are laughing, or just feeling better about themselves because of what you are saying, those same folks will tell you to write a book. So I did. I wrote a book. I wrote the most awesomest book in the history of book writing! (2) I wrote this book, and I will write others, for so many people that it would be impossible to mention them all.

This book, in particular, was a labor of love for two groups of special people:

1   Actual quote from a supervisor's observation report!
2   hyperbole – intentional exaggeration or overstatement.

For the teachers that care

You underpaid, under appreciated, over achieving, hyper dedicated, slightly insane bastards, I salute each and every one of you.

*(Notice I said "the ones that **care**." Some of you don't. You're stealing money and staining the reputation of a noble profession. You know who you are. Get out. Now.)*

For the students

For *my* students, who have shown, time and time again, that you can handle the truth, and even laugh at it once in a while. I am, and will always be, here for you; and for *any* students out there that know that laughing and learning are not mutually exclusive.

For Oprah

Oprah, baby! I know **this** one will never make your book club, but I'm willing to sit on the couch and defend myself anyway! Call me! (3)

The stories and observations in here don't follow any particular chronological order, and I'm sure I forgot some of the funny stuff that happened during my two decades in the business of boring

3   verbal irony - total sarcasm, as in saying something that you know will never happen.

people; hopefully, the ghosts of classrooms past will haunt (or E-mail) me and help me rectify those omissions.

Speaking of my stories, it may seem (given the nature of my anecdotal record) that I spent the first fifteen years of my teaching career cursing copiously, threatening students, giving administrators migraines, and engaging in funny stuff. Not true. I spent at least a few of those years misinforming black, Hispanic, and inner city white kids so as to "keep them down" and narrow their employment opportunities. Seriously though, if you read this book SLOWLY it would take you a few days. Even if you were my sister Molly it would take you a month, max. I have spent, to date, about 28,576 HOURS in front of students, I must have snuck a few moments of teaching in there *somewhere.*

On a somewhat related note, you'll notice that, at random points throughout the narrative, I identify certain literary techniques (allegory, alliteration, metaphor, etc.) This is in honor of my students, who never fail to ask me "do [authors] really use that shit on purpose?" Yes, they do, and here's your proof.

Another thing you'll notice is that I footnote a lot. That's because there are several voices competing simultaneously for time in my head, so when I have a "side thought," you get that (in smaller font) FOR FREE!

This book could have been 1,000 pages long and I still would have had a ton of material left, so I chose the stories and ideas I thought would translate best into print. My co-workers and friends (all three of them) swear that I should do an audio book so I could tell the stories using "all the voices and sound effects." I'll make a deal with you, guys – if I make $1 profit off this book, I'll look into the audio thing. At this point, I'm just glad people like listening to my stories. I think being a good storyteller is a key component to both stand up comedy and teaching which, in my case, is the same thing. If you like my stories, tell me. If you really like them, give me a good review on Amazon, Barnes and Noble.com or whatever, that way I can read it when I'm feeling insignificant and suicidal. (I'm a high school English teacher, so that happens about once a month.)

⇒))(◉)((⇐

Finally, several people "in the business" told me that this book should "do well" as teachers are a "great target demographic" because they *buy* books instead of *borrowing* them from other people to read. I didn't write this book to become a millionaire or to get out of the classroom, I wrote it because I *had* to. (4)

That having been said – if you spent your hard earned money on this book, I thank you from the bottom of my heart. I'm just happy you spent your time reading my stories, as your time is more valuable than any amount of money. You guys rock, and I hope we meet someday so you can teach me something.

Step

---

4   Not because of some inner desire to express myself. I wrote this so that when my students bitch about a 15 page research paper, I can point to this and say "300 pages in 3 months, now play like a shepherd with a noisy bunch of sheep and shut the flock up!"

Every Journey Begins
with a Single Step

"Take a look at my face, I am the future. How do you like what you see?"

-Alice Cooper (I Am the Future)

They let this guy teach our kids?

Yes, they did, folks – and they still do. That's why it took so long to write this book.

You won't know it while you're reading, but I'd leave off in mid-sentence, and by the time I did homework with my three kids, ran to the Rite Aid for materials for their science project due tomorrow, escorted to them to whatever practice they had that night, helped coach the team, marked essays in between the running, responded to parents' requests while sitting on the toilet (thank you Verizon Network,) made insightful comments on students' papers so they knew I took the time to really READ their work, entered grades, created lesson plans, corresponded w/ counselors, administrators, and coaches while DRIVING (thank you, Blackberry)went to musicals, games, debates and such so my students know I care about them outside the classroom, copied, texted, called, wrote, edited, typed, collated, graded and created new and [hopefully] exciting lessons for my students, etc. etc. etc. etc. etc. etc. etc. etc., days had become weeks and I had forgotten about being an author in deference to being a teacher, a dad, a coach, and a husband.

You'll notice the order of those titles. Any good teacher knows that sometimes the children in our classrooms take up an inordinate amount of our time, sometimes at the expense of time spent with the children we raise and/or coach. Our spouses are often the ones left alone while we agonize over "why those little bastards can't remember how to **X** after we went over it **Y** times in class!" If you're nodding your head right now, maybe getting a bit misty-eyed, I have good news for you – you're a good teacher, and I have yet to meet a good teacher that wasn't a good parent. We're usually good marriage bait, too, overlooking the fact that we think we know it all when it comes to raising kids; after all, "I deal with this all day." Go ahead and laugh, you know you've said it.

Why Are All the Good teachers Crazy is a painfully funny look back at some of the stories from my formative years as a teacher that I have been asked to tell again and again, often by the people involved. I've changed names and fabricated elements so that the stories retain their humor and reality, while simultaneously keeping identities safe and me out of jail or the asylum. (Basically I mixed and matched stuff so as to create plausible deniability in the event somebody tries to prevent me from earning a living doing the one thing that I was born to do.)

I taught for roughly fifteen years at a private school specializing in the care of children with special needs. Don't start with that shit – I know that ALL children have special needs, but you know what I mean so ***zip it*** and let me finish my touching soliloquy on the puberty of my teaching career.

Having no formal training in special ed., I was hired as an English teacher, for which I did happen to have a veritable war chest full of training, diplomas, and certifications.

None of which did me a damn bit of good once the first kids got off the bus.

What kept me in front of the classroom, out of jail, away from drugs, and into the limelight was something else entirely. The seething hatred I harbored for most of the teachers that littered my academic path. That's right, kiddies, I became a teacher because

I though most teachers sucked. One of the aforementioned tools of inspiration, a Catholic nun that thought copying whole passages from a literary text was more important than actually reading and *thinking* about the material reading in a literature class actually said to me: "if you can do a better job, MISter Stepnowski, by all means, do it."

So I did. Fuck you, Sister Vincent.

Just as powerful a fuel source were the all too rare teachers that understood that they were teaching *human beings*, men and women that really embraced the art form of the teaching profession. One of the aforementioned angels of inspiration, the head of the secondary education department and one of my graduate instructors, actually said to me: "teaching is a subversive activity, and you, MISter Stepnowski, could do *a lot* of damage to the status quo if you gained access to the young minds of America."

So I did. Thank you, Dr. Amato.

And so we begin our journey into…what's that? Yes, as a matter of fact I did say "fuck you" to a Catholic nun. Do I think that's appropriate? No, but it's funny – and everyone that ever endured a Catholic education *thought* it at least a few hundred times, so at least I'm honest. That's as good a triumvirate as any to encapsulate my educational odyssey up to this point: funny, inappropriate, and honest.

I can hear some of you now: "They let this guy teach our kids?"

Yes, they did, folks – and they still do.

And so it begins.

July 17, 1989

It all started innocently enough. My dad drove me to my first teaching interview back in the summer of 1989. 6'3" 260 pounds of unemployed English teacher in a black double breasted suit, shoulder length hair pulled back into a well manicured, "early-in-his-film-career-Steven Segal" ponytail, and my resume', letters of recommendation, and professional certificates at the ready. Did I mention it was 95 degrees in the shade? Well it was. Remember, 260 pounds, long hair, black suit. I get uncomfortable just thinking about it, and that was over 30 years ago. At any rate, my heat stroke was replaced with intrigue as I spied a man in seersucker shorts (ask your grand pop) and a white tank top sunning himself outside the school. He had a phone line running out to a landline (ask your dad) and had a glass of lemonade next to him.

"I'm looking for the director of education," said I.

"That's me," he replied jauntily.

"Quit fucking around and take me to the principal. Now." I snarled.

"Richard Long, director of education for the Moorzakunt Approved Private School, at your service," he laughed as he stood and studied me. He shook his head and laughed again, "you might be just what we need, come on inside where it's cooler."

"Just what we ...hey, Mr. Long, right? This is a *teaching* position, right?"

He smiled at me the way a cobra would smile at a mouse that asked if his nest was a warm place to spend the night. "Technically, it most certainly is a teaching position."

Weirder by the minute, but at least the air conditioning made it bearable.

After he gave me tour of the facilities, he asked me if I had any questions. I figured I had already lost the job with my "quit fucking around" line so I swung for the fences:

"What's your curriculum like?"

He stifled another laugh. "Curriculum? If they're learning, I don't care what you're teaching."

O.K. Good answer. "What's your policy on getting close to the kids?"

He didn't even hesitate a second "if you mean sexually, that could be a problem, but emotional attachment is a necessity when you teach these kinds of kids."

Sick sense of humor coupled with a healthy dose of realism, check.

"Finally," (I figured I should ask since I was dying in that suit) "what's the dress code?" As God is my witness, I'll never forget his response: "whatever you can move fast in."

My hand shot out to shake his. "Mr. Long, you probably hear this a lot, but *I am your man.*"

"Actually, I never hear that," he chuckled menacingly, "and we'll see soon enough."

As I climbed into my dad's Bronco he asked immediately

"Well?' (dad always was right to the point.)

"I don't know. I'll be right back."

Re-entering what would soon become my home for the next 15 years I apprehended Mr. Long as he was returning to his prime tanning location.

"Looking for the director of ed.?" he asked.

Smart ass, I like this guy.

"No, I met him, now I just need to know if he gave me job or not."

Only now, upon reflection, do I realize what a pompous ass I was, and how that helped me.

"Yeah, you'll do for now, how's 18,000 to start sound?" (Don't laugh, it was 1989, I was 21, and I wasn't going to be a bartender my whole life.)

"Sounds like we have a deal. One more thing...Richard Long? Dick Long? Are you serious?"

"Serious as a heart attack, he smirked."

Back to dad's Bronco. I knew what was coming.

" I hate to bother you with such a trivial detail after I drove you to a job interview, but do you, perhaps, have a job?"

I was so amped, even the sarcasm dripping off my dad's dashboard couldn't affect me. "Yeah, the principal, Richard Long, just hired me."

Dad's eyebrows raised. "Dick Long? For real?"

"Yeah," I smirked, full of myself as only a 21year old twit could be "I know where the big dick is here, and pretty soon he'll know who's got the balls."

Thank you very mulch.

September 6, 1989

My first Day as a full time teacher! I could barely contain myself as the busses pulled in to the Moorzakunt Approved Private School, named after Eastern European behavioral specialist Friedrich Moorzakunt, a leading figure in the development of child psychology. I looked to my immediate left and shrugged slightly as Mr. Long appraised me with a look of mild curiosity. The first bus pulled to an abrupt stop and the first young mind for me to mold stepped off. Approximately 5'2", black, with a wool hat on in September. He looked me up and down and asked "Your mom know you work here, bitch?"

I looked to my immediate left for some help.

"Hi, Adrian." deadpanned Mr. Long. That gave me some ammunition for return fire:

"Your mom know she named you after a girl?" That got a few laughs from the rest of the urban whirlwind that was flying out of the assorted short busses. Adrian was not pleased.

"Bitch, you best get the fuck outta my way and know who you dealin' with."

A 400-pound bench press with a degree in English Literature

blocked Adrian's path and whispered into his ear "that's the second time you called me 'bitch', there will *not* be a third." "Bitch you better back up offa me before I…"

> Grammar note: that thing with the three periods is a punctuation mark called an ellipsis; that lets the reader know that something else was said in that particular time. Adrian did say *something* after the third "bitch" but I never really heard it clearly, as his little ass got launched (a pretty respectable distance, I might add) over the nearest picnic bench and into the new mulch surrounding the swings.

I turned to Mr. Long to inquire about my termination and saw him chuckling and looking, along with two other gentlemen, approvingly at my inner city humanoid discus technique.

"You'll do just fine." They collectively agreed. Confused, excited, and full of adrenaline, I turned to the next young boy coming my way.

"Hi, I'm Mr. Stepnowski"

"I hear you big dog," he shot back quickly, "and whatever that nigga Adrian said, I officially say the opposite."

I laughed out loud and asked for a name.

"Kenny," he said, "you new here I guess?"

"I guess so." I replied.

"I'll show you around when you not teachin', but right now I gotta tell everyone not to mess wit' the big white boy."

As he sped away, he turned, laughing, "and that Adrian got fucked up… A-gain."

Mr. Long and company suggested that if I was done making friends, I might want to find my way over to the trailer and start actually earning a paycheck. If first contact with the natives was any indication of social skills here at M.A., I couldn't wait to see what passed for education…

(quick quiz: what are the 3 dots called?) Very good, an ellipsis…even though I saw you turn back the page.

How Mr. Stepnowski died on his first day teaching.

So, having hurled a young man into the mulch and remaining a teacher, I ventured forth to the trailer, an actual two room trailer sitting on top of, near as I could tell, cinder blocks. I sure as hell wasn't getting underneath to check the structural integrity, but even a blind man could tell that this thing looked like shit.

Smelled like shit, too; more on that later, I promise.

"Smells like shit (hmph), don't it?" sniffed Mr. Steve Kovack the guy that was going to be sharing this dorm room from hell with me. Steve always had a small dip of chewing tobacco lodged in his lower lip, and the mildly annoying habit of breathing through his nose forcefully (hmph) two or three times per sentence.

"Yeah, among other things." I denounced. "Oh, well, first thing we'll do is clean 'er

up a bit."

Kovack looked at me like I just suggested we let Marilyn Manson baby-sit the kids.

"Um, (hmph) these kids ain't big on personal hygiene, let alone cleaning up somebody else's mess (hmph.)"

I looked at Steve like I didn't give two fucks what these kids were "big on."

"Good luck with that (hmph.) Let me know how it works out

for you." He chuckled, in a way that – as an arrogant 22 year-old – I took as a challenge.

"I'll tell you *now* how it's going to work out." I boasted, moving eye to eye with him, "It'll work out fine because I *say* it will."

The first things the 20 or so worst students at Moorzakunt Academy saw when they barreled in the door were two very large (me at 6'3" 260 and Kovack at 6'5" 240) men in a stare down. The idea that one of those old Marvel comic "The Thing vs. The Hulk" comics was about to be reenacted quieted them down considerably, and shook them just enough for me and Steve to come to our senses and seize command. We both held up our lists and started shouting names, escorting our stunned students into their respective rooms.

Weeks later, when I was no longer Mr. Stepnowski and Steve had become re-baptized as well, we laughed long and hard over many Heinekens recounting how the betting had begun in earnest on day one at M.A. who would win in a fight – the really tall red head with the buzz cut and no neck or the evil looking motherfucker with the long black hair. (hmph)

But I digress, as usual.

Once I got my first ever classroom full of students under control, I engaged in the time- honored tradition of writing my name on the board. In perfect block lettering (1) I wrote

Mr. Stepnowski

---

1   I have been complimented, too many times to count, on my blackboard/ whiteboard writing skills. The most common "compliment" is that I write like a girl…in a good way." I blame my borderline OCD and years of having to explain *what that word is…no, that one, no the one under the thingy. What? Yeah the question mark; what's the word under the question mark?* It just became easier to write it VERY NEATLY the first time, believe me.

"Gentlemen, my name is Mr. Stepnowski, and for the next nine and a half months…"

"These niggas ain't gonna remember all that." came a voice from the front row.

"Come again, Mr…?"

"Walter Plains," responded Walter Plains, "call me Walt, and these niggas ain't gonna remember no last name that long."

Ah! My first challenge! The metaphorical crossroads that I knew I would face early on in my virgin career as an educator of the youth of tomorrow. So, would I take the tried and true path of resistance, telling the students that I was in charge and that they had better learn to remember my name because I was the teacher and blah, blah, blah…"

Or

I castrated the last six letters of my last name off the board with a dramatic swipe

Mr. Step

And asked, ever so politely but with just a dash of menace, "will these niggas remember *that?*"

"Aw, hell yeah," laughed Walter, and the rest of the class loosened up and we started talking about my plans for getting the room clean before we started learning anything academic.

14 young men looked at me like I just suggested we let Charles Manson baby-sit the kids.

Before the boys had a chance to protest, I jumped into action as though what I were doing was the most natural thing on Earth.

"You four, get into that red Nissan Sentra out there, and we'll run around the corner to Rite Aid and get some cleaning stuff, you three go ask the maintenance guys for some mops and brooms and stuff. What? I don't know, FIND the maintenance guys. Ask the principal or the secretary. The rest of you start moving everything to the back of the room so we can clean and move things as we go."

Everybody sort of shuffled around and looked at each other until I asked, a bit louder than intended: "Is this too difficult to understand? I mean, are we fuckin' special ed. here, because I'll get some of the smarter kids to help me later if..."

"Yo mothafucka, we ain't no special ed.," challenged Hakim Butler

"Well then, Hakim," I growled, hovering over him, "why aren't you in my car yet?"

———— ((●)) ————

It should be noted that approximately five hours, and one delicious lunch courtesy of yours truly, later, our half of the trash trailer was the cleanest, best smelling, and most educationally decorated (2) classroom in Moorzakunt Academy.

It should also be noted that I was summoned to Mr. Long's office three seconds after the last bus left for the day.

"Are you out of your goddamned mind?!?" He gently inquired "You *took kids off campus*, in *your* vehicle, *without* a signed waiver, *bought them lunch* with your money, sent them on a maintenance scavenger hunt *with no notes or permission slips*, had them *perform housecleaning* services, called them special ed., and *threatened* them, *with profanity*, to comply?!?!? What the *hell* were you thinking?!?!?"

"Boy, that's a lot of italics," I thought.

2   Thanks, Dawn, for buying me a bunch of scholastic posters and such long before I ever though of such things.

"I'm sorry, Mr. Long, really. I didn't know I couldn't do all of that stuff, and the guys just went along with it. Our room is immaculate, we gave the remaining cleaning stuff I bought to the maintenance guys, and part of their homework is to write about..."

"Whoa, wait a second," he interrupted, "what did you just say about homework?"

"They have to write about..."

"You gave them *homework?*" he asked, incredulous, as evidenced by his use of italics again.

"Yeah, I had a bunch of note books and folders I bought at Staples, and I told them to..."

"And they agreed to do it?"

"I love this guy, but if he interrupts me *one more time*," I thought, employing some italicizing of my own.

"Yes, they seemed pretty excited about it, actually."

He laughed and shook his head. "You are certifiably insane, but if they turn in that homework tomorrow, we'll call it even. Just talk to Kovack about proper procedures."

I looked at him seriously. "Why don't *you* tell me about proper procedures."

He returned my look with a knowing glance. "Trouble in paradise already? O.K., when you want to transport a student off campus..."

When we were done he bid me a fond farewell and said he couldn't wait to see what I did for an encore.

"See you tomorrow, Mr. Stepnowski."

"Step" I said.

"Excuse me? What happened to Mr. Stepnowski?" he inquired.

I answered as honestly as I could.

"He's dead. It was pretty painless but, alas, he is no more. The guys sort of re-christened me Mr. Step and the 'Mr.' seems pretty optional already."

He shook his head again. He would later tell me that he was thinking, "this guy is either going to be one of the best teachers I ever hired or the most entertaining train wreck he ever witnessed."

I am proud to say that, in my humble opinion, I was both.

Before I move on with our story, I would like to point out the moral of this story:

I broke almost every rule in the book, but I was honest and forthright with my students, and I treated them with respect and trust. They rose to my expectations, I acquiesced to some of their reasonable demands, and TOGETHER we became the *new standard by which others were judged.*

It can be done.

By the time we were sharing our Halloween candy, the "Mr. " had, indeed, disappeared from my name and I had become, and would remain, to everybody in the world except Dawn and the kids, simply "Step." I often joke that in a few years I'm going to (in Prince-like fashion) become *the artist formerly known as Step,* and sign my name with some sort of weird symbol; maybe a hybrid of the Islamic symbol for infidel and a semicolon.

"Hey, Step," crunched Charles, in between munches of Snickers and Tootsie Rolls, "you musta thought this place was pretty fucked up when you first got here, right?"

"Yeah, Step," Bartram agreed, with M&Ms falling out of his mouth, "I remember your face when you knocked bulldog out, like 'I can't believe this shit!'"

Bulldog, aka, Joe McFadden, nodded approvingly, mouth full of something sticky.

I'll spare you the full details but Joe was the first of many students to put his hands on me in [what *they* thought was] a threatening manner. His quiet acknowledgement of what he *got* being not at all what he *expected* but what he *deserved* was a look I have caused, unfortunately, several times throughout my illustrious career.

"True dat, Step," confirmed Rayshown, who claimed he couldn't eat any of the candy because he was a Muslim," we was takin' bets on how long you was gonna last."

"Really? Who bet that I would last the year?"

One hand went up.

I was stunned.

"Adrian?! *You* bet that I would last the year? I thought you hated me, especially after our encounter on the first day of school, and your little run-in with the dumpster right after that." (long story)

"Yeah," the class roared together, "when that nigga said you was gonna be here for a long while we fell about the place!"

I grew serious for just a moment. "So, Adrian, why'd you figure I'd last?"

He shrugged, obviously put off by the attention, "I dunno. You changed since you started here."

"Agreed," I said, trying to get him off the hook by offering him an answer, "I think I was Mr. Frank Stepnowski when I started here, with all the junk that came with that. Now I'm just Step, with all the new awareness that comes with that."

"So what happened to Mr. Frank Stepnowski?" Bartram laughed.

We'll give Adrian the [almost] last word on this one.

"That nigga dead."

———— ◄(●)► ————

And that's how Mr. Stepnowski died on his first day of teaching.

No tears, please. I don't miss him. He was a self-important asshole that thought he learned everything he needed to be a good teacher at Temple University.

Step is a bit of an asshole, too; but at least he knows that teaching is like bartending – 5% making drinks and 95% dealing with people. Don't understand? Ask some teachers, then ask them who died early on in *their* career.

I'd love to hear some of those stories…

The ODDyssey

I think of all the education that I missed
But then my homework was never quite like this.

- Van Halen (Hot For Teacher.)

Toilet coffee and gator bites.

September 29, 1989

It was NOT a good week for Richard Lovington; he drank used toilet water and got bitten by a gator. Lest you feel sorry for him, I can assure you that he deserved everything he got. Rich Lovington - other than sweetbreads, there was never a more misnamed item on Earth, as he was neither rich nor loving. What he *was* was a lazy, racist, homophobic, mean-spirited teen-aged white boy that refuted any attempts to educate or improve him morally with an elegant "go fuck yourself" or "suck my dick." I was not flexible enough to do the former nor motivated to do the latter, so I settled for trying to educate the boy in my classroom, a two room trailer with no real heat or air conditioning that I shared with one other teacher and 26 severely emotionally disturbed young men.

So in walks Lovington, late (as he was every day,) and he grabs my travel mug (as he did every day.) I warned him not touch my stuff (as I did every…Oh, you get the point!) and he would proceed to ignore me and take a huge gulp of my coffee, while 13 young criminals wondered why I hadn't killed him up yet.

"Why ain't you killed him yet?" asked Kenny, my tour guide from day one and one of my best students.

"Some things are worse than death, Kenny."

He smiled, "this is gonna be good, ain't it Step?"

I just smiled

"Hey Step," Kenny pleaded, "do me a favor?"

"Yes, Kenneth?"

"If I ever do something that makes you smile like that, kill my ass, please."

My smile this time was much warmer.

"No chance of that, Kenny. Now, about young Mr. Lovington."

But first, a word about Mr. Kovack, the man with whom I shared a stinky two room trailer with no heat and no air conditioning. Kovack never, ever, requested for maintenance to come and clean his room. Part of it was that he knew the young man who did room maintenance was a drug addict who worked sporadically at best, but part of it was that he believed, and I quote:

"I gotta put up with their shit all day, so they can smell their shit all day."

I almost felt compelled to point out that he would have to smell it too, but I figured that level of dedication was best left alone.

Needless to say, there was a veritable laboratory of body functions floating in Mr. Kovack's bathroom toilet…

Wait a minute, you're thinking, *this chapter started with you warning this brat not to drink from your travel mug and now you're describing the unspeakable contents of a special ed. toilet. You didn't do what I think you did, did you?*

I did.

12 young men in my room, and 13 from Mr. Kovack's, all with criminal records as long as my arm, laughed until tears came out of their eyes. Mr. Kovack and I shook our heads and chuckled at the irony of the moment. Richard J. Lovington projectile vomited outside and wished that he had listened to his teacher.

Now you would think that this was the worst thing on Earth that could happen to young Mr. Lovington, and that he would, at least, learn to listen to me.

And you would be wrong.

The worst thing to happen to Rich Lovington would go down only two short weeks from that day; and it would happen because he refused to accept my advice when he chose to antagonize Larry Barnes - a severely retarded young man affectionately known as "gator" due to his signature response of biting antagonists – I cautioned Mr. Lovington with the following pearls of wisdom:

" Normally I'd smack the crap out of you for abusing a boy like Larry, but my spider senses tell me that you're going to reap what you sow."

I was fairly sure of myself on this one as Larry had taken to growling "MMmmmmmmm, I'ma bite you" under his breath when lurking near Richard Lovington, who responded to my warning with …

Go ahead guess, you've got a 50/50 shot.

"Go fuck yourself Step" (Did you get it? Good for you!)

Now I'm no slouch down south of the border [insert the beautiful laughter of my wife here,] but I still couldn't manage to fulfill that request, so I pleaded once more to Rich that he leave Gator alone and "pick on someone his own size."

He didn't, and Larry bit him. Hard.

It happened on a beautiful day, and we were outside the 'classroom' getting ready to walk to the gymnasium. Lovington was leaning on the wooden railing and talking loudly about the "retards" walking off campus to the deli, where they picked up their lunch order every day.

Larry Barnes head came up slowly, like the scene of Captain

Willard coming out of the water (1). How his jaw opened so wide I'll never know, but it took a medical unit and several officers to unhinge the vise-like clamp of Gator's teeth from around Lovington's hand and the wooden railing. The screams of Richard Lovington will haunt me forever.

O.K. That's a lie, I laughed my ass off when it was all over.

I was stunned for a moment when Gator bit him, but I really did try to break Larry's "grip" on Rich's hand once the aforementioned chomp was executed. And Rich's scream was singular, before he passed out from the pain.

What I will remember forever is the smile on Larry Barnes' face as they led him into the police wagon, a trickle of blood from mouth to chin, like a freckled mulatto vampire. "MMmmmmmmm, I told you I was gonna bite you." he reminded his unconscious nemesis.

It should be noted that within mere moments of the last emergency vehicle leaving the school grounds, we were back in class reading a short story by Dino Buzzati.

Such was life at Ye Olde Moorzakunt School House.

---

1   My reference to Capt. Willard is an allusion, which is a reference to another story, movie, etc, without actually saying the name. In this case, I'm comparing Larry's "rise" to a scene from the movie *Apocalypse Now*.

Seventeen vaginas hang on the wall

(Sing to the tune of *99 bottles of beer on the wall*)
"Seventeen vaginas hang on the wall
Seventeen vaginas hang,
If one of those pussies gets torn down in the hall
Sixteen vaginas still hang in the hall."

Once more, with **feeling**! I'll wait...

O.K., now that the audience participation of our show is over, I suppose I should explain the genesis of that little ditty. It all started, as most things did at Moorzakunt, with me trying to be a real teacher.

"Biology quiz today!" I announced, like I was giving out winning lottery tickets.

The various responses I received were not, in fact, the kind of responses you would get from winning lottery ticket recipients; however, I was undaunted, because I had a *plan*.

By now my guys had been with me long enough to know that I never did anything without a reason, so they grumbled and bitched quietly as they read over the quizzes. By the way, when I say "guys" I mean the thirteen young men (and Jessica, who would probably hunt me down and kill me if I referred to her as a young lady) that comprised my self-contained class for the 90-91' scholastic year. So anyway, once the unlucky 13 started actually *reading* the questions on the quiz, they realized that we had just gone over the exact questions, word-for-word, a few minutes prior to the quiz. You might ask, "what good is a quiz if you just gave them the answers?"

Clearly you haven't been paying attention. I SAID, less than four sentences ago, that I never did anything without having a reason. Now if you'll quiet down, I'll finish my story.

The baker's dozen of maladjusted youth couldn't have been happier. They all aced the quiz; for some of them, that was the first perfect score they could ever remember "earning" in any class, ever.

(Note to future teachers. You simply cannot underestimate the power of a good grade, a sticker, and a short note praising the student. Even if you have to manufacture said grade like a synthetic protein bar, do it. You will be, in most cases, pleasantly shocked at the power of the self confidence resulting from your academic legerdemain.)

I marked the quizzes in front of them, putting Power Ranger stickers on each one.

Note to post-elementary students: do NOT, when teachers put stickers or your paper, say shit like "that's gay," or "this ain't first grade" because, in addition to being grammatically and politically incorrect, you'll look like a real douchebag when you get your next good grade back and you ask, like a puppy looking for his chew toy,

"What, no sticker?"

At length, I had them done. 13 quizzes, adorned with stickers and great grades in bright red marker. The future criminals of America were happy, but they were soon to be euphoric.

"Into the hallway, bring the two-side tape" I commanded triumphantly.

<hr>

Then, with various staff members looking at me like I was taking a piss on the Vatican, I hung all of the papers neatly in a diagonal procession along the hallway, so that each students name was prominently displayed. Trust me when I tell you that, at some point, I had to pull each of those kids out of a trance as they stared proudly at their now displayed work. Of course, not everyone shared my enthusiasm and optimism.

"You can't hang shit in these hallways!"

"You're fuckin' nuts, this isn't elementary school."

"Are you crazy, those papers are gonna get destroyed!"

These, and many other responses, did I endure once I started displaying work in the halls.

Little did the doubting horde know that I fully intended for those papers to get destroyed.

Once.

As if on cue, an unwitting pawn thrust himself into my psychological chess game in the form of one Jason Secoda. It broke my heart for young Jason to be the sacrificial lamb, being that he shared the name of one of my favorite people. Alas, to make an omelet, you've got to crack a few heads. Jason was being dragged to the "time out" room where he could chill out and re-examine his inappropriate behavior, which, in this case, involved calling

Ms. Graves in room 14 a bitch and spitting at her. So here cameth young Mr. Secoda around the corner frothing, cursing, thrashing and, upon seeing the nice papers on the wall, seeing an outlet for his frustration.

The behavior management personnel (think "school bouncers") had been under strict order from yours truly, *not* to interfere with the first lamb silly enough to fuck with the work of the wolves. They didn't, he did, and I intervened,

"Wow, Lamar, shame about your quiz." I regretted.

That remark, combined with the soothing sound of Jason's fury (and ripping paper,) got Lamar, and the rest of the class out of their collective seats, fast. The thirteen biggest, baddest, wolves in Moorzakunt APS stared at their tattered triumphs. Then they stared at the lamb that scratched their self-esteem.

A real lamb would have had a better shot with thirteen real wolves, and the sounds that came out of young Jason at that point ensured that, from that point on, ALL work hung in the hallways would be safer than tofu in a tiger cage.

It was around this time that Mr. Long's sister, who was functioning as vice principal at the time, chose to make an ill-advised comment to Mr. Kevin Caper.

Cape was one of my best friends, and a great health / phys. ed teacher. Cape was, quite possibly, the fastest white man I'd ever seen, but even his vaunted speed couldn't outrun his occasional lapse in judgment. Like the time he planned to show *The Miracle of Life* to his health class, so they could "learn about how babies were made."

I offered to cue up the movie in the VCR for him.

Now you're only a few chapters into this book, and you know better than to trust me with such delicate matters, so don't feel bad for him for not seeing this coming. I did, indeed, cue up a movie, which, *technically speaking*, involved activity that could lead to childbirth.

But you want to hear about the vaginas on the wall, so let's get to it.

Ms. Long was constantly reprimanding Mr. Caper about one thing or another; I think it was simply a manifestation of her unspoken lust for him, and I told him so. His response was vaguely Richard Lovington-ish. (see previous chapter)

Anyway, on his particular day of ball busting, I was in the back "office" of my classroom, which Caper used once a day for health class, when Ms. Long asked him "why he never hung papers in the hallway like Step."

I perked up like a spring daisy.

"Yeah, Cape" I purred, "I keep telling you to hang up the kids' work."

The murderous look in his eyes was superseded only by the look of contempt on Ms. Long's face.

She hated me too, but I had already entrenched myself into the good graces of the Moorzakunt board of directors like a tick at that point, and she had no shot of getting me removed.

"Yes, ma'am" Caper bristled, "I'll get right on that."

And he did, folks. Yes he did.

I have to tell you, every time I recount this story, I laugh out loud remembering the sight.

Since Cape taught health, he seized the opportunity to display the work of his diligent delinquents by seeking out, with predatory speed, an anatomical workbook/coloring book.

You see where this is going, don't you?

I came in several days later and nearly choked on my coffee.

There, in all their beauty, were 17 beautifully colored, diagramed, and graded workbook pages dedicated to that part of the female anatomy that has led greater men than me to their downfall. Simply put, there were seventeen vaginas hanging on the wall.

When I ran into Cape at the sign-in desk, all I could manage was "Genius. Absolute fucking genius. You're dead, you know."

We both burst into laughter. By that point all the other teachers asked what was so funny and we told 'em, so everybody was in on the joke. Everybody except the students who, truth be told, did exceptional jobs coloring and labeling their pussy projects. Based on the variety of shaving options displayed in the hallway, Cape and I agreed that some of the little fuckers were getting more variety in their down time than we were. He smiled wickedly, and we both waited, like kids on Christmas morning, the arrival and subsequent hallway rounds of Ms. Long.

She arrived, and her reaction did not disappoint.

"Whhhaaaaaat is THAT?!?" demanded Ms. Long

I couldn't resist. "You mean THOSE?"

The look she gave me would have melted a perfectly good fudge pop; alas, I was not the target of this particular would-be homicide. Long ripped into Cape right in front of his stunned, and (truth be told) offended, health class.

"MISter Caper, explain yourself!"

And he did folks. Yes he did.

"Aren't they great? The guys…"

"Ahem!"

"…the guys AND JESSICA worked really hard on them so we could get something out on the walls, like you requested." As God is my witness those last three words came out so sweetly that I nearly sought immediate dental attention. Instead, I stood right beside my devious buddy, smiling in a now-what-the-fuck-you-gotta-say-girlfriend? sort of way.

Ms. Long was about to blow. The vein in her temple was

prominent enough to give a heroin addict a hard on. I thought to myself that now would have been a good time to chill out. Yes, now would definitely be a good time to chill out.

"We're starting the MALE reproductive system tomorrow, and the guys can't WAIT to get to work on…"

Clearly, Mr. Caper did not get the mental projections I was sending his way. Good thing, too, because, on my deathbed when I'm asked the top ten hardest times I've ever laughed…

The entire class, Cape and I included, burst into hysterics.

Ms. Long, as you might imagine, did not share our enthusiasm.

"You…will…remove…those…assignments…from…the   … wall…**NOW!**"

When she said the word "assignments" she made a face like she'd swallowed a bad oyster. Once her mandate had been laid down, she turned abruptly and stormed down the hall to the front office, no doubt to tell her brother Dick about our vaginanannigans.

No doubt.

The phone rang less than five minutes later, prompting a collective "uh oh" from the melancholy bunch that were, oh so carefully, taking down the prohibited pussies from their prominent placement. (2)

Caper bit the bullet and answered.

"Hello?"

"I swear on all that's holy…"

"Mr. Long, I can explain…"

"Shut UP and let me finish, you idiot. If you EVER do something like that again without telling me first, I'll fire both of you. The look on her face must have been priceless, and you morons didn't think to involve me? Sister or not, she gets on my last nerve sometimes"

Cape landed, catlike, on his feet.

2   All those "P" words? That's alliteration, folks! The repetition of initial consonant sounds, used to create a nifty, poetic effect.

"You got it, Mr. Long, sorry. Hey, I was gonna work on the male reproductive…"

"Don't push it, Caper."

"Yes, sir."

Cape hung up the phone and smiled triumphantly. I, however, was not about to let him get too full of himself.

"This all could have been avoided if you taught more like me, you know."

His middle finger was the last thing I saw, as he strode confidently back into class to bitterly disappoint a group of urban predators who already had colored pencils and markers picked out so that they could shade and color, with subtlety and panache', 17 dicks.

By the pricking of my thumb, Shakespeare for the dumb (and dumber.)"

"My ass! This used to be Yorick! I knew that motherfucker! He was funny as shit! And he used to carry my ass when I was little " (3)

Such was Shakespeare as performed at Moorzakunt Academy.

"Excuse me?" you say. "Aren't these kids a bit, um...*unrefined* [euphemism for stupid] for Shakespeare?" you ask. While I admire your euphemistic honesty (and I do, really) I think perhaps you is a bit *misguided* [euphemism for clueless] regarding this issue.

I hung papers in the hallways the DAY they told me I couldn't. I had my guys mentor little dudes in the school when they told me they couldn't be trusted with *toilet paper*. My wife made them Thanksgiving dinner and brought them to our **house** to eat it! Shakespeare, folks, ain't shit when you look at it in that context.

This is not to say I don't have mad respect for the bard. I do, believe me. I didn't "get him" when I was studying in high school or college, but since my immersion into the written language as a teacher, reader and writer, I can tell you (in the words of one Tyree Junkins) why old Will transcends time and genre:

"Dawg was all *about* the sex, violence, and dirty dealins' yo!"

---

3   Translated, brutally, from William Shakespeare's <u>Hamlet</u>. *"Alas, poor Yorick! I knew him, Horatio, a fellow of infinite jest, of most excellent fancy. He hath bore me on his back a thousand times..."*

I simply could not have said it better myself, yo.

Oh, did I mention that we performed Hamlet for the entire school?

Hamlet. Us, at a school for severely emotionally disturbed kids.

I **dare** you not to keep reading.

———————— ⊸«⟨●⟩»⊸ ————————

The excitement that permeated the halls of our beloved Moorzakunt Academy leading up to our performance was roughly akin to the thrill that NASCAR fans have prior to a big race at Talladega Motor Speedway; that is to say, everybody was drooling with anticipation over the potential for some serious fucking carnage.

You'd think, with that kind of pressure, that my special ed. Shakespeares would be shaking in their fake 19th century Renaissance Italian boots. And you'd be wrong. Despite the fact that we were about to re-create one of the most important plays in all of English literature on a tiny stage in a tiny gymnasium in front of 100 tiny kids with every conceivable learning disability, emotional problem, or both, despite the fact that we had to get it done with one week of preparation, and despite the fact that we had to get it done in under 45 minutes (the maximum time we figured this bunch could sit still without utter chaos,) despite all of that, and more, my thick-headed thespians were ready to rock n' roll.

"Let's do this shit on the real, ya mean?" shouted Josh

"I feel you dawg, I'ma blow this shit UP!" asserted Tyree

"Dese niggas gonna be all up on dese nuts when we drop this shit." articulated Will to which Messiah [real name, I kid you not] finally intoned, " it's on like Donkey Kong."

I know how hard Shakespeare can be to read, given the language barrier, so allow me to translate:

Josh: "Do you all understand, as I do, that it's imperative that we get started?"

Tyree: " I, for one, understand completely, and suggest that we perform at our very best!"

Will: " Our audience will be sure to embrace us once we've enthralled them with our
performance."

Messiah: The anticipation I feel at this moment is vaguely similar to that moment of anxiety just prior to engaging in that wacky video game involving a primate, some barrels, and ladders."

Did I mention that, to accommodate the attention span of my ADHD ensemble that I threw in the witches from MacBeth, the sisters from King Lear (two of the guys *wanted* to put on dresses, more on that later,)and Othello because Billy thought it would be hilarious if the only white kid in the show played the most famous "black" part in Shakespeare? I didn't mention that?

Well, I did.

My thoughts at the time were roughly the same as they were just prior to curtain: "Who the fuck is gonna know?"

"Weren't the witches in *Macbeth?*" inquired Mr. Kerrygan, mere moments into the play.

Fucking gym teacher. This guy's idea of heavy reading is the Dick's Sporting Goods advertisements in the Sunday paper and he knows that I'm mixing metaphors? Everybody's a critic.

Well, almost everybody.

The retarded kids and autistic kids thought our performance

was amazing, and cheered loudly throughout the performance.

Lest you think I'm trying to be funny, I'm not. Any young man or woman I've ever taught will tell you that only two things are absolutely off limits in my presence: you don't speak without reverence for my son Cain, who died in his infancy, and you don't *ever* make fun of a person with any type of disability. I am crystal clear on this. Cain's death hurt my wife profoundly, and anybody noble enough to navigate this world with an additional burden is worthy of respect. Failure to respect the volatile nature of either subject will result in profound suffering at my hands, and I do not give a *fuck* what anybody *thinks* they can do about it.

———————◖◉◗———————

Momentary gravitas aside, the kids in the audience were eating our fractured fairy tale up. When Rodney Ramirez came out with the skull for the famous "to be or not to be" soliloquy, I thought the doors were going to blow off. It would have been one of my fondest memories as a teacher had it not been for the fact that I was totally distracted by the fact that Rodney was not wearing the Hamlet costume we made, nor was he in possession of the paper mache' skull that the art department made; rather, he was wearing a bona fide (and expensive looking) Shakespearean ensemble and holding, with all the appropriate flourish, *a very real human skull.*

"Alas, poor Yorick… " was all I heard before the little voice in my head (the one that often spoke up in moments when my teaching license was in serious jeopardy) petitioned:

"Where, exactly, did the costume come from?"

Then the other little voice (the one that only crept forth from my deeper consciousness when the industrial sized shit was about to hit the factory sized fan) queried:

"To hell with the costume, where the FUCK DID THE SKULL COME FROM?!?"

Several moments later, every one of which made me feel like I was bleeding internally, Hamlet defeated Laertes, the witches danced, and the King forgot his lines so he just fell (off the stage) and died. Such ended the Moorzakunt players' inaugural performance of Hamlet.

The crowd, it should be noted, lost their fucking minds.

Then, in what was one of the coolest things I've ever seen, the "actors" mingled with, talked to, and *signed autographs for*, the younger and more learning-disabled kids. I actually heard one of my knuckleheads tell a beaming little boy with Downs Syndrome that if he worked hard and believed in himself, he could be an actor someday too! Mr. Long almost choked to death on his beer and peanuts when I told him that story some days later at one of our frequent happy hours.

━━━━━━◅《◉》▻━━━━━━

All kidding aside for a moment, the momuMENtal self esteem boost that my guys got from performing for, and being worshipped by, the younger kids, left an impression that lasted longer than an everlasting gobstopper. (4) If such undertakings didn't threaten to deprive me of both my sanity, my life savings (you don't think the *school* financed this thing, do you?) and my teaching license, I'd have done it more often.

4   Candy referenced in Roald Dahl's classic <u>Charly and the Chocolate Factory</u>,. It's
     a candy that lasts a *really* long time.

That being said, the look of pure, unadulterated joy on the face of the "disabled" kids' faces during the play led me and the boys, some months later, to organize and oversee *The Half Hour Odyssey*, (5) acted entirely by autistic, retarded, and handicapped children, and directed entirely by my collection of severely emotionally disturbed miscreants. Without a doubt, one of the greatest thirty minutes of my life, I cried (discreetly) through most of the performance.

P.S. – If you're going to give me shit about the terminology, (retarded, handicapped, etc.,) don't.

Don't ruin a beautiful thing with your issues. There's plenty of stuff to give me shit about in this book, find something else.

P.S.S. – The authentic Hamlet costume came courtesy of Billy's "lesbian aunt who worked for a costume place in Center City, Philadelphia." (His words.)She thought it would be a great surprise.

It was, and I will forever be thankful that she cared enough about our little project to contribute to it.

Oh, the skull?

Wow.

That's a fucking story in and of itself, believe me.

Maybe in the next book.

---

5   Inspired by The 5 minute Iliad, a book by Greg Nagan that everyone should own.

Conflict and Opportunity

I have endured some very serious tribulations throughout my two decades as a teacher, and I have earned more from those trials than I ever did sitting in a classroom. With apologies to those whose expertise lay in the field of Chinese philosophy, here's a lesson I teach all of my students, regardless of age or level, about conflict and opportunity.

———))(((———

Google *Yin Yang* and take a look, you're going to learn a valuable life lesson just by looking at it.

See where the white area is at it's fullest? That's when things are at their best, relationships are going well, success is plentiful, and your mind is at peace. Unfortunately, as you well know, that's when problems start, and these problems are represented by the dark spot in the center of your happiness. This is when jealousy, grudges, and complacency sneak into your life, insidiously trying to undo all of your hard work. One of the problems with success is that as it increases, so do the forces determined to suppress it. Sometimes those forces grow to the point where darkness becomes the majority of your day-to-day reality

See where the darkness is at it's fullest? That's when things are at their worst, when loved ones seem distant, failure is everywhere, and your soul is at war. There is beauty in these moments; however, as you never really know whom your true friends are until you have nothing to offer them but a share of your burden. That bright spot, located in the deepest citadel of the darkness represents those true friends, loyal family members, and moments of opportunity. Like the proverbial "light at the end of the tunnel," true light and awareness can only come to you once you have been tested by adversity. Within conflict lay the seeds of opportunity.

Here are some of my own moments in the darkness, and the sources of light that shone though them.

Cain

It was Friday, March 10th, 1995, and I couldn't wait for school to end. My wife Dawn had just given birth to our first child, my son, Cain. It was near mid day and I was clock watching, because, after three days in the hospital, Cain was home and the nurse was coming to the house for a routine follow up visit, so when I got home, I could spend the entire weekend kissing Dawn and staring in awe at Cain. I figured it was never too early to start reading to him, so I already had some books picked out, and I would take him for a few walks, identifying all the things in his new world by name: tree, car, clouds, doggie...

"Frank, I need to talk to you."

—————————«(◦)»—————————

The voice of my dear friend Don Studwell snapped me out of my daydreams. Given that he never called me Frank, usually preferring bud, buddy, Frankie, or something equally informal, I was suspicious. Once we got into the hallway, and I fully embraced Don's body language and facial expression, suspicion gave way to serious concern.

"What's up Donnie?"

"Your son is very sick, and I am going to drive you to Saint Christopher's hospital right now so you and Dawn can make a decision about his future."

⚈⚈⚈

Looking back on that moment I must, once again, thank you Don, for being honest, plain spoken, and calm. I don't remember much about the car ride to the hospital, but your strength was instrumental in getting me there, and for that I am forever grateful as well.

⚈⚈⚈

I will spare you the details of the ten days that followed that Friday, but I will tell you the truth; my son Cain died from a congenital heart defect on March 20th, 13 days after he was born.

⚈⚈⚈

I tried to be strong for my wife, who lost her first-born child. I tried to be strong for my family and my wife's family, who were devastated. I tried to be strong for our friends, who were in shock that something so impossible could happen to Frank and Dawn. I tried to be strong, even demanding that I carry his coffin with my own hands, but after we came home from the funeral, and I sat, listening to my wife crying upstairs, something broke inside of me.

But this is a book about teaching, and Cain's death taught me how fortunate I was to have the support and love of people around me.

The day after the services, I received a message from Stein Yelnats, the man who signed the paychecks and controlled my future at Moorzakunt Academy. It was memorable in its simplicity.

"Take as long as you need, you'll be paid for any time you miss."

You simply do not last in this business without that kind of support.

I believed that I put everything, mind, body and soul into my job, and that I deserved that sort of faith in my work and my person. However, business is business, and I was truly touched that the boss thought less about "the bottom line" and more about me as a human being.

I could have stayed out and collected money for at least three months.

I went back to work one week later.

I believe there's a lesson in there somewhere.

To sleep, perchance to dream…sometime, before the year 2000?

After our son Cain died, my dear friend Mr. Long came to visit me and Dawn; he was kind enough to bring his older brother Bill along with him. As laid back and forgiving as Bob was, Bill was intense and demanding. I will always have fond memories of our battles on the basketball court as he tried to school the young punk and I tried to show the old guy who was boss.

This visit was not about intensity; instead, Bill was beautifully open about the fact that he, too, lost his first-born son, and he was very honest about the experience and how he and his wife managed to live with their grief. It turns out that Bill and his wife had several more children fairly quickly, and he told me that there would come a time when "you will be so busy raising the children that are here that you won't have time to grieve so much for the one that is gone."

I wasn't sure I believed him at he time, but he was 100% correct and I can never thank him, or Bob, enough for making themselves available to us in our time of darkness.

Maybe we listened too intently to that "had several more children fairly quickly" part, maybe we forgot that Dawn's father was one of 13 children and my father was one of 17 so we were genetically disposed to reproducing like rabbits, or maybe we just couldn't keep our freakin' hands off one another...

Either way, Samantha, Mason, and Frankie were among us within three and half years of my meeting with the Long brothers.

Oh, by the way, Samantha had colic and chronic ear infections, and Mason had reflux problems. Suffice it to say, we didn't sleep for two years, and by the time Frankie arrived, we were outnumbered, sleep deprived, I had lost my hair, Dawn had lost her mind, and sex had gone from our favorite full contact activity to a dirty word that led to chronic exhaustion. I'm sure none of you have ever felt that way so I won't belabor the point.

Oh, by the way, Dawn worked NIGHTS during those years in Hell, so if the kids didn't sleep, then I didn't sleep, and I was forced to face the animals I taught on low batteries.

AUTHOR'S NOTE: Dawn is reading over my shoulder and mentioning [loudly] in my ear that she was alone <u>all day</u> with the kids. Clearly, *she doesn't realize that I'm trying to elicit pity from the reader here!*

So where was I?

Right, I was lacking in sleep, you knew that.

But what you didn't know was that, one time, I fell asleep *standing up, while teaching.*

"DAMN Step!" howled Tom Nannygoat, "You fell asleep standing UP! That is messed UP!"

"How long was I out?"

"Few seconds," laughed Lamar, " but that shit was intense. You was talking, the you started mumbling some nonsense, and then you was out.'

"Damn, that's messed up."

"That's what I'm sayin!" shouted Tom

So I resumed my lesson, and about five minutes later, IT HAPPENED AGAIN.

Needless to say, my guys were in hysterics when I came to a few seconds later. Lamar actually had tears in his eyes.

"That shit gets funnier every time Step. I'm sorry, but you was like, 'once you understand the relationshmummmmumanummmm' and you were *out,* eyes all rolled back in your head and shit."

"Damn. I'm sorry guys, just consider me a walking birth control advertisement."

⊷•((◦))•⊶

Remember that spot of white in the darkness? One of them spoke up.

"Step, for real,' suggested Tyree, "why don't you take a nap and we'll just do some quiet shit." The rest of the guys nodded in agreement.

I repeated that, just to show my well-meaning Stepchildren the insanity of the suggestion:

"Yeah, I'll just go to sleep in front of a room full of previously incarcerated youth and trust them to do 'some quiet shit.'"

Know what I saw when I was done talking?

A bright light in the darkness.

Actually, that was just a metaphor. What I really saw was 13 guys nodding like bobble heads, thrilled at their own desire to help the old guy get his shit together. However, the idea of leaving 13 special ed. kids basically unattended while I counted sheep, and bribing them to stay quiet by promising them lunch, would be crossing a line that even I couldn't cross.

"How was you're nap Step?" petitioned Charles.

"Musta been good, you were snoring," observed Tyree.

"Alright guys, put the magazines and Playstation away" said I, "stretching and rubbing my eyes, "we're going to lunch."

Line crossed.

Lunch is served.

Light up the darkness.

"The truck was totaled, Step was not."

Saint Patrick's Day; I had just finished work and, unlike the majority of my co-workers, I was headed home rather than indulge in the usual alcohol-drenched festivities that usually accompany the day in question.

As many of the younger guys and gals I've worked with will tell you, that's a regular occurrence with me; I've always felt that, psychologically, if I'm working out while you're out drinking, or still sleeping, or relaxing, it might keep me relevant and dangerous instead of settling comfortably into flabby, dull-witted compliance. So I usually say "sure, I'll meet you all there," and sneak home instead to punish myself for my own good.

This is not to say I avoid all happy hours and get togethers. I'm no prude, and I understand how important a few beers with friends can be to the morale and camaraderie of those you fight the good fight with. I just happened to have three young ones to go home to on this particular day, and I wanted to get a workout in, then pick them up at...

Why is my horn blaring? Blood? on the windshield? Where...

What? Blacked out. Again. No. No more, get out of the truck.

Whoa! A cop screeches to a halt on front of me. Too close, or maybe my depth perception is off, after all I'm busted up pretty g---

"Huh? No sir, I don't know what..."

"NO! GodDAMN it, I'm here, I'm here. No, sir, I wasn't cursing at you, I just don't want to black out aga..."

"I have the driver of the other vehicle," I hear him say, "This one is alive."

"Wha...what?" I ask, suddenly very focused, is somebody dead? Are there any kids? What happened?" I scream, near tears at this point.

The officer, still seemingly unaware that he was addressing a smashed up victim of a car crash who was on the verge of blacking out, rattled off a string of by-the-book facts, the only parts I catch are single male driver, taken to Cooper Medical, injured but alive...

Once I hear alive, I collapse back into the truck and, moments later, I hear a heated exchange between ambulance people and the officer, something about my condition and the way he was treating me.

"You tell him," I think, "I'm gonna give him the finger when they pull me out of this truck, then...

Lights in my eyes. Questions. Something around my neck. I don't need a stretcher! Can't you see how strong I am? I don't need...

⸺⊙⸺

Shit.

O.K., relax. Where am I? You're on a bed. You're in a hallway. A hallway? Too many beds, not enough nurses. That's good, you remember. All the stuff you're wife talks about when she complains about the hospital. Good. What else do I remember? What song was on the radio? Invincible, by Pat Benetar. That's ironic. Good. Very good. Nobody really fucked up could remember what irony is. Shit, my students don't remember. My students! My papers? Where is my bag?

I sit up, my neck is on fire. I look around, nobody talking to me, my shoes and my bag are nowhere to be seen. O.K., I'm getting this thing off my neck and then...

"Whoa, young man!" says an elderly doctor, putting his hand firmly on my chest and settling me back to a laying posture as he reattached the neck brace.

"Doc," I growl "tell me what's going on, or I *will* get up and I *will* find out."

"Okay," he began, "let's start from the beginning."

AUTHOR'S NOTE: I was scared, and I was an asshole. If you're the gentleman who calmed me down and spoke to me on that day and you somehow remember me amidst all of your other memories of helping people, know that I am very sorry for being such a punk, and thank you for being the only person who would talk to me, even though I wasn't "your case."

(Hey doctors and nurses, there's a lesson in there, too.)

What I know:

The other guy stalled on the Betsy Ross Bridge. Once he got his car started again, he stayed in the middle lane, and (apparently) stalled again. I have no recollection of the impact, but apparently I hit him head on. My head shattered my windshield and my chest pushed the entire steering column into the dashboard, my legs/knees obliterated anything that was left of the console. I had a shit load of things wrong with me, but I guess being disoriented and alone gets you put out on the curb if you're not dying, and that's where I wound up. I actually had to ask a security guard to go back and look for my bag (and all of my teaching stuff.) He bought it out just as my brother –in-law George pulled up, with three very scared little kids in the back seat.

What I did:

I didn't want the kids to be afraid, so I started asking them about school and stuff, and I was giving them a bubble bath when my wife finally came home from work that night. Say what you will about me folks, I am one hard to kill motherfucker.

What I was told:

Apparently, I had called my wife and told her I was in an accident, that her mom needed to pick the kids up, and that she should stay at Temple and teach her class that night. I told her that the truck was in bad shape as well. (This was all news to me. I didn't remember shit.)

Rita, one of the ladies that I taught with at the time was in the police line driving by as I got out of the truck the first time, and *everybody* at M.A. knew about what happened by the time 1st period the next day.

Stein Yelnats, the same guy that called me after Cain's death, called Dawn to tell her that, once again, I could take as long as I needed, and money was not an issue.

My guys, bless their hearts, were extremely upset, worried that their father figure was going to abandon them the way so many other people had. I received a call the day after the accident from the principal at the time, asking me to "speak to them." Apparently, the guys were sitting, silently, in the room, threatening massive violence if anyone went in there and "try to take my place."

A whole day of silent vigil? That's 23 hours more than I was worth, but I knew I had to talk to them, and I knew I had to get back, even against doctor's orders.

I called the class and one of my guys, I think it was Josh, answered.

"Put me on speaker phone. Can you guys hear me? Good. Listen closely."

"You all right Step?" " Somebody said you wasn't' coming

back!" "Tell them not to put anybody in here!" When you comin' back? Etc. etc."

I waited for the onslaught to stop then, when they realized no sound was coming from the phone, they quieted down, all of them offering some version of "sorry, we'll shut up now."

"You're education is the most important thing, I always tell you that, right?"

"But Step…"

"RIGHT?"

"Right."

"Give me one more day, then I'll have the weekend, and I'll be back on Monday. In the meantime, you act like I'm there, let somebody teach you, and don't give me any more grief to come back to, 'cause I'm dealing with some shit as it is, know what I mean?"

"So you're coming back on…"

"MONday. I just said that. Please don't make me repeat myself, my freakin' head hurts."

"Sorry," chimed the children of the Corn, "Hey Step…"

"Yeah?"

"We're sorry. We just didn't want nobody tryin' to take your place. You know they want to break this class up and all. What we're trying to say…you know, you don't hafta come back if you ain't, you know…"

I let the tension hang for a minute, figuring I'd crank up the drama, AND remind my current, ball-busting principal (I heard her in the background) who *really* ran the show

"Are you listening to me?"

"Yeah, we're here."

"The truck was totaled....*Step* was not. See you Monday." (1)

And I hung up. Shame, too, because Dennis Champeen later told me that the shout that went up was positively thunderous, and my little angels exploded out of the room, almost trampling the principal in the process. Any questions about my well-being were answered with a loud "The truck was totaled, Step was not!"

I went back on Monday, four days after I French kissed the windshield, totally violating every medical professional's advice.

Well, almost every medical professional. My wife just shook her head and sighed.

"I know they need you, and I know what a stubborn ass you are, just be careful."

That's why we're still married.

Of course, my wife was (and usually is) part of that light that illuminates me when the darkness threatens to overwhelm me, but Mr. Yelnats offering to pay me until I was better (and trusting that I wouldn't abuse that offer,) my students sitting vigil for me, and the empathy and assistance of my co-workers when I returned to work, were just a few more bricks in the wall that have surrounded and protected me over the years.

Nobody lasts in this business without tons of support.

Are we clear?

Good.

Much love to all of you.

One black belt, two black eyes, and some sneaky black ops.

Remember a few pages back when I referred to myself, in typically humble fashion, as "one hard to kill motherfucker?" You

---

1   I realize that referring to myself in the third person is a total violation of my own "no self-important asshole" policy; however, I was feeling indestructible and loved to the max, so cut me some slack just this one time, okay?

do? Well Rorey Bussey and Dennis Tosten, put that to the test long before I did the chest bump with my steering column.

Many moons ago, in the B.C. (before kids) era, your humble author was something of a martial artist, having earned several "degrees" and participated in international tournaments, *Toughman* competitions, and early qualifiers for the fledgling UFC. No fight, however, was worse than my very first black belt test, and my master instructor (Master Tosten) and my fighting coach (Master Bussey) seemed determined to make sure that I knew I earned every stitch of that baby. I'm pretty sure my size, my intensity, and my big mouth had something to do with that.

"I really want the old kind of test, you know, a real gut check, nothing like the new, politically correct, worried about hurtin' people test, blah, blah, blah…"

What…the…hell…was… I… thinking?

At 8 pm sharp, a baker's dozen of legitimately badass instructors awaited me in the basement of the Kenpo karate school I attended, determined to give me the "full experience" of earning my first black belt.

If Snoop Dogg was in attendance, I believe he would have quipped:

"Damn, dawg, they beat the bullshizzle outta that white boy!"

I went to work the next day knowing that I had earned my promotion, largely because I was bruised and lacerated down to the sub atomic level.

Mr. Long took one look at me and asked, with out even cracking a smile,

"Dawn didn't like the way you folded the clothes?"

Smart ass, I still love this guy.

"Go home, Step. You look like shit, and if I let you teach looking like that, I look almost as bad as your face. I'll cover you for the day.

And he did.

The principal himself taught all my classes for the day, and never reported me as missing a day. Do you know how fucking rare it is to have an administrator leave the office and jump in the trenches for you.

I do.

You da man, Bob. Always were. Always will be. Moorzakunt Academy without Mr. Long was like Yin without the Yang.

An afterthought: the darkness teaches, too.

As I was writing this chapter, I thought, several times, to myself:

"A lot of people are going to think I'm full of shit here. When you put it all together in a few pages like this, it seems barely believable."

If you're one of those people, I understand your trepidation; however, everything here is absolutely true, and I could have given you a LOT more, believe me. The bottom line is that you understand that when the elephant sized shit hits the industrial sized fan, you need to remember that you will get through it, and all of those selfless acts and all that support and instruction you provided while you were "off the clock" will come back to you like the loaves and fishes. It might not happen today, it might not happen tomorrow, but it will happen.

Obviously, there is no way I could thank *all* of the people that helped me survive and thrive in the face of adversity, but I think I did my very best to do so when the moments arrived. If I didn't, I'm sorry. Know that I really do remember all of the people that stood by me.

You are all the wind beneath my wings

O.K., that last part was comPLETE bullshit, and if you ever hear me talk like that, please contact the authorities, tell them aliens exist and that they've taken over the body of the 37th funniest author you've ever read. (2)

Before we get back to stories with more characterization and less pontification, I thought you might be interested to know that sometimes, when things seem to be at their best, and the darkness rears it's ugly head, it can (even at its most vile) educate and improve you just as effectively as the good stuff.

Case in point: A few days after I had returned to work following the death of my son, I happened to be taking one of my young men to the "time out" room, largely because he was antagonizing the entire class. His mom was in the hospital, leading to a ton of misplaced anxiety, you know the deal. I figured I would walk him down there, sit down and talk with him for a few minutes, and he could come back when he was chilled out. Simple enough, right?

Sean and I entered the "time out" room, said "hello" to Don and Steve, who knew the routine by now (although they were still treating me with "kid gloves" since my return.) I sat down opposite Sean and, trying to ignore the comments and insults of the other kids in the "time out" room, we started talking through the situation. One of the little angels, Dominic Tryal, refused to stop hurling insults and profanity at all of us, to the point where Sean actually asked:

"Dude, can you stop for, like, half a second so we can talk."

Dominic sneered at him, and spat:

"Your mom."

---

2   Oh come on! The forty seventh?! I'm at *least* as funny as Stephanie Meyer and that guy at number 45!

— 56 —

Normally, the standard "your mom" is a classic, like the little black dress or the traditional tuxedo, it's timeless; an insult that transcends generation and socioeconomic status, and I would have given young Mr. Tryal props for his reliance on the classics. *However,* given the circumstances, (with Sean's mom in the hospital and that being the reason for his misplaced aggression) Dominic's two-word rebuttal was ill timed, to say the least. Steve helped me restrain Sean and lead him to another room, just as Greg Guildenstern and Marc Rosencrantz (two more of the awesome staff at M.A.) came in to chat.

When I came back into the room, I couldn't help but reprimand Dominic for his completely ignorant behavior.

Little did I know how low young Mr. Tryal was willing to go.

———————

"Dominic! Sean's mom is sick, in the hospital, and I was trying to talk to…"

"Fuck his sick ass mom, I don't care about that shit!"

"Tryal," I fumed, trying to stay under control, "if you're going to walk around this school   saying anything that comes to your mind, eventually, you're… "

"Man, shut the fuck up, ain't nobody listening to you."

"Fine, I was simply trying to…"

"Fuck you ***and your dead ass son.***"

———————

Yes, you read that right. He actually *smiled* and *laughed* when he saw the expression on my face and the faces of Don, Steve, John and Marc.

He wasn't smiling and laughing for long.

————))(((((((————

I still have a little chip in my left knee from where Donnie finally took me down. The other three guys, thank goodness, were strong [and compassionate] enough to stop me so that my extended hand was mere inches from Dominic, who was trying to squeeze his suddenly reticent body into the masonry. I am positive that if I had been allowed to reach him, I would be incarcerated today.

But the learning experience, courtesy of that little black spot inside my healing Yin, as provided by the impossibly ignorant Mr. Tryal, took hold, and I stopped struggling and spoke:

"Guys, it's okay, let me go. I'm not going to do anything."

They weren't buying it, and I think it was Greg that said,

"Sorry Frankie, but there ain't no fuckin' way we're letting go right now."

"Guys, I swear on Cain's name, I'm done."

Four men who cared very much about me, but had been conditioned to be suspicious, looked at each other, debating. The rest of the inhabitants of the "time out" room, especially Dominic, were very vocal in their suggestions that I should remain restrained.

————))(((((((————

A decision was reached, and I stood in front of Dominic, surrounded, but not restrained by, four men ready to pounce. It think it's fair to say you could have cut the tension with a knife.

"Dominic…thank you."

Confused looks all around.

"Thank you for showing me that to you, and I'm sure almost

everybody else, my son's death, and the pain it caused me and my family, is just an idea, something that you don't feel, so you don't care."

He opened his mouth,

"Don't apologize. I know you didn't mean it; you can't *possibly* be that callous. None of you can," I said, looking around the room at the other kids. "I'm sorry if I scared you." I looked Steve, Marc, Don, and Greg in the eyes: "And I apologize to you guys for being a maniac, but I learned something here, and I think it was important that this happened as early as it did. Now I know what to expect, and not to take it personally, ever again, no matter what the circumstances are."

———————

The lesson:

So, as you see, gentle reader, the darkness teaches just a well as the light, you just have to know how to use it. To this day, I am, according to my co-workers, one of the "coolest" people (under fire) they've ever seen.

Because I know how bad it can get.

Because I never take it personally.

———————

...and if you're out there, "Dominic Tryal," (obviously I changed your name,) you know who you are, and you know what *almost* happened on March 28, 1995. I hope the unselfish actions of four men, and the forgiveness of another, helped you become an instrument of forgiveness yourself.

He blinded me…with science!

My fellow teachers, guardians, and role models, lend me your ears,

I come today, not to bury the kids we influence, but to recognize that they are, by nature of their age, mentally fucking unstable.

Do some research: Add a prefrontal cortex that continues to develop through your mid 20s to a tsunami of dopamine receptors, sprinkle in and the normal hypersensitivity of a kid, and you've got a humanoid organism that is going to regret many of his/her impulsive decisions.

Don't take those actions personally, any more than you would take the random acts of the universe (loss of a child, car crash, etc.) personally. Instead, figure out where you are in the Yin and Yang. Are you in the heart of darkness, or knee deep in the good times?

What lurks behind the trials you are facing? Most importantly, what can you LEARN from them? I can't help but look at life that way. I am, after all, a teacher.

Thanks for letting me share this stuff with you, I hope you got something out of it

Dodgeball Abuse + Taco Bell - Seagulls = A Nice Desk Chair

Eric VanDiesel hated me.

Maybe hate isn't the right word. Eric loathed God for creating my parents and despised them for giving birth to me; he would have gladly sacrificed the entire population of California if it would just be kind enough to sink into the ocean when I was vacationing there.

So how, then, did Evil E. come to be one of my best students? And why did young Mr. VanDiesel present me, as a gift on the day of his graduation, the desk chair that I still use to this day? To answer that, we must rewind a bit, so everybody make those wiggly things with your fingers and do your best "flashback" noise, 'cause we're going back in time.

⟾⦿⟽

(You there! Yeah, you; the lady reading in the tub in Pennsylvania. *Very* nice flashback noises!)

⟾⦿⟽

Eric VanDiesel came to Moorzakunt Academy via the Philadelphia School System, so he was already getting a sub-standard education and used to incompetence when he got here; unfortunately, he possessed the all-too-common combination of far too little education and far too high self-esteem. Any teacher will tell you, this particular formula of equal parts stupid and cocky, with a dash of ignorance usually results in what I like to call the *major asshole cocktail*. Hands up, how many of you know these people?

Wow, that's a lot of you. (1)

Eric, because of his age and the particular alphabet soup of letters in his diagnoses, was placed in the room of Miss Debbie Tombs, a wonderful, maternal woman who actually *taught* her students and reinforced, as best she could, proper etiquette and respect. It was often joked that when the kids "outgrew mom" they got shipped around the corner and down the hall to "dad" [yours truly] for harder work and a firmer hand.

Even though Debbie and I disagreed many times on what she saw as my "overdoing it" when it came to discipline, I still respected her a great deal and I must say that the students I got from Ms. Tomb's room always came in much better prepared for my academic onslaught than any other additions I received. I just thought she was a little....soft, shall we say? on her flock. I always called her kids "the flock" because they were like sheep: they always traveled as a group, were a bit sheltered, and bleated loudly any time the slightest difficulty arose.

Oh, yes, and they were food for the wolves.

I was sitting outside with the wolves, teaching different cloud formations and weather indicators when Eric VanDiesel made his first appearance with the flock. As Debbie walked her sheltered

---

1   I can hear you from here, people. So to clarify: I have a Master's degree +15, dual certification, and am a published author, so I am an *entirely* different type of asshole, thank you very much.

shitheads over to the "basketball court portion" (2) of our campus, Eric made it a point to wander dangerously close to my "outdoor learning area, strutting like a peacock, flexing his pasty, slightly larger than linguine noodle, arm, showing off his Celtic cross tattoo that looked like your four year-old niece drew it in permanent marker. He smirked, staring at us with his best "hard guy" look. Years later, Eric would tell me that he was a big fan of the HBO series "Oz," and he was trying to emulate Ryan O'Reilly, an Irish character who tried to "out-tough" the inmates of the violent prison where he was incarcerated.

The wolves were, to say the least, amused.

"The FUCK he looking at?!"

"That bitch ass little white boy better walk on before he gets FUCKed up!"

"I'ma whoop his ass 'till his face looks like a cummingalotofus cloud."

"That's *cumulonimbus* cloud, Randy" I corrected, "but good job getting back to the lesson. Now, when you see clouds like that..."

"Who the new white boy? " interrupted Elvis Segura.

Suddenly, a hush fell over the inquisitive pack of lupine losers; most likely due to the homicidal look on my face. I *do* so hate to be interrupted, and they damn well knew it. I took a deep, non-murderous breath, and spoke crisply and briefly:

"I don't know who the kid with the bad attitude and the bad tattoo is and, for the record, I do not GIVE A SHIT either, he's one of the flock so he'll be one of us someday. Now if you don't mind..."

Duly chastised, the wolves returned to scanning the sky and

---

2   The whole "campus" of M.A. was about the size of a real high school parking lot so, with buildings and stuff taking up most of the room, certain areas were divided up into specific activity areas; it was like trying to divide one bedroom up with your two siblings. "These two square feet are mine, all mine!!"

listening to the lesson, although I caught them all, on more than one occasion, glancing over toward the basketball nets and the loud-mouthed new kid, no doubt thinking "yeah, one of us one day, if we don't kill that muthafucka first."

————))((()))((————

He second time I encountered Eric VanDiesel I was alone, having walked Karen Artsyfartsy, an autistic savant with stunning powers of calculation but crippling trust issues, to the nurse. The Mariannes, Short and O'Connor, (two angels of mercy that taught the most profoundly handicapped kids) let me escort her from their contained class. Karen always let me walk her from place to place if I happened to be around and, over time, she learned to trust some of my guys as she did me. Say what you want about me, folks, but I inspire trust in people almost as much as I inspire nausea.

So, leaving Karen in the capable hands of nurse Vermicelli, I breezed into the hall and smack dab into Eric, who looked me up and down like he was deciding which square inch of me disgusted him the most. I figured I would introduce myself, perhaps dispelling any wrong impressions this young man might have in the process. I extended my hand.

"New guy. Nice to meet you, I'm Mr. Stepnow…"

"Yeah, mm-hmm, Stepnowski. Oh, wait," (rolling his eyes and making little quote marks in the air with his fingers), "*Step*. Right? Not impressed. Don't care. Just stay the fuck outta my way and you won't have any problems."

————))((()))((————

Ladies and gentlemen, I am not prone to gratuitous self-

WHY ARE ALL THE GOOD TEACHERS CRAZY?

promotion but I feel that, to properly set the mood for the rest of the chapter, I must tell you that (in the context of my position at Moorzakunt Academy at the time) Eric speaking to me like this was roughly equivalent to Richard Simmons going into the 1976 Oakland Raiders locker room and telling the inhabitants to step off before they got hurt.

I folded my hands in dramatic fashion, smiled the way the cobra does when she realizes the bird she's chasing can't fly and whispered, ever so sweetly:

"Yes, sir. I will do my very best to stay out of your way, sir. Sorry to bother you, sir."

(Eric would later tell me that *that smile* scared him worse than anything up to that point in his life.)

I smiled to the point of hurting myself at the thought of telling my baker's dozen of destruction about my little dialogue with young master VanDiesel.

"That mottherfucker said WHAT?!?!?" screamed Tyrone in disbelief.

John shook his head, laughing, "Oh HELLLLL no!" amid a cacophony of comments, all of which centered around the time-tested theme of *thou shalt not writeth checks with one's mouth that thou cannot casheth with thy hands.*

Larry Dallas, one of the recent transplants from Ms. Tombs class; an all-around hellraiser who looked for any opportunity to create random acts of senseless violence, finally asked the question that was on the tips of everybody's tongues:

"What are we gonna do about this asshole, Step?"

My reply was not what they expected at all.

"Nothing."

"NOTHING?!?!?!" came the severely over punctuated reply.

"Nothing. I'm sure Eric VanDiesel will come around once he's been here a while, now finish up your lunch so we can finish the chapter on the Revolutionary War that we started yesterday."

Stunned, confused, and hostile, my obedient pack of thirteen wolves finished their lunches in virtual silence, and I knew all too well that all of them wished that they could substitute their peanut butter and jellies or Italian hoagies with some nice tender Irish mutton.

━━━━◆◆◆◆━━━━

At this point, I must confess to having been very immature and vindictive. While I *said* all the right things, and *acted* consummately professional in response to Eric's repeated and flagrant disrespect (he mouthed off to me *and* Ms. Tombs several times without provocation after the original incident,) I knew that preventing my guys [and girl, sorry Jess] from *immediately* retaliating would be like slapping around a bunch of wolverines, locking them in a small closet with a case of Red Bull, and *waiting*. I am, in hindsight, truly sorry.

Just kidding, I'm not really sorry at all. The eventual repercussions for his repeated insubordination taught Eric about accountability and social awareness, and helped to mold him into the fine young man that he eventually became.

That's my story and I'm sticking to it.

Dodge ball was big in gym class. East to play, easy to monitor, and the nurse's office was only ten feet from the gymnasium. Every so often, gym teacher John Wang and one of his revolving gym assistants would allow classes to combine for some truly memorable dodge ball debacles.

Much the same way a prison guard might tell another one to "take a break" while the former promises to "keeps an eye on the

━ 66 ━

area" while a well deserved retaliation of some sort takes place, I came to the gymnasium bearing gifts; specifically, coffee and doughnuts. I happened to know that John was as much a sucker for powdered jelly and apple fritters as Shannon G. was for caffeine. They swiftly secured their booty in the gym office and commenced munching and slurping. I offered to watch Ms. Tomb's gym class while they feasted.

"Munch, munch, slurp, slurp"

"Oh, by the way, I'm bringing my guys down, too. O.k?"

"Munchity munch, chew, chew, slurpity slurp"

"I figured you would be cool with it. By the way, extra apple fritters in there."

"Munch munch, I ruv appa fittas, munch munch."

"Slurp, munch, any maw cweme? Yeah ats wat Ahm tawkin bout! Slurp, slurp."

Gym teachers placated.

Dodgeballs distributed.

Classes combined, me in charge.

———◦《◉》◦———

I just happened to throw ALL of the potential projectiles to my guys [and girl] to start the game.

Then I blocked the door.

Nice.

With fire in their eyes, the wolves looked at Eric, then to me. "Well?"

I looked at Eric, the *only* one of the terrified flock that didn't know what was about to happen; as evidenced by his looking at me and beginning:

"This is bullshit. Now give us some of those balls before…"

While he was talking, I held my hand up, dramatically, and snapped my fingers.

I haven't seen that many red balls hit something Irish since the entire sunburned collection of North Wildwood lifeguards ran naked though the O'Flynn's Pub during the summer streak of 1989.

It was beautiful in it's brutality. Misplaced aggression and poor self-esteem channeled into the eradication of false bravado and reinforcement of the social hierarchy. Freud, and the Marquis de Sade would have been proud,

Eric was reduced, in mere seconds, to a slobbering little cumulonimbus cloud of new-found humility and bodily functions. Mission accomplished, my class and I retreated to our classroom to finish our algebra packets, leaving the rest of the flock to sweep up Eric and thank their lucky sheep stars that they weren't singled out for dodge ball deconstruction.

John and Shannon emerged from the gym office in sugar and coffee comas to find a slightly damaged kid with general swelling and red noodles for arms crying violently and vacating the gym. Apparently, he thought he was going to run into my room and beat up everybody.

He was, medically speaking, fucking nuts.

"You're fucking nuts," John Wang told him, last remnant of apple fritter falling from the corner of his mouth, "you're lucky that's *all* they did."

"For real," added Shannon G., you can't go around here bullying and talking to people the way you do, es*pecia*lly Step."

———⟫(《》)⟪———

Eric, for his part, still didn't get the message. (What follows is a rough translation given to me by one of his classmates, and one of my finest snitches, who was concerned about Eric's safety – for obvious reasons.)

"Fuck you you fucking chink, and you can suck my dick you dike bitch!! You're all a bunch of fucking pussies, and I'm gonna show all of you, watch! Now get the fuck offa me you fucking faggots! I'm gonna run out of that bitch's class as soon as we get back and I'm gonna grab a pair of scissors off her cunt desk and stab that motherfucker's eyes out then I'm gonna hack apart the rest of the niggers and spiks in his class!"

Charming.

Obviously, Eric never made it to my class that day, mainly because he didn't really want to. As the saying goes, "Cowardly dogs bark the loudest," and E.VD, as I came to know him, was smart enough to know what awaited him if he ever *really* crossed the line.

Not that he didn't put a foot over it now and again.

And this is a good time to teach the concept of Newton's Third Law of Motion, which states that "for every action there is an equal and opposite reaction."

Action: Eric spit at Danny Coyle from the bus one day.
Reaction: Donnie Amato, Danny's buddy, waited in Ms. Tomb's bathroom until Eric needed to use it. Don't know if Eric had to go #1 or #2, but he sure as heck #2'd himself when the door shut.

Action: Eric lied to Ms. Tombs, completely fabricating a story about how some of my guys jumped him and stole all of the money his mom gave him for the week. [It was later discovered he spent it all on weed]
Reaction: Weed: taken and flushed (in *front* of Eric.). Story: disproved. Eric's ass: kicked.

I could go on and on, but I'll get to my favorite one.

Action: Eric continued to be a belligerent pain in the ass for Debbie Tombs and every other teacher, counselor, and administrator for the entire 1994 year, with particular venom spat in the direction of my lovable self and my cuddly little wolf cubs.

Reaction: Guess who found out on orientation day, 1995, that he was a member of Step's class?

I'll give you three guesses.

Wow. You guys are good.

I had been told the day before during teacher orientation, so I was fully prepared when, after having to be restrained and dragged, screaming, to my room, Eric finally stood, sweating and hyperventilating, in front of us. Everybody was seated, hands folded, at their desks. I sat, legs folded, at my desk and just pointed to the five words written neatly on the board.

Welcome to Hell, Eric. Maybe.

E.VD never got past the first three words, and he tried to bolt out of the room.

Key word: tried.

The entire school was in full support of the "Stepification" of Eric VanDiesel, including the behavior management team, who were waiting outside the door and dumped Eric, unceremoniously, back into my room like lumberjacks outside the ring in a WWE wrestling match.

Once he realized there was no escape Eric, to his credit, climbed into the only open desk (by design, right in the eye of the storm,) composed himself, and asked what the "maybe" part of the note on the board meant.

I waited for almost a full minute (I know, I know...too much drama. Again, I was young and immature)

"It means," I said, barely above a whisper, "that for you to survive in this class, you need to check your ego at the door,"

"Check your ego," echoed Anthony

"beg forgiveness for the dumb shit you did last year,"

"Beg forgiveness," snarled Tyree and Keoni."

"and understand that, like Vegas, what happens in Step's room stays in Step's room."

"Understand?" sneered Maxwell.

Eric gave it a minute to sink in, then stood up and spoke. I remember what he said, to the letter, to this very day:

"I apologize for being a dick. I can't promise that I won't be a dick again, but I know you'll discipline me if I am. I realize that I'm low man on the totem pole in this class, and that I disrespected you, Step, so I am willing to do whatever it takes to be a proud member of this class. I will keep my mouth shut and my ears open, and I just ask that you tell me the right thing to do before you whoop me for doing the wrong thing by accident."

Then he sat down and waited for the verdict.

Keoni, who I always referred to as "the Polynesian Punisher," spoke up (good thing, too, because I was temporarily speechless.)

"I think *some*body changed over the summer."

Jarren added: "Maybe, maybe he's just scared shitless."

"Either way," I added, breaking the tension, "he came with his tail between his legs and his heart in the right place. I hope, for your sake Eric, that the man in front of me right now is the next evolution of the boy that we grew to know and hate last year."

"I am, sir."

"Good, I don't want to know why unless you want to tell me; and that's for another time anyway. Right now, let's get our shit together and get started."

"Awwww, work on the *first DAY*, Step?" cried the chorus.

Charles rolled his eyes and deadpanned: "This is his SECond day back to school and, yes, we have work to do."

You'd think they might have heard that before.

And so it was that Eric VanDiesel made the metaphorical leap from counting sheep to running with the wolves. He turned out to be one of my favorite students, and was involved in several of my more amusing anecdotes. However, it was his surprisingly candid admission of his biggest fear to a room full of predators, and the subsequent torture I heaped upon him, that will be E.VD's enduring legacy as far as I am concerned.

"Spiders. I *hate* them little fuckers. All hairy and eight eyes lookin' at me and...BLECCH!"

Joshua Kates shook his arms like a scared little girl as he visualized his arachnidan nemesis.

We were doing one of my infamous *let's learn about each other and thereby become more tolerant and empathetic toward one another* exercises while we had some "down" time between lessons.

NOTE to NEW TEACHERS : Always a good idea to break up your lessons with some student movement around the room, or at least with some deviation from the material. Most kids can't really focus hard on one thing for a long time (3) and getting to know each other exercises can be

3   *You're* kid can? Good for you. Tell her to invent a cure for cancer, then spend some of her millions on copies of this book for all of her alpha friends

disguised as, say, a normal freakin' conversation where you share some information about yourself and encourage the students to feel safe enough to do the same.

"Yeah, I'm with that," I agreed, "anything with multiple eyes and hairy legs is pretty creepy."

"Know what I hate?" blurted Trumaine.

"Pray tell, what?"

He stood up and started, in that nasally voice of his. Think an exaggerated version of James Cagney, or Dave Chapelle doing Rick James:

"I hate talkin' in front of people. Muthafuckas be like 'you need to talk' and I'm all like 'I ain't gotta say SHIT!'" I'm scared shitless 'bout getting' up in front of people and talking...all nervous and shit thinkin' 'I don't want to be doing this shit' the whole time I'm doing that shit. I ain't gonna do it, even if I have to. I hate talking in front of a room full of – what? Yeah. Public speaking. I hate that shit."

Silence as fourteen kids who, according to their paperwork, couldn't discern subtlety, allowed the Optimus Prime-sized irony to settle in before moving on.

"Aaaaaany way," Keoni saved us, "what 'bout you E? Whatchoo scared of, brudda?"

"I am absolutely terrified of seagulls. When I see one, I'm paralyzed with fear. When I was a baby, my mom took me to the Jersey shore. This was before the divorce happened and I moved in with my dad. So I'm sitting on my mom's lap, and she hands me a Rice Krispy treat..."

(insert a wave of comments about how much my idiots love Rice Krispy

treats and a bunch of offshoot comments about other delicious snacks before I could regain control and get Eric back on track.)

"...so I'm gumming my Rice Krispy treat, loving life. You know, the beach, my mom, my Rice Krispy treat, it was perfect. Until a giant seagull (4) swooped down and pulled it right out of my hands and devoured it right in front of me. I've been terrified of them ever since."

If I may be perfectly honest, I thought Eric was being ironic and funny, and I had to cover my mouth to keep from laughing. It wasn't until later that I realized how serious he was.

I know what you're thinking, gentle reader. Seagulls, are you shitting me?

I know, and he *told* that shit to a group of unstable teenagers with wicked senses of humor.

Crazy right?

Not as crazy as the idea that immediately formulated in my head upon learning of Eric's phobia of *larus occidentalis.*

———⋘◉⋙———

Eric VanDiesel loved Taco Bell.

Maybe love isn't the right word. Eric wanted to name his first child Glenn after founder Glenn Bell, and he wanted to be buried in a casket full of cheesy Gordita crunches. One of the perks of being me was that every principal that came through Moorzakunt Academy was given specific instructions by the CEO that signed the checks to leave me do whatever I had to do to keep the number of incidents down and the test scores up — and part of that meant <u>letting me take</u> my guys, when they earned it, a few blocks away

4   Giant seagull? Maybe to a baby E.VD it *seemed* like a giant breed of waterfowl, but it was probably just a big seagull.

to the Franklin Mills Mall food court. The four or five "runners" would take the orders, hop in the truck with me, and we would be there in five minutes. Once the eagle had landed, the boys knew they had ten minutes to D.O.G.(Disperse, Obtain, and Get your ass back in the vehicle.)

The choices were myriad: Arby's, McDonald's. Burger King, Saladalley, Pizza Hut, KFC and, of course, the beloved home of the chalupa, Taco Bell. If we went off campus 70 times, Eric ate Taco Bell 69 times. I remember, going there one Monday only to find that Taco Bell had burned to the ground on Friday night. If camera phones were around then I would have a photo of Eric on his knees, hands outstretched like the movie poster for Platoon, screaming "Noooooooooo!"

On this parTICu-lar day in November, I had some plans of my own. Once everybody was back in the truck, I cruised over to the section of parking lot behind the Burger King. Out of eyeshot if you were driving in via our entrance, I knew from driving around the Mall that an army of seagulls set up base camp back there, fighting for scraps from the B.K. dumpster. Josh was my point man, keeping Eric distracted in the back seat while slipping me a few fries, which I threw onto the room of the truck, as I had taken the liberty of putting down the windows.

Within seconds, my black Ford F-150 was covered, I mean COVERED in white plumage. We were all laughing our asses off until Billy and Tyrone yelled over the laughter:

"Step, something's really wrong with Eric, yo!"

Eric was actually curled into a near fetal position and was rocking and talking to himself, thereby freaking out everybody in the truck.

Driver included.

We sped back to Ye Olde Moorzakunt Academy and exploded out of the truck like a well smacked piñata. I took momentary notice of the fact that there was about a quarter ton of seagull poop decorating my [previously] black vehicle before pulling Eric out of the truck o' doom and getting him into the classroom. Once he was de-traumatized, he did several things:

1. Commented on my heritage, sexual preferences, and sanity with a Scarface-like string of profanity.
2. Politely requested that I never make seagulls swarm the truck again, unless he was *not in* the truck at the time.
3. Asked me what my greatest fear was.

Whereupon I did several things:

Gave him a pass on the string of insults. Hey, I deserved that.

Explained that I really didn't think he was serious about the phobia, and I thought I would help him goof on the guys. Clearly, I was wrong, and I apologized.

Told him that my greatest fear was that I would lose control, torture and kill one of my students, probably one that tried to retaliate on me for a prank gone wrong.

Now that the scavenger bird debacle was behind us, it was time to think about what to get Eric for Christmas, and it would involve a trip to the Jersey Shore.

No, you sick bastards, I didn't capture a seagull and put it in a box! I just traumatized the kid by accident, so this would have to be funny without being psychologically scarring. I own a shore house in North Wildwood, New Jersey with my in-laws, and my mother-in-law decorated it in true beach fashion with wooden knick-knacks. You know, sailboats, lighthouses, and seagulls…

When E.VD came in the day before Christmas he was surprised to find a box on his desk wrapped in Garfield Christmas paper (he had also admitted to loving Garfield, for which we gave him an untold amount of grief.) When he opened it he couldn't help but laugh.

After all, how many kids get their own 24"wooden seagull, complete with Rice Krispy treat sticking to it's bill, for Christmas. There was also a note that was part funny ("Don't be afraid of me, Eric, I was just really hungry that day. Please, share this tasty treat with me as a sign of our solidarity.") Part serious, (sorry, you don't get this info., too personal.)

Everybody laughed, E. called me a sick bastard, and the rest is history. I'm sure young Mr. VanDiesel will pop up at other points in this novel.

What's that?

Oh, yes…the title of this chapter mentions a desk chair, doesn't it?

Well, Eric VanDiesel finally graduated, and (as with most of my guys) it was pretty emotional. When you teach kids with emotional problems, abandonment and trust issues, and all the other baggage that they carry, valiantly, every day; when you interact with these kids on a very personal level, talking to them more than just about any other adult on a day to day basis, the final separation is always an emotionally intense affair. Many of you out there are shaking your heads. Hurts, doesn't it? It's kind of like driving your kids to their dorms at college, you're thrilled for their progress, their accomplishments, and their potential, but you're also terrified that you won't be around to protect them any more, and that the big bad world will besiege them at every turn.

Such it was with E.VD. There were the prerequisite pictures, the occasional tears, and the annual parents/guardians that tell you that "he/she could have never done this without you."

There weren't a lot of people there for Eric; two, actually, but even so he made a pretty hasty retreat from graduation. I figured he had a party to go to, or he might still harbor some resentment deep down inside from all the shit I gave him while turning him into a man.

Nothing could have been further from the truth.

Eric showed up on the last day of school, (graduation was the night before the last day) and before I had a chance to ask him what was up, he dragged a huge box into the room. The fact that none of my remaining wolves so much as blinked let me know that this was a planned event. I was asked to step out of the room, *my* room, for about 15-20 minutes, I figured whatever was in the box – rabid chimpanzee, 1,000 mouse traps, giant seagull stuffed with Amazonian fire ants, thermonuclear device - I probably deserved it.

In hindsight, I did not deserve it.

When I was summoned back into the room, I was greeted by 9 smiling faces surrounding one bad-ass, super-comfy, desk chair. Black and silver, a nod to my love of the Oakland Raiders, oversized, with all the cool adjustable thingies…a veritable pleasure cruise for my ass and back.

I was, as always, erudite and verbose.

"Wow…that's…wow. *Wow.*"

Eric, bless his heart, let me off the hook or else I probably would've kept on mumbling like a shock treatment patient.

"Step, I hated you more than any human on Earth a few years ago. Now…"

This time, bless my heart, I let Eric off the hook before we *both* started crying like little girls at a Jonas Brothers concert,

"I know, E., I know…me, too."

—————◦《》◦—————

Epilogue:

Every year, no matter what school, what classroom, somebody will say "damn, that's an awesome chair, where'd you get it?"

To which I will reply, "well, there's an interesting story behind this chair, want to hear it?"

"Sure."

"Eric VanDiesel hated me…"

Playing Frogger on the Highway with The Thing.

If Patrick Starfish (from <u>Spongebob</u>,) and The Thing (from <u>The Fantastic 4</u>,) had a baby, Billy Flynt would be the result. The combination of the Thing's densely packed physique and notorious temper, combined with Patrick's innocence and dullness of wit, made Billy a volatile combination; the metaphorical ticking time bomb that we sometimes successfully diffused.

Sometimes.

Sometime, Billy go BOOM.

Usually that involved an overturned desk, a grunted "fuck dis shit" and an angry Irish kid that looked like The Thing running out of his classroom and off campus. As a matter of fact…

The first time I talked to Billy was in the middle of Interstate 95, with cars and trucks whizzing by us. The problem? We weren't *in* a vehicle.

Remember the video game *Frogger,* where you were a frog that jumped back and forth, on a crowded highway, doing your best to avoid get shmushed? Well Billy and I were doing the live action Frogger, the one where you actually die if you don't make it across the road. A lot of honking, a lot of cursing, a lot of cajoling and negotiating, and one very, VERY close call with a Ford F-250. Later, Billy and I walked back to campus, having bonded via near death experience. And he wasn't even in my class yet!

We'll come back to the details of our highway hijinks later but, for now, we'll focus on Billy Flynt after he had joined the STEPchildren.

As I mentioned Billy, though lovable and hard working, came to me with well below age-appropriate academic levels.

Fuck. I just caught myself justifying, and trying to word things technically so as to avoid hurting feelings. If Billy were reading over my shoulder, he would tell me just to tell it like it is.

(Actually, he would be asking me what justifying and technically mean…there, that's more like it.)

Billy was dumb as a box of rocks when he was sent to my room. A box of rocks with a volatile temper that was prone to throw desks and teachers; hence, report to Step's room effective tomorrow.

———— ((◉)) ————

"I got sent here 'cause they're scared of me," announced Billy on day one.

"Ain't nobody scared of you here, white boy," replied the welcoming committee.

"Fuck dis shit, I'm outta here," grunted Billy, and he took off, power walking down the hall. (Swear to God, first day, and I'm already getting the 'fuck dis shit' and the stomping out of class!) This, as a wise man once said, was when you separate the men from the boys, so I held my hand up to stop my wolves in their tracks from going into pursuit mode. They instantly understood:

The boss was going to handle this one all by himself.

I won't repeat *exactly* what I said to Billy after I caught up with him in the hall and he informed me that he was "going to get da FUCK outta there and there wasn't shit I could do about it", but it went *something* like this:

> "William, my good man, I am deeply wounded. I thought we had a 'moment' during our little outdoor escapade on I-95, but clearly I was mistaken. I would very much appreciate it if you would be so kind as to return to class before I'm forced to reprimand you in a manner unbecoming a gentleman of my stature." (1)

It worked.

Clearly, my smooth approach and non-threatening demeanor made Billy see the error of his ways. At any rate, Billy was back in class with the quickness, and the wolves, having seen this movie before, made the newest cub feel at home, talking shit about other teachers, talking about dumb shit at M.A., and other topics sure to elicit laughs and feelings of camaraderie. Now that I think of it, my guys were better at making scared, inferior kids feel comfortable and ready to learn than any of the lame ass child psychologists we EVER had at dear old Moorzakunt.

Once we were ready to get down to the business of learning, Billy was ready.

Kind of.

We were covering World War II in history, and I had set up the dramatic moment when the U.S. entered the war:

Me (in full dramatic voice mode) "And the U.S. declared war on December 8, 1941.

Following that, the Allies…"

Billy: "What did they have against December 8 ?"

---

1   And if you believe that I have, in the words of my buddy Pete Nardello, some prime real estate in Darfur you might be interested in.

Me (perplexed) "What? What does that mean, Bill?"

Billy: "Forget it, just forget it."

Me (resolved) "Fine, once the U.S. entered the war effort....
damn it, Bill, what do you mean what did they have against..."

and suddenly, it hit me; and I knew I had a story for my book.
"Bill..."

"Step, don't..."

"You thought...that the United States of America...

"Step..."

"declared war **on a day of the week**?"

"Ho-o-o-ly shit!" announced Eric, who got it before the rest
of the class, "you think that the U.S. wanted to fight the *day* of
December 8th?!?!"

The rest of the class caught on, and much laughter ensued. I
wasn't letting Billy of the hook with this one. (Sorry, but this was
a classic)

"Hey Bill, the good thing about *this* war... "

"Step..."

...you've got 364 days to get ready! I mean, Thanksgiving dinner
is over, time to start getting READY FOR WAR!"

"GodDAMN it Step!"

"Ah, shit, Bill this is a classic. I, personally, would wage war on
September 6 this year. Fucking back to school! Who needs it?"

"For real," chimed in Josh, "I don't want to go to my sis's sweet
16 party on April6th..."

"This means war!!!" yelled the class.

More war was waged against various dates, and (eventually, after
at least one "fuck dis shit,") Billy started to laugh along with us. The
rest of the boys figured that Billy would be good for at least one
classic line a day.

I'm happy and proud to say that Billy was embraced by the guys and eventually became part of the family. This is not to say that there weren't some throwdowns. Let's not forget, we're talking about 13 testosterone driven young men with learning disabilities and self-esteem issues here. One of the classic battles was Billy vs. Keoni, the Polynesian powerhouse. By the time I got to the art room, it looked like one of those old Marvel comic The Thing vs. The Hulk battles had gone down. Ironically, the Hulk (played this particular afternoon by Keoni) had green paint splattered all over him. (2)

I'm also happy to say that Eric VanDiesel, he of the big brain and seagull phobia, took Billy under his wing and tried to keep the big guy calm and help him with his work. I figured it was because they were the only two white Irish kids in a class with 10 black and Hispanic kids and one other white kid, Josh, who thought he was black. Of course, Josh also thought he was going to marry Angelina Jolie so reality was a vague concept for out resident "Crip."

Actually, Eric and Josh were the ones that restrained Billy from what could have been one of his most catastrophic outbursts. Actually, it took Eric, Josh, Charles, Pee-Wee, Trumaine and yours truly (plus some quick thinking) to prevent what came to be known thereafter as the "Biggie Mistake."

We were on one of our infamous lunch runs, and the whole gang decided that they were going to Wendy's; even Eric, the Taco Bell connoisseur himself. So the out to lunch bunch are putting their orders in while their teacher marks papers in the front seat of the truck, clock and engine running, when Charles explodes out of the door.

"Step, Billy's goin' the fuck OFF! Josh and Eric got him, but…"

I never heard the rest as I blew by Chuck and into the home of the Frosty.

2   That's called artistic license, kids. The paint was actually yellow, but see how my version gave the story a little extra "flava?" I know you felt it.

(mmmmm…Frosty. Maybe a double and some fries….)

Sorry, lost myself for a moment. So I run into Wendy's and, in the few seconds I had, assessed the situation. Let's call it "when fast food goes wrong."

LET'S PLAY 'YOU BE THE TEACHER!'

Read what I saw when I ran into Wendy's.

Decide, in under ten seconds, how to handle the situation.

Gooooood luck.

What I saw

Billy is being held back, barely, by Eric and Josh, the latter of which is *laughing*.

Pee-Wee and one of the Wendy's employees are chasing each other around the salad bar.

A VERY large, angry looking Wendy's employee (with a large wet stain on his shirt) is coming over the counter, presumably to kill Bill.

Trumaine is trying to pick up the lone female clerk (unsuccessfully) in the midst of the chaos.

There are several bags of food on the counter, and one of the Special offer displays has been ripped down from the ceiling.

Now *you* decide what to do. (No peeking!)

———— ((◦)) ————

I screamed to Trumaine "Get in the truck, NOW!" snatched Pee-Wee and threw him toward the door, moving right into the path of the big dude that was bearing down on Billy. (Fortunately, I was little bigger and a lot smarter than the advancing burger bagger,) I flipped open my wallet and yelled "police matter! You three, assume the position!" whereupon Billy, Josh, and Eric put their hands behind their heads and spread 'em. I turned to the dazed and confused fries flinger and shook his hand,

"Thanks you for calling us, sir, we've been trying to catch these guys for a while. I'm going to put them all IN MY TRUCK and take 'em down to the station NOW."

My guys are dumb, but they ain't stupid, and they broke for the truck like Olympic sprinters, I commanded the chicken sandwich champion to "guard the registers!" and as soon as he moved to the counter, I was out of there like a 260 lb ninja.

————

Elapsed time: 1 minute

Hurt children: none (not counting slapping Billy upside the head once I found out the

cause of the near rumble)

Cost of lunch for seven people: $0

————

So how did you do?

No you did *not* do exactly what I did! Liar liar pants on fire!

Ok, Ok…if you *did* just what I did. Explain *why* you did what you did.

Thought so. You big fibber. Now, allow me to explain the method to my madness. Pay attention, this is major teacher awareness stuff here.

————

I knew Charles was the smartest kid of the bunch (rarity), so I knew he would stay outside to cut down on collateral damage. I also knew that Trumaine was a "grubber" (food fanatic) so I knew he would grab the bags of food on his way out. Furthermore, I knew that Pee-Wee was a "pussy" (pussy) so he wouldn't need much incentive to get out of the way. In addition, I knew that the guy attacking Billy was a Wendy's employee (moron) so I could baffle him temporarily while the three foolish white boys hustled their ass out of Dave Thomas' restaurant.

Once we got back to campus, we laughed that nervous laughter that comes from narrowly avoiding disaster, ate our lunch, and discussed how the little motherfuckers were going to earn the money I was going to drop off anonymously to Wendy's for the food we took. *That* put a bit of a damper on things. Finally, I asked what started the whole fight.

Ready for this?

Once the other boys had placed their orders, and Trumaine had begun his 34th unsuccessful attempt to woo the one female employee at that particular Wendy's, it was Billy's turn. Bill noticed the circular advertisement twirling over his head letting you know that you could "BIGGIE SIZE" your meal for an additional 39 cents. (Meaning you could "upgrade" the size of your combo meal from the standard artery clogging size to the monster, die-within-the-hour size for a quarter, a dime, and four pennies.)

Problem: All that was on the advertisement was a BIGGIE soda and a BIGGIE fries and the words **Biggie Size for 39cents!**
Bigger Problem: Billy asked for the 39 cent soda and fries combo.
Atomic bomb sized problem: The big clerk, no rocket scientist himself, used this opportunity to flex his limited intellect by

asking Billy "what, is you retarded or sumthin?"

Nuclear warhead sized problem: Billy replied by tearing down the ad, shoving it in the aforementioned employees face and saying "Ah, DUH, it's right here, you big black dummy."

Ah, Billy, you crazy kid, every place my guys went in for about a month following that incident they asked for some variation of the BIGGIE combo, much to the chagrin of young Mr. Flynt.

By the way, I did go back, pay for the food, and explain the situation. Also, I don't think all Wendy's employees are morons, now the Burger King people...

Well, now that I've ensured that I'll never get a Whopper again without "special sauce," I can tell you what happened when Billy and I were playing Frogger on that fateful day on interstate 95.

Billy was in Ms. Queensryche's class, an amazingly diverse bunch of crazy kids and reluctant learners. Admittedly, Billy was a bit "big" for that class, but his prehistorically low academic levels made him the perfect fit for Lisa's little family of Biggie-sized kindergartners. The perfect fit...if it wasn't for that whole "throwing desks and running out of the room" thing.

On the day of our first chance encounter, Billy had one of his moments of hyperbolic frustration. (That means he got pissed and really over-reacted.)

More than a decade later, at the Ozzfest in New Jersey, I ran into Ms. Queensryche and we laughed about our experiences at M.A., and she told me what happened on the day Billy and I hit the highway. (We also showed each other our tattoos, but you get none of *that*, you cheeky monkeys!) She told me:

"Man, Billy was in was of those moods. Every question I asked him or anything I asked him to do, he just mumbled 'fuck dis shit' or 'leave me alone,' so I worked around it, like you do, you know?"

"Yes, I know, although I doubt that a lot of people would 'get it.'"

"So anyway, it's almost time for lunch, and I tell the guys and girls to get their money and order forms from the basket, like we do every single day..."

NOTE: If any teacher (or parent) story prefaces their story with "like we do every single day," that means that somebody was going to get into trouble by forgetting, violating, or disrupting something that has been common practice for months, possibly years.

"...and Billy says to me 'you get my stuff' and I say 'no, Billy, you have to get your own money and form, remember?' and he explodes 'Yeah, I remember! Whaddya think I'm STUPID? Just do what a woman is supposed to do and get my stuff.' So I yell back at him 'William Flynt! That is unacceptable behavior, now apologize. Well..."

"Yeah, I know the routine," I laughed, "Fuck dis shit, desk overturned, out goes Billy?"

Lisa laughed, "yeah, at least he was consistent. But how did you wind up going after him, I called the behavior management team."

"I just happened to be in the vicinity." I shrugged

"Lucky you," she remarked, with all the sexy sarcasm of a tattooed metal chick that teaches special ed.

NOTE: Don't judge a book by it's cover, kiddies. That boring lady math teacher might be rocking out and flaunting her killer body, tattoos and piercings when you're not looking.

But I digress; back to the story at hand. Once Billy emerged from Lisa's room in full "I'm gettin' the hell outta here" mode, I happened to be in the vicinity, having taken my young pups outside for some community service. As we were cleaning up around the campus swing set, Charles pointed out Billy lumbering, Thing-like, toward the gate that led down Revolutionary Road and dangerously close to Interstate 95. Nobody in their right mind would run out *that* gate.

"That no-neck mothafucka goin' right out the back gate, Step." observed Lamar.

"Want us to get him?" inquired Mike, as the wolves prepared to hunt.

━━━━●((●))●━━━━

It was at that moment that I felt my age hanging around my neck like the proverbial albatross (3)I realized that the young men under my aegis weren't offering to get Billy out of *courtesy*, they just *didn't think I could run him down myself* anymore.

"Fuck that" said my ego, which hadn't aged a day since achieving full blown asshole

status somewhere around 21 years old.

"I got it," said I, who had, in fact, aged, but was still a bad ass machine of pursuit, so suck me sideways, father time.

Billy, just exiting the gate, couldn't help but notice the defensive end with the long black hair starting in pursuit of him, so he took off running straight for the median that would put him right in the middle of four lanes of oncoming traffic, with me to the rescue.

"Suck on *that*," whispered father time into my ear.

---

3   Did you catch that allusion, students? Albatross? Rime of the Ancient Mariner? No? Jesus, do you fucking kids *ever* pay attention when I'm teaching?! Wait a minute, YES. Thank you, Taylor Corgan, at least SOMEbody listens to me.

Fast forward a few seconds and sprints and we find ourselves where we began this chapter, with young William and I prepared to engage in some pithy dialogue whilst casually avoiding several hundred thousand tons of angry vehicles bent on modifying our stunning good looks.

"Hey Bill," NNNNEEEEOOOW, "you think maybe," WHHOOOOSSHH "we can talk about this, while we walk back to school?" SCCREEEECHHHHONNK!! "Sorry!"

"Nah, I'm goin' home." SCCREEEECHHHHONNK!! "Fuck you too! Go back Step, I ain't goin' back" NNNNEEEEOOOW "to that school."

"God DAMN it Billy!" NNNNEEEEOOOW NNNNEEEEOOOW "That last truck was a Ford F –250," WHHOOOOSSHH, "Know how I know that?"

" Cause of the size of the tires?" SCCREEEECHHHHONNK!! "Shit!"

No...because I could *READ THE FUCKING EMBLEM AS IT WHIZZED BY MY FACE!!!!"* NNNNEEEEOOOW WHHOOOOSSHH SCCREEEECHHHHONNK!!

Now grab my hand, and let's go. NOW!"

Apparently, the combination of my homicidal rage, coupled with Billy almost getting smeared a few times himself, was enough of a combo platter to get us the fuck outta Dodge (no pun intended) and back onto the sidewalk, which I would have kissed if I hadn't been bent on ripping Billy's head off.

"Billy," I bristled, "I don't care if anyone saw us skipping hand in hand off of the highway. That's how happy I am to be in one piece. Now would you mind telling me exactly what the fuck that was all about?!"

"We weren't holding hands." he said, looking embarrassed that I'd even *said* it.

"Wow." I thought. "Thank God I don't have to teach this blockhead."

—————⊃«❮❍❯»⊂—————

I know, I know…when I look back on it now I realize just how much I fucking jinxed myself.

But hey, Billy and I had many more heartfelt moments than we did confrontational ones; they weren't as funny, but they're enough to make me smile fondly when I do recall the funny ones.

…like playing real-life Frogger with The Thing.

Intermezzo - A message to those who think teachers are overpaid

A message to all those people who think that teachers shouldn't be paid more because: they have weekends and holidays "off," they're "done" by 3:30 in the afternoon, they don't warrant pay for physical endangerment, etc.

Go.

Fuck yourself. (1)

---

1   Actual, grammatically correct sentences. The only requirements for a sentence are a subject and a verb. "You" is the (understood) subject pronoun, and the verbs are self evident. If you knew that, thank a teacher; if you just learned something, thank *this* teacher.

My choose are black.

January 21, 1991

It was my 23rd birthday, and coffee had just shot out of my nose.

One of my students, who I will call Hector Alactacos, because his name was Hector Alactacos, had just, very unselfishly, given me a story that would become one of my "most requested" when gathered with friends and associates.

We were gathered in Room 3, having just returned from the gym. "We" was myself, and thirteen juvenile delinquents ranging in age from 16 to 19 with vocabulary levels ranging from the 2nd grade level to about the mid 8th. Of course, we didn't have any books to accommodate that sort of disparity in learning levels. Oh wait, I almost forgot, we didn't have any vocabulary books at all! Silly me! Thank God for Kinko's, who were nice enough to bind and print (at my expense, of course,) twenty or so copies of a vocabulary book that I had created and typed the previous summer, but I digress...

So there we were, packed like stinky sardines (1) in a classroom that you could fit in the average public school classroom three

---

1   simile- comparing two unlike things using the words *like* or *as*. For example, reading this book is *like* a breath of fresh air. (I hear you laughing, and it hurts me deeply.)

times. Me and the unlucky thirteen, celebrating my birthday with a game of *"spell it and use it in a sentence."*

"Step, man, do we hafta do vocab now man?" whined Tyree "we just ran ball for a whole period, yo."

I countered, "Yeah, yeah, I know. I was there, remember? I was the big white guy posting your skinny ass up all day. Now sit down and choose up teams."

"Come on, y'all," chimed in Will Bunson, "the sooner we sit down the sooner Step opens the window, and the more we play the better chance that Trumaine or Hector'll say something stupid."

Truer words had never been spoken

The class sat. The teams were chosen. The windows were opened. It was on like Donkey Kong.

"Receive!" shouted Josh, my resident Crip." R-E-C-I before E-V-E! I <u>receive</u> that check every month. What nigga?! What?! I got mad skills, son!"

High fives all around on the red team. (for those of you familiar with gang affiliations and their colors, yes, I made them the *red* team *just* to fuck with Josh, who was so excited at the moment that he almost forgot.)

"I hate to break up the party," I chimed in, " but *I* before *E* except…"

"Fuck! *I* before *E* except after *C*!" lamented Josh "I knew that shit!"

"Evidently not," I said. "No points! You're up pink team!" (for those of you familiar with male teenage juvenile delinquents yes, I made them the *pink* team *just* to fuck with all of them.)

Hector Rodriguez stood up.

"Choose"

Hector pondered the word like you would ponder a trigonometry problem without a calculator.

Hector: "Choose....choose...C...H...U"

Me: "O"

Hector: "C, H. O...S

Me: "O"

Hector "I said that"

Me: "O, then O again"

Hector: "Oh, C,H,O then O again........C,H,O then O again........Z?"

This went on for some time; meanwhile the young criminals of America association yelled, teased, and generally made a shitload of noise while Hector hacked through his vocabularic nightmare. Finally, he spelled it and, as I took a long sip from my brand new travel mug...

"Choose, C-H-O then O again S-E. Choose."

He looked around in desperation, his eyes resting on the Jordans loosely tied on his feet.

"My choose are black!"

Hector beamed.

Then coffee flew out of my nose and mouth as the room, for one pregnant pause, went silent.

Then it exploded, with Will Bunson taking the lead amid the laughter, screaming, and general chaos.

"Oh my God, Step, I know I got some learning issues, but that's some B building (2) shit right there. PLEASE tell me I'm not on the level with this motherfucka right here!"

Hector was one righteously indignant Puerto Rican with black choose.

"My choose ARE black **jese' !**"

---

2   (B *Building was the building at Moorzakunt APS where the developmentally and mentally handicapped students were given special attention and education in an isolated, therapeutic setting.)*

"SSSSHHHHHHooooooes you wetback mothafucka, SSSHHHOOOOOeees!"

"That's what I said, you black ass bitch!!! CCCHHHHHOOOOeees, my choose are black, my laces are black, my hair is black, my hoodie is black and you're ugly ass nigger face is black!"

I had been busy cleaning up the coffee and admiring Hector's run-on sentence capability, but even amid the tsunami of profanity that occasionally engulfed our classroom, words like "wetback" and "niggER" were not allowed, period.

"ENOUGH!" I thundered, loud enough, and with enough potential menace to temporarily halt the "negotiations" that were about to commence over those particular racial remarks. Suffice it to say, the next hour or so involved a lot of passionate conversation, a few frayed nerve endings on my part as thirteen inner city kids *talked* and *listened* (under threat of dismemberment) about how to express anger and frustration without violence.

<hr />

Eventually, we would get back to learning. Biology, or current events, or whatever the fuck could get them back on task, learning and laughing – until tomorrow, when I'd have to do it all over again, like I was never here.

That night, I munched on birthday cake and tried not to act as drained as I felt, I though to myself, "between the comedy and chaos, how long can I continue to do this?"

NOTE : when this scene is acted in what is sure to be the screenplay based on the novel, I would request that Mr. Washington bring the proper pathos to the moment .You can do it Denzel! King Kong ain't got nothing on you, baby!

Gangsta Graduation

O.K., I'm going to tell you right off the bat, ALL of the names in this section have been completely changed. Not slightly altered, more like *Tranformers-Autobot-into-a-helicopter* changed, for reasons that will become readily evident once we are under way. That having been said, we can get under way.

One of my all time favorite students did not start as one of my all time favorite students. As a matter of fact, I truly disliked the little bastard the first time I met him. I shall call him Roberto Chavez, for three reasons: One, his name was certainly not Roberto Chavez. Two, **Roberto** Clemente was a man of rare character and maturity, as my young friend eventually became. Three, Julio Caesar **Chavez** was always my favorite fighter, even though he weighed about as much as my thigh on any given day, and this young man was quite entertaining in the bare knuckle boxing department, if I do say so myself.

Sobriquet shenanigans aside, young Roberto was presented to me, as so many young men were at dear old Moorzakunt Academy, as a "rehabilitation project." (Euphemism for "kid that need a MAJOR fucking attitude adjustment.) In this particular case, Mr. Chavez made repeated inappropriate sexual comments to Ms. Tombs, and then called her a word that rhymes with runt loudly and often in between threats of physical violence. Ms. Tombs was a wonderful, albeit maternal and forgiving, 115 lb woman.

I was not. (1)

So here comes Roberto, dragged by the behavior management team, to my humble classroom. Home, if you'll recall, to the biggest, baddest, and most loyal [to me] monkeys in the Monkey House.(2) Roberto made the category 5 hurricane mistake of announcing, upon entrance:

"You don't know who I'm related to, you can't touch me, and I'm not afraid of you motherfuckers."

Fourteen *verrrrry* anxious eyes turned to their leader, awaiting the equivalent of the gesture Pilate gave the centurions before that whole 39 lashes thing. (3)

I waited, letting the tension build; even the behavior management fellows waited around, anxious to see what would happen to a kid who would dare throw gasoline on the fire that was "Step's class." Roberto, truth be told, looked unfazed. (He would later tell me that he was shitting himself, but he didn't want to appear weak. I told him that he put on one hell of a show and that I apologized again for how it ended. He understood.)

When the silence had become almost unbearable, I solicited, quietly:

"Say that again."

He proclaimed, with a barely perceptible reduction in bravado:

---

1   Nor am I still, as of the writing of this book.
2   Spare me the racist bullshit. Monkey House is an allusion to a fantastic book by Kurt Vonnegut that fits this particular metaphor beautifully.
3   For those of you unfamiliar with the biblical reference, my boys wanted a sign to beat the living shit out of this impudent little Hispanic chap.

"You don't know who I'm related to, you can't touch me, and I'm not afraid of you motherfuckers."

I smiled. Then I purred, like a cat about to eat the canary (4)
"They're not here, yes we can, and yes you are."
"No, I ain't, and none of you are gonna do shit."
Fourteen verrrrrry hostile eyes turned to their leader, with a look that screamed "say the word **now** or we're gonna do it with or with**out** you're divine fucking permission."
I held up my palms dramatically as if to say "it's out of my hands."
The behavior management guys left.
I folded my hands.
The Monkey House exploded,
And Roberto Chavez learned three things in thirty seconds:
We don't care who you know.
We can, and will, touch you.
Fear can be learned just as respect is earned.
Little did Mr. Chavez realize, as I scooped what was left of him into the bathroom for cleanup and re-programming, that he would soon be the lead dog on my little Iditarod sleigh of justice. As you might expect, young Roberto Chavez, having basically challenged the manhood of a room full of young men who don't take kindly to that sort of thing, endured a rather tempestuous first week as a new member of Mr. Step's class.

Eazy-E and DJ Yella (not their real names, could you tell?) were particularly affronted by our young Puerto Rican compadre'; in part because "they didn't like his attitude" and partly because of another reason that I should have noticed immediately.

Roberto, for all of the three days I knew him, was wearing colors

4   Students! That's a simile! Did you catch it? Good for you! You're like sponges. There's ANOTHER one!

WHY ARE ALL THE GOOD TEACHERS CRAZY?

that more or less announced to the world that he was affiliated with a certain "organization of Latino individuals that find themselves to be particularly regal in nature."

Comprende?

Yes! He was connected to a Latino gang! One that was most certainly not friendly with the one E and Yella claimed to represent. How connected? Holy shit, folks, THAT little slice of intel is the coup de'grace of this whole chapter, so you're gonna have to wait for it.

———— ((•)) ————

O.K. Back to the classroom, where Eazy-E and DJ Yella were making a game out of how many pencils they could accurately fire at the back of Roberto's ever-reddening face. I wasn't in any hurry to stop them, or any of the other guys, as a certain amount of non-injurious hazing was necessary to properly welcome any new recruit into our little brotherhood of the misunderstood and disenfranchised. Since Mr. Chavez had a nasty habit of referring to people in less-than-gracious terms (wow, I'm using a lot of hyphenated words in this chapter,) I returned the favor by christening him "dog shit."

"Dog shit, pick up that pencil."

"Don't speak to me in that tone of voice, dog shit."

"If you take issue with that, d.s. (shorthand for dog shit,) we can re-create you first day here."

Et cetera et cetera ad nauseum until I received a phone call from Ms. Chavez, the fiery female responsible for producing this young man and, would later learn, nurturing the heart that would make him a man among boys.

"Hello, is this Mr. Stepnowski?"

"Yes it is."

"This is dog shit's mother."

———— ◦«◉»◦ ————

"Now, humble reader, you're probably thinking what I was thinking at that moment, something along the lines of "Oh shit, what do I say to that?" But what separates me from you, I hope (for your sake) is that I have been subjected, in my teaching career, to tens of thousands of insults, derogatory comments, disparaging remarks, and threats of varying degree. Therefore, I have a mammoth library of sharp, quick-witted comebacks for just about any occasion. Simply put, I possess a veritable Batman utility belt of ready-to-go comebacks that is perpetually available.

None of which came to mind when Ms. Chavez introduced herself as dog shit's mother.

———— ◦«◉»◦ ————

While I took a moment to land on my metaphorical feet and assess how much I admired this woman's directness and confrontational nature, I simply solicited:

"Excuse me?" (in the righteously upset tone of voice of someone who didn't understand why he was being cursed at.)

"This is Ms. Jennifer Chavez"

SIDE NOTE: I named you after Jennifer Esposito, *Ms. You-know-who-you-are*, because that's who you looked like the first time I met you. Very distracting, I must now admit, when a stunningly beautiful woman reprimands you. I have gone out of my way to replicate such a moment with my wife on a near weekly basis.

But I digress…

————))(((————

"This is Ms. Jennifer Chavez, and I have a few questions for you, Mr. Stepnowski."

"O.K., but can you clarify something for me first, Ms. Chavez?"

"Certainly."

"Did you say something about, pardon my language, dog crap when you first spoke?"

(Don't laugh, fuckers, I could have won a Golden Globe for my confused yet concerned affect)

"Yes, Mr. Stepnowski…"

"Call me Frank, or Step."

"No, Mr. *Stepnowski*. Now, as I said, I have a few questions for you."

NOTE: Any cobra that tells you he doesn't **love** the challenge when the mongoose comes at him fired up with self-righteous rage is one lying, cold-blooded reptile.

"Ssso you sssaid - *Jennifer*." I hissed, "I'm all ears."

————))(((————

Later. MUCH later. Much, MUCH later, at Roberto's graduation, Ms. Chavez confided in me that when I called her Jennifer that day on the phone she wanted to reach through the phone and (I'm paraphrasing) "rip my fucking arm off and beat me to death with it."

Ah, say what you will, I *am* a hit with the ladies. Now back to the phone…

———————))((———————

"No, Mr. *Stepnowski*. Now, as I said, I have a few questions for you."

"Ssso you sssaid - Jennifer." I hissed, "I'm all ears."

"I understand that you allow your students to hit Roberto?"

When she said "students" it sounded like she was throwing up a little in her mouth

"Really? That's interesting. Go on."

"Well, is it true, because if it is, then I'd…"

"Ms. Chavez (I was suddenly all formal) if this is going to be, as I think it is, a fairly lengthy conversation where I'm to be accused of a lot of things that have *no* basis in reality, I'd like to hear them all first, so I can dismiss them and get back to teaching the young man at this school that take **accountability** for their actions without trying to discredit the people trying to **correct** the behavior that **led** to the aforementioned actions!"

"Excuse me?"

(The irony that she was using the same "give-me-a-minute-to-recover" line that I did was not lost on me, and I hope you caught it, too. You did? **You** are one smart cookie!)

"I SAID…"

"No, I heard you. Well, then. Here are the things that Roberto has told me…"

———————))((———————

Some 5 minutes later (how the fuck could this kid remember

everything we did to him for three days and manage to forget his homework?) she was finished and it was my turn to launch my defense:

"Yes, Ms. Chavez, it's all true. I allow my students to physically discipline each other to maintain order. I encourage it, in fact. I refer to your son, and the rest of the students, in terms that are politically incorrect and profane. I create creative punishments for inappropriate behavior, many of which involve ridicule or public shaming, and I threaten to ostracize them from the group, along with its protection and benefits, if they dare to tell anyone outside our class. I do all of these things, Ms. Chavez, and that is why I still have a teaching license, why I've won multiple teacher of the year awards, and why I'm continually asked to come to the homes of my students and their families. Clearly, it's all true."

HATER ALERT! If you're one of the clueless tools who read this book and wants my teaching license revoked for behavior unbecoming a professional, yadda yadda yadda, feel free to use the above paragraph as a convenient summary of the stuff I did that was inappropriate. I deny nothing unless it is something I fabricated of which the aforementioned may or may not be. If that's too hard to comprehend, get a teacher to help you, dickwad.

My students, who were listening intently and (stunningly) quietly, since the phone call was forwarded to my room, were very impressed with how I managed to confess to everything and yet make it seem impossible that any of it ever occurred. They were also taking a very keen interest in young Mr. Chavez, who had broken the first commandment of "that which happens in Vegas stays in Vegas."

The phone call ended with me reassuring Jennifer [in a voice that would have given Willy Wonka cavities] that I would continue to work tirelessly to establish a rapport with her son, and that I would continue to maintain a dialogue with her, because "parents are the main educators in the lives of their children." (They love that shit)

She apologized for inconveniencing me, and we ended our phirst phone phight.

I hung up, and smiled at Roberto, who by now knew that running to mommy was not the course of action that he should have chosen to undertake, and I let him know it with style, grace, and subtle verbage:

"You, dog shit, are *dead.*"

Fast-forward three years. Young Mr. Chavez is now 18 years old, and ready to graduate.

He has become one of my favorite students and, if I do say so myself, a responsible young man who I could trust to "re-educate" younger, more troubled kids with the perfect balance of menace and compassion.

Seems I learned a bit over the three years Roberto and I prowled the zoo together. My guys learned along with me, and they became mentors for many of the young men and women that were admitted into Moorzakunt Academy. Although they were a polarizing bunch (some teachers didn't want "hoodlums" and "gangsters" mentoring their kids,) they remained tightly knit and, dare I say, more intelligent than some of the judgmental pricks that I just mentioned.

Aaaaaanyway, graduation day had arrived for Roberto "pooch poop" Chavez, and I was about as proud as a non-parent could be of a kid. Graduation was a small, albeit intimate thing at Moorzakunt. Our whole student population rarely exceeded 200 students so graduation was a small scale event; usually less than 75 parents, teachers, and administrators, in a small basketball gym that was decorated like a high school dance, sitting in folding chairs and witnessing (for most) the last academic graduation that they would ever see. Many of our kids were the first in their families to graduate, and most of the audience looked like they just stepped out of an episode of "Cops" and into our humble graduation ceremony. Lest you think I'm being sarcastic, I tell you that some of the greatest memories I will ever keep from my teaching career happened at those graduations.

I was talking to Ms. Chavez about the time Roberto alerted me when a kid had brought a gun to school with me in mind. (True story – maybe I'll use that for a chapter in the next book,) when something happened that I will keep with me forever.

———

"Yes, it has been interesting, Ms. Chavez. No doubt about it."

"Are you kidding! Call me Jennifer, after everything we've been though, Step!"

No, Ms. *Chavez*. Now about your son."

"You mean *our* son."

"Wow. I'm honored. I always felt he was like a son to me..."

"No, you fool. *Our* son."

And with that she smiled nervously and pointed just over my shoulder.

How I could have missed the rumble of activity that greeted the arrival of MISTER Gustavo Chavez (and the police officers that were escorting him, handcuffed, into the gymnasium) I still don't know. Maybe because Ms. Chavez looked like Jennifer Esposito…

Now I'm a fairly big guy, think NFL defensive lineman big. But Mr. Chavez, at about 5'9", had more muscle in his neck than I did in my whole back. He looked like, if he chose to, he could have made short work of the handcuffs (and the three guards surrounding him.) He also had more tattoos than Lil' Wayne, (in the late 80's when it wasn't so common.) He said something to one of the guards and they brought him over to me. The buzz in the room made it slightly less obvious that my heart was pumping like a wolverine on crack.

At any rate, I now gazed, with a mixture of awe and intrigue, at Roberto's father, Jennifer's husband, and my…

"Hermano."

Apparently, that means brother in Spanish, but Mr. Chavez' accent was so thick, and I was so overwhelmed by the moment that I missed it. Fortunately for me, he understood my look of *"I'd really like to respond I'm not sure what you just said, sir,"* and smiled.

"Brother." Ms. Chavez mentioned in my ear, "he called you brother. Hello Gustavo."

———— ((O)) ————

Mr. Chavez nodded to his wife, with a look that betrayed his tough exterior and gave a flash of an impression that he was sad. Sad to be away from her (I didn't blame him) and sad that he [I would later learn] needed a special dispensation just to be at his son's graduation for an hour. After he and Ms. Chavez touched hands, he turned to me and said, in a mixture of broken English and hand gestures that was as loud and clear to me then as it is in my head to this day:

"Roberto has become a man. That was MY job. Mine. But I was not here to do the job. My wife tells me all that you did. Roberto tells me all that you did. You helped Roberto. You helped my son become a man. I thank you, Mister, and if you ever need it, the name Gustavo Chavez is one you call friend, yes?"

"Yes, and I thank you sir."

We shook hands intensely (his grip, as you might expect, was vice-like) and he smiled sadly and nodded before being taken to his seat, watching graduation, and spending a few minutes with Roberto and Jessica before going back to prison.

That day, I can tell you, I will *never* forget.

⸺◉⸺

Yeah, yeah...I know. You want to know what gang, who Gustavo was, and all that shit. Sorry, folks, I'm dumb but I ain't stupid. I put the names and times of this story in a food processor. I even added and removed a few things to protect all concerned (especially the privacy and dignity of the "Chavez" family.)

Suffice it to say that I fucked with, came to be friends with, and helped graduate, the son of a man who was (so I am told) *very* high up in the power structure of a Latino gang, and his beautifully confrontational wife. Apparently, I could drop that name in certain circles and become invincible or instantly deceased. I don't think I'm likely to test that particular hypothesis any time soon. I prefer to think of them all and just be glad I knew them.

That O.K. with you?

It is?

Thanks.

On to the next story.

Oh, you're gonna love this one...

Pee Pee Cold

Every so often God, or the Gods, or the cast of High School Musical, whomever you happen to worship, play tricks on us, just to let us know how insignificant we are in the grand scheme of the universe. Such a trick was manifest in the form of one Stanley Beckford's penis.

Stanley's tremendously titanic tallywhacker (1) was the source of many a legend before I arrived at Moorzakunt Academy and, having seen the oft remarked upon one eyed wonder worm with my own eyes, I can verify that it did indeed live up to the near mythical proportions assigned to it. But I'm getting ahead of myself.

I first met Stanley Beckford (whose last name I have changed because he looked like model Tyson Beckford; this I will swear on the heads of my children as you simply can not make this shit up) when he ran into me (literally) whilst running away from the two ladies who taught in the special education annex of Moorzakunt Academy.

Oh, did I mention that Stanley, he of the haughtily heralded hammer of the gods, was (as per his "paperwork" circa 1990something) severely mentally retarded? I didn't mention that?

Well he was; and, unless your last name happens to be Diggler

---

1   Remember alliteration students? The repetition of consonant sounds in a string of words? Let's see how many times I can use alliteration in this phallically fascinating fixture.)

(2), he was going to the Olympics with a MUCH bigger javelin than you; a dichotomy which prompted the following touching observation from one Billy Bashwinder:

"That's fucking God's little joke right there, a Corvette body with a Hyundai engine!"

I punched Billy in the arm for that, hard enough to leave a mark for several weeks and make him (a kid who was no stranger to getting hit) cry.

Before you call DHS on me, even Billy knew he shouldn't have said it. As I made very clear in an earlier chapter, you simply do not make fun of mentally challenged people around me or I will hurt you. Now, can I please get on with the story of Stanley's super-sized schlong?

Thank you.

So Stanley runs into me while I was looking up during a lesson on photosynthesis (don't ask me how I remember this shit) and when I recovered enough to ask him if he was okay, Maryanne O'Connor and Marianne Short ran up to me, breathless.

"Two breathless Mary Annes and no Ginger, what's a guy to do?" I quipped, amazed at my own polished pop-culture delivery.

"Shut...up...Step" they gasped, not amazed at all at my lame attempt at humor.

At this point I noticed that Stanley, who I had seen around the school property, seemed very nervous and, more to the point, was clutching at the groin of his Jordache jeans.

"He's got ladies underwear ads...stuffed in there." huffed O'Connor, recovered from her sprint after Stanley who, at a very lean 6'5", could run like the wind; if the wind had a positively ponderous pecker.

---

2   Main character from the movie Boogie Nights, huge pecker, only *his* was the product of special effects (sorry Mark.) Stanley's was an act of God – the Roman god Vulcan from the looks of it.

"He's got *what*?"

"He's got...oh, never mind, just get them out of there."

I know, folks, I know. I thought the same thing

"Are you out of your fucking *MIND*, O'Connor? You want me to reach in and get ladies

lingerie ads from the Sears catalog out of a special ed. kid's crotch? You CANnot be

serious."

"Well WE can't get 'em!" Ms. Short declared, like it was the most natural thing in the world.

I am not often speechless, folks, but this was a special occasion. I looked up at Stanley, who looked like a dog who had just pissed on the Persian rug, and (since I was speechless) turned up my palm and gestured in a way that said "give-up-the-granny-panty-ads-or-die" Must have worked because, much to my chagrin, I soon had a musky wad of plus-sized middle aged women in white undergarments in my hands. (3) Stanley loomed nearby, looking suitably remorseful, the Mary Annes hovered nearby, looking suitably content, and Mr. Long (I would later learn) sat nearby, looking out his window, suitably impressed, and singing to himself "you just might make it after aaalllllll."

I, by the way, couldn't find anyone that wanted to relieve me of the 6" diameter spitball of lingerie ads that had been so precariously close to Moby Dick.

I would encounter Stanley many more times throughout my wanderings about Moorzakunt's sparse school grounds, and he was always an awesome kid who, despite never speaking beyond a few incomprehensible mumbles, always conveyed a warmth and happiness that made me happy just to be around him.

But, as the reviews of this book have made abundantly clear,

3   It has been one of my life's dreams to use that sentence. Dream fulfilled. One more off the bucket list, baby!

you sick bastards don't want to hear the *nice* stuff, so I'll get back to the object of your phallic fascination.

Jade Vermicelli was the school nurse at the time I first encountered young Mr. Beckford, and she had a rather intriguing story to tell about our young protagonist. Oh, yes, she did.

It seems that Stanley needed to use the lavatory one day and, finding the ones nearest to the gymnasium locked, ran in the nurse's bathroom to relieve himself. Jade thought nothing of it, as the nurse's bathroom is often invaded by folks looking for a clean potty and the best hand soap on campus. After a few moments, nurse Vermicelli heard Stanley moaning in what sounded like pain. When she went to the door to inquire about Stanley's welfare, the only response she received was a repeated three-syllable refrain: "pee pee cold! pee pee cold! pee pee cold!"

Righteously concerned that one of our special ed. students might be hurt in some way, nurse Jade made an executive decision on behalf of the student and opened the door. She saw the source of Stanley's discomfort right away. Oh, yes, she did. Even as she told me the story, her eyes grew wide in a sort *of I-know-it's-sick-to-speak.... admiringly...of —it-but-you-weren't-there-and-if-you-were-you-would-have-to-admire-it-too* sort of way.

Stanley's pee pee, dearest reader, was cold because HE was sitting on the seat and IT was hanging in the toilet water.

Go ahead, boys. Go sit on the shitter. Get the little fella as "robust" as you can. Let him hang. (I'll wait.)

Not even CLOSE, is it, champ? I know, I barely touched the water myself. (4)

———————•《◉》•———————

---

4   Remember hyperbole? Well, that's some major fucking hyperbole right there, kids.

The "pee pee cold" story was campus-wide in the blink of an eye, and soon every guy on campus was complaining about his own pee pee being chilly every time he took a piss. The divine irony of a group of professional grown men aspiring to be like an innocent kid with severe learning disabilities was never once lost on me.

The fateful day when I finally bore witness to the leviathan love log myself happened against my better judgment. I am *not* in the habit of checking out other men's equipment, even when the equipment in question is a preposterously proportioned pee pee; nonetheless, the teaching profession calls upon one to do things that are beyond one's comprehension on an almost daily basis.

I was working detention with one David Mullet.

Dave, if you're out there, I almost used your real name because I figured you were one of the only ones that wouldn't sue me, knowing how much we went though together.

So there we were, running detention together, 20+ of the worst kids in Moorzakunt crammed in a little, hot room with two very large men bent on making their last 90 minutes prior to the weekend totally miserable. Dave, who was a powerlifter, and no stranger to student confrontation, had made it a point to have a copious amount of Chinese food and a two liter soda for lunch, knowing full well that it would give him nuclear capability gas. I, being well aware of this incoming assault, drank a quart of whole milk with my three or four peanut butter and jelly sandwiches.

I am lactose intolerant.

Let the games begin.

Forty-five minutes into detention, and 20-plus hoodlumsand thugs are gagging and begging for the powerlifting pair of hysterical laughter to "open a goddamned window, please!"

Mullet and I were having none of it, despite the fact that we were, indeed, making ourselves nauseous with our neurotoxic flatulence.

(NOTE: **None** of those kids were in detention next week, so sit on **that,** behavioral modification specialists.)

It was during this positively ancient Roman entertainment that our boy Stanley appeared behind the building, in full view of every idiot in the room.

Looking for any distraction from the olfactory nightmare that Mullet and I were unleashing, all the detention kids crowded around the window, trying to get Stanley's attention, to no avail. Then Stanley whipped it out and started peeing.

And all Hell broke loose.

————))(())((————

20 plus oppositional defiant youth got a front row view of Stanley's celebrated super-sized celibacy sausage, which prompted the following astute acknowledgement from one Billy Bashwinder:

"That's fucking God's little joke right there, a Corvette body with a Hyundai engine!"

Much laughter ensued, except from Billy, who was shortly thereafter rubbing his arm and crying a bit.

"Take a look," said Dave, like it was the most natural thing in the world.

"Have you lost your fucking mind?" I inquired earnestly "Take a *look*?!"

"We have to, man, and you're closer to the window." Mullet replied, obviously enjoying my anxiety and confusion.

"Why, pray tell, do we *have* to?" I demanded, numbly ignoring the chorus of "holy shit,

look at that thing!" coming from the window.

"BeCAUSE," Childs purred, "if he's STIMulating himself, we're contractually

OB-li-gat-ed to stop him. Now please just see if he's pissing or whackin' off."

———————————

You know, something, folks, I bought it. To this day, I don't know if that bastard was lying to me or not. Hey Dave, if you're out there laughing your ass off reading this:

Bless you for buying the book

Much love to you and the family.

A pox on your pecker, you ugly wart on a salamander's tongue!

So I moved the throng of nasally violated morons from the window and took a quick look. Stanley was, indeed, finishing up a urinary incident of impressive duration. Then, with practiced efficiency, he sheathed the sword.

Do you really want to know?

You do?

Fine.

———————————

There wasn't enough blood in Vlad the Impaler's castle to give that monstrosity an erection. I know rhinoceroses that would weep in comparison. Stanley, I pray that there is a heaven, and that you will someday be allowed to wield that weapon of mass destruction with eternal aplomb.

1 severed ear = 2 front row seats.

Kenny Vango was one of the very few kids at Moorzakunt Acedemy that lived with both of his biological parents. This, as you might expect, was a source of great pride for him. As emotionally disturbed as Kenny was, and he was every bit the emotional train wreck as his counterparts, he maintained a certain ambivalence to the chaos around him because he was, in his words "a normal kid from a normal family." It would not be an understatement to say that Kenny wielded that little piece of information like a righteous hammer, and he didn't care whose fragile psyche he smashed in doing so. Then one day, as has been know to happen in normal marriages across these United States, Mr. Vango and the soon-to-be (once again) Ms. McGill decided that their marital commitment was no longer something they wanted to maintain, and that young Kenny and his sister would soon be splitting time twixt houses in Philly and Bensalem, Pennsylvania.

———————⫸⫷———————

Kenny Vango, to put it succinctly, lost his motherfucking mind.

———((•))———

On Friday, Kenny was a fairly compliant kid with a mild learning disability who got into the occasional fight, spit at the occasional counselor, and forgot his homework; one of the basic llamas in the zoo that was Moorzakunt Academy. When he got off the bus on Monday (after his parents broke the news to him over tacos at *Chi Chi's* on Sunday) he was a large chimpanzee on steroids and speed.

"What's up Kenny?" I inquired, innocently enough, expecting the usual Monday morning eyes down/mumble/shrug combo.

"Fuck you pussy, get the fuck outta my face." and then he deliberately bumped me on the way by, spilling hot coffee on my beloved Oakland Raiders sweatshirt.

My buddy Donnie Jagger, a five foot six, impressively moustached man with 19" arms who worked for the behavior management team (think "school bouncers") glanced at me with equal parts concern and dread.

"Something's up there, bud," he observed, "that is *really* out of character for Kenny."

"For sure," I agreed, glancing unhappily at the coffee stain on my sleeve, "I'll give him some space and see if he spills on his own before I approach him about it."

Don couldn't help himself: "looks like he spilled already."

"Go fuck yourself midget" I laughed.

But we both knew something very wrong had happened to Kenny, we just didn't know at the time it would result in me inadvertently tearing part of his ear off.

I figured we would start the day with some literature. I was given a good amount of autonomy regarding my curriculum given the nature of my students, and the fact that a lot of them passed the CAT tests when they were given every year. It was a dreary Monday. I already knew that at least Kenny was out of sorts, and he probably wasn't the only one. (My guys tended to come back from two days in their home environments in foul moods.) So I took the advice of one of my graduate teachers, Dr. Anthony Amato: "When in doubt, read to them."

A quick word of thanks. If you're out there Dr. Amato, thank you from the bottom of my cold black heart. There have been too many times to count, in classrooms, with my own children, and in various other settings, where the simple act of reading to the individual or crowd (complete with the "voices" and "effects") turned chaos into a peaceful, learning experience. Bless you Dr. Amato, may your house be free of cobras and mongooses.

I was reading Holes (great book, good movie) to the class and stopped to probe for the vibe of the class via some comprehension questions:

"Tyree, why do you think Zero doesn't talk?"

"I don't know, man, he unhappy about somethin'."

"Can you be more specific?"

"Nah"

"Alright. Kenny…"

"I ain't answering shit, leave me alone."

"That's the second time you disrespected me today Ken, there will not be a third."

"I don't give a FUCK! (tears welling up in eyes at this point) I don't!"

What followed was me trying to deal with the elephant in the middle of the room (1) while various members of the class woke up and started questioning Kenny, which led to me escorting (wrestling) him, physically, out of the class to avoid the various fights that almost started when he told everybody to "suck his dick." Once the behavior management team had Kenny, and I got Rodney to a counselor (he was having a really bad day, too, and Kenny totally set him off,) I fielded a million questions about Kenny and Rodney with various euphemisms for "I don't know yet" and got back to reading Holes just as the bell went off and my guys got to go to gym.

It was 9:15 a.m. Mr. Caper and Mr. Basil, our gym teachers, knew I was dealing with something so they said they would be fine without me, which was good, because Tyree, Adrian, and Eric were asleep in my room, and it's always best to let sleeping (emotionally disturbed) dogs (that were probably up 'till 2 a.m dealing drugs to support their fatherless households) lie.

I had just rolled up the sleeve of my sweatshirt to examine the slight burn on my forearm that Kenny's earlier "coffee bump" had caused when I heard the commotion come blasting down the hall, with Kenny's voice above the chorus of chaos.

"Get the FUCK offa me you fucking ASSholes or I'll sneak(2) you too!"

---

1   the elephant in the room is a metaphor for some giant issue that everybody knows is there but tries to avoid. I know, ridiculous right? Just deal with the pachyderm problem and then move on.

2   sneak (sneek) v. – to sucker punch, to strike without warning, to clobber an otherwise unsuspecting victim thereby setting off a chain of events that will invariably get you "snuck" back while simultaneously putting a teacher's license in jeopardy breaking up you and the previously snuck party.

I glance at the clock.
9:25 a.m.
Gonna be a long day.

———⸙———

We pick up our story some thirty minutes later, after finding someone willing to cover my class, getting the natives less restless, and trying to communicate with Kenny in a semi-civilized manner. We are now in the "time out" room; basically, a trailer set off from the main building with a padded floor, protective mesh over the windows, and video cameras, where out of control kids are taken to "reflect on their actions" and generally cool off in the hopes that they can be "reinserted into the learning environment."

Me: "Dude, something obviously happened over the weekend. You've always been a fairly good kid. You've never been disrespectful like this. You know that I care about you, Kenny, after all the things I've done for you, all the shit we've been through, I think I deserve an apology, or at the very least an explanation about what's going on. It's just you and me here so it's safe to tell me whatever's on your mind."

Kenny: "Fuck you, fuck this place, leave me alone and suck my dick." (then he threw a chair at me.)

10 a.m.
Gonna be a long day

One thing I learned from my dad who, despite being a very real, living version of a Clint Eastwood movie bad ass, loves to garden:

Sometimes you have to trim the dead branches so the whole bush can grow.

———⇒»«(◉)»«⇐———

That being said, I had to leave Kenny in a state of misplaced rage and isolation so that I could get back to 12 other young men who needed my help. By the time I got back to my class, Gabriel Okay, my Nigerian friend and resident computer guru of Moorzakunt, had seen enough of my little cherubs:

"Deez leetle pieces of sheet ah craziah den *my* little pieces of sheet! I don't for de life o' me know how ya deal wit dat bunch of aneemals all day long."

(You'd be amazed how cool insults sound with a Nigerian accent)

"Thanks Gabe, you the man."

"Ow is Kenny?"

"A work in progress."

"Good luck wit dat. De rest of ya, remember de fahmula."

Formula? I checked the notes on the board and realized that in my absence Gabe took the half hour or so and taught my leetle pieces of sheet *the Pythagorean Theorum!*

"Later Mr. Gabe!" cried the aneemals.

Immediately, 12 versions of "What up with Kenny?"

"Guys," I begged, "I am fried and it's only 10:15, and we have to get a few chapters read, plus review for the test on the skeletal system. If we get that done by noon I'll run you guys off campus for lunch. Deal?"

"What page we on?" came the chorus

Food.

Motivatus maximus.

At some point, the CEO of the school, realizing that the principalship at Moorzakunt was a revolving door after Mr. Long's departure, basically gave me autonomy to teach what I saw fit and reward/punish with the same autonomy. He then told all the new principals as they came in to "leave Step the fuck alone." God bless you, boss. Know that I always did my very best to reward your faith in me.

So we got our chapters read, reviewed for the science test, and make a quick run to the food court of a local mall for lunch.

Guess who was being loaded into a police car when we returned?

—— ((◊)) ——

If you work with these kinds of kids long enough, you come to realize that while they are openly disrespectful, hostile and profane on the outside, there is often a wounded kid inside that, (once you've made him/her feel safe around you) becomes fiercely loyal and empathetic. For that reason, most of my guys dropped their lunches and ran into the midst of the cops loading Kenny into the wagon.

"What did he do?"

"Y'all ain't gotta be rough wit him.

"Kenny, keep ya head up nigga." (Note: Kenny was white.)

I gathered my flock, told them I'd take care of it, got them safely back to class, and talked to the police, who were visibly impressed with the love and concern the guys showed, and how quickly they acquiesced to my demand to get in the building. I told them that lunch had a lot to do with that. Once we had a minute to talk, the officers told me that Kenny had launched into a tirade that involved kicking the mesh over the windows hard enough to break them, and then he kicked and bit members of the management team that tried to restrain him.

I stuck my head in the back of the wagon and saw a kid, openly weeping now, whose whole world had gone from quasi-normal to shattered glass in a few short days.

"Ken, I'll come down to the station after work and make a statement that you're not usually like this. I'll see what I can do for you, but we have GOT to talk when this is all done."

"Okay"

"In the meantime, I'll call your mom and dad if the office hasn't already."

"I don't give a fuck" was all I could make out before he started kicking the seat and crying openly again."

As the wagon pulled away, I checked my watch. Almost 12:45. My eyes traveled to the coffee stain on my sleeve, and it hit me that it was only about 4 hours old. A little over two hours left and then a trip to the station in Philly to make a statement. One small consolation,at least I knew what was wrong with Kenny.

———((•))———

I'm not going to punish you with the rest of the details of the day, so here it is in a nutshell:

1. Get class under control, finish lunch
2. Deal with principal who publicly blamed my absence from campus for Kenny's outburst
3. Defuse class full of emotionally volatile students who now want to kill principal.
4. Teach history and grammar, with some conflict resolution and life skills writing thrown in there for good measure

5. Drive to police station, make statement, gather information.

6. Get home, call Kenny's dad, get the story about the impending divorce.

7. Call Kenny's mom, now at a different phone number, get similar details.

8. Sit on the floor munching recently delivered pizza, thinking "at least his mom and dad have similar stories, their divorce might not be as messy as my parents' was"

9. Get half assed workout in, trying to clear head for tomorrow. Unsuccessful.

10. Mark papers, watch 11:00 news, pre-read chapters for tomorrow and make notes.

11. Bed, sometime around midnight. Proceed to sleep restlessly.

Sound familiar? You must be a teacher! Bravo!

The rest of the week was *predictably chaotic* (3) until Friday afternoon, when the student population either enjoyed rewards (gym activities, video games, etc.) or punishments (detention, clean up duty, etc.) based on whether they earned appropriate points for the week.

Kenny, despite a MONUMENTAL effort on his part to "keep it together" all week, which included volunteering (with a slight suggestion and some financial assistance from yours truly) to pay for new windows, was placed in detention, even though he earned just enough points to stay out.

I could see storm clouds gathering around him as he read the list. I told him that he wasn't going to be in detention, that I would

---

3   oxymoron – two words that shouldn't go together: predictably chaotic, jumbo shrimp, Icy Hot, honest politician, overpaid teacher, …you get the point, right?

talk to our principal, and that he should calm down and keep it together as he had done for most of the week.

Know what they say about "good intentions paving the way to Hell?" Sometimes "they" really know what they're talking about.

At this point, I will exercise some artistic license in "re-naming" because I don't want you to seek out and destroy the principal in question, who demonstrated total heartlessness and lack of understanding for [what I will loosely refer to as] one of his children.

"Mr. Dooshbagh," I pleaded, "can we please keep Kenny Vango out of detention this week? His parents are going through…"

"No." Dooshbagh cut me off, "He broke school property and he will serve detention."

"If you'll give a minute of your valuable time," I choked back some vomit in my mouth,"I can explain why that might not be such a good idea for the mental health and welfare of…"

"Detention. And we're done here."

I swear to you I could feel my incisors growing in my mouth. For Kenny's sake; hell, for my sake, I had to try one last time.

"At least let him come to whatever activity I'm covering, that way I can take full responsibility for his actions and we can get to the weekend without…"

Dooshbagh cut me off. Again. This time with a *cat-that-ate-the-canary* smile.

"He *is* in *your* activity, and you're almost late for detention. Room 7. Good-bye."

The door slammed in my face.

There was an "understanding" of sorts with every principal that I never worked detention (4) , largely because my students, being the biggest, meanest kids in the school, under my supervision, were almost always dealt with "in house" by me, freeing up the behavior management team from what could be serious physical altercations all week. Furthermore, my guys would often *help* the team chase down some of the faster more reckless younger kids, and "talk" to them afterwards. Almost always resulting in a quickly reformed, sincerely apologetic youth.

This understanding was on temporary hiatus in Mr. Dooshbagh's eyes. Eyes that seemed determined to engage me in a power struggle over his version of control and mine. Obedient to the cause, I walked into Friday afternoon detention. 21 of the worst of the worst, locked in a 15' by 15' room for 90 minutes on a Friday afternoon, with all the anger and misplaced anxiety at a fever pitch.

All of the kids shit themselves when I walked in. A variety of comments flooded the room, all versions on a theme:

"What the fuck is Step doing here?!?"

I silenced all of them with a look that could have softened stainless steel.

Did I say *all* of the kids shit themselves? I meant all but one.

Kenny sat in the corner like a wounded animal, his eyes conveying equal parts disappointment in, and hatred for, me. Alas, you only hurt the ones you love. A cliché that was about to become manifest in the very room that neither Kenny nor I should have occupied.

Within the first few minutes it was evident to every kids in the

4   I know I was working detention in the previous chapter but, as I said, these
      stories aren't in chronological order.

detention room that something bad was going to happen between this angry, defiant, haunted white kid that was never in detention, and the large, clearly agitated instrument of righteous cruelty that was trying his best to keep a lid on a boiling pot for an hour and a half.

It started, if memory serves me, with Chris Johnson asking to use the bathroom. The bathroom breaks for detention kids were counted and monitored, even though the lavatory was five feet away. I agreed, but as I opened the door for him, Kenny tried to push by Chris and I, saying "I need to go first." He was looking for a confrontation, and I knew it; fortunately, so did Chris, who was much bigger and a frequent flyer in Friday detention.

"Get him away from me Step."

"Go to the bathroom, Chris." I replied, eyeballing Kenny hard, "and I'll handle this

without your help or permission, clear?"

"Whatever, but dude's been looking for a fight since he got here."

"Fuckin' right!" Kenny sneered, "I'll beat the shit out of anyone up in this bitch!"

I honestly think a special education battle royale would have exploded right them if the look on my face and my body language didn't scream *this guy is going to snap any second and you will know he did from the trail of dead bodies littering the hallway.*

Seconds pass like hours when a bunch of angry kids filled with misplaced anxieties are forced together in a hot, crowded room; especially when one of them WILL NOT STOP taunting the whole stinking lot of them!

"Bunch of bitches. You won't do nothin' etc.etc.etc…" for what seemed like forever until I couldn't take in any more. I am still embarrassed that I let my professionalism slip, but my nerves had reached their breaking point. Just as Harry Johnson and Chris Johnson (no relation) were about to pounce on Kenny due to his incessant bullshit, I let him have it:

"ENOUGH!" I thundered, loud enough to stun everybody to a temporary halt," Kenny, you're not the only kid in the world whose parents broke up. Shit, you're one of the few kids in this school who even KNOWS both of his parents, so **GIVE IT A FUCKING REST!"**

As 19 really troubled kids nodded in agreement, Kenny glared at me with just the wrong mix of desperation and utter contempt. Then he charged me.

The primal scream that came out of Kenny sounded like he was exorcising all of his demons at once; and he looked at me like I was the cause of all of them." Think that sounds overly dramatic? Check with *any* special ed. teacher you know and ask them if they've been on the receiving end of that look or that sound.

I'll wait.

See, I told you I'm not making this shit up.

So Kenny came at me, fast and hard; too fast for any of the kids to react and too hard for me not to take him seriously. Nonetheless, he was still just a wiry 15-year old kid and I was, to put it mildly, not.

I caught him coming in and with a fairly elementary move, spun him into a corner, where he stood, embarrassed and infuriated. As any special ed. teacher knows, any type of violence is a catalyst to these kids, and Harry Johnson and Bartram Walker started shoving each other in the opposite corner, distracting me just enough that Kenny could come crashing into me full speed, arms flailing and mouth spitting.

More annoyed than hurt, I brought my hands under his armpits and hurled him backward. I finished breaking up Harry and Bartram, the latter of which waked over to Kenny's sobbing body, laying next to a metal bookshelf that had the faintest trickle of blood running down the side of it.

"He leakin' (bleeding) Step."

You know those scenes in the movies where everything slows down and everything you see and hear gets distorted? I was having one of those moments.

But only for a moment.

I shot over, cradled Kenny into my arms and flew to the nurses office. Kenny's bleeding head, and the very uncommon look of fear on my face were enough for her to drop [literally] her latte' and spring into action. As I stood there, recovering, Bartram walked up next to me and handed me something. I looked down at the tiny object in my hand.

"Do you know what this is Bartram?" I asked quietly, "my teaching career."

"No it ain't " he cheerfully replied, "That's a piece of Kenny's ear that I found on the floor."

"No way" you're saying to yourself.

Yes way. I was handing the school nurse, as if she could do something about it, the top third of Kenny's ear which, it was later discovered, caught on one of the shelves when I threw him out of the way after he attacked me in the midst of the fights breaking out in the detention room.

The odd thing was, I wasn't thinking about my job at that point. All I could think about were all of the fucked up events that led up to this moment, and I felt guilty that I hadn't done more to prevent this from happening. That kind of ridiculous guilt in the face of a fucking avalanche of ignorance and lack of caring is a burden that every decent teacher knows all too well.

Anyway, Kenny went to he hospital, the kids from detention

helped me clean up the room in dead silence, and everybody got on their busses and went home for the weekend. I was on my way back to the nurse's office to call Kenny's parents (no cell phones back then, kids) when Mr. Dooshbagh asked me "how was detention, I trust you enjoyed it?"

Then it occurred to me. This fucking moron *had no idea*. How was that possible? Didn't the nurse tell him? Didn't he see the *ambulance* in the parking lot? How was it possible that he *didn't know*?

I would find out a bit later in the year exactly how that was possible; suffice it to say that Mr. Major Dooshbagh became one of many principals that didn't last out the year at Moorzakunt Academy. But I've already dedicated too much time to that useless twat, so back to the real hero of this chapter.

Kenny wasn't there when I got to the hospital, but he was when I got to his house. So were his mom and dad. Kenny greeted me like the past seven days never happened.

"Hey Step, like my new earring?" he laughed, showing off the heavy bandaging.

"Very nice," or something lame like that, was all I could manage. I went right up to Mr. and Ms. Vango.

"Can I speak to you both outside."

"Don't bother." Said dad. Mom nodded in agreement.

"Fine," I said, trying not to choke up at the thought of the only job I ever wanted to do dying a lonely death in a courtroom. "But understand this. You *know* me. You *both* know me. And you know that while I may have had a lapse in my professionalism I never have, and never will harm a kid, especially your kid. Sue me if you want, take my ability to teach, but…"

"Step," Ms. Vango cut me off, "stop."

"I'm sorry, but it's important that you know how I feel. I'll go now."

"Step," she and Mr. Vango almost laughed at my discomfort, "we said don't bother 'cause we knew what you would say. We know all you've done for Kenny, and we know how seriously our problems have affected him. Thank you for working with him and putting up with our mess, we would never dream of suing you, and we don't think any less of you. Please give us that much credit. We're going to try to work something out so that this doesn't tear Kenny up so bad."

"That explains his drastic mood change. He wanted to kill me a few hours ago."

———◦«◦»◦———

"We heard," they answered in tandem, "sorry about that. Again, our problem spilling over onto you."

The only response I could manage was to look at the coffee stain and say

"Yeah, literally."

Even now I wince at the inadequacy and lameness of that response, but my head was buzzing with all of the information I had to process, the fact that I still had a job, I wasn't getting sued, Kenny was O.K., and all the other events of the day. I was having an out of body experience until I remembered that I had to pick up my girlfriend from work at 6:30 and I was going to be late.

"Um, I'm really sorry, but I gotta go, I have to...I gotta go. Thank you for being so cool about this. Thank you. You know I love your kid. I gotta go." (5)

5   To the best of my recollection, that's what I blabbered leaving the house. I honestly don't remember, I was pretty fucked up (mentally) at the time.

I Picked Dawn up at work, took her to dinner, and starting telling her my story. Somewhere in the middle of my amusing anecdote, the reality of the whole day hit me and I started crying quietly but profusely right there in the middle of Pizzeria Uno. I guess I recovered quick enough to finish my individual Sporkie pie, let Dawn pay the bill, and drive home. I guess I slept soundly that night, but I had to bartend on Saturday and Sunday nights, then it was back to the asylum on Monday. Better get my story ready and practice it enough that it sounds matter-of –fact by then

The good thing about a place like Moorzakunt, or any place filled with volatile teens and crazy adults, is that, if you give it a minute, some major issue will come along and eclipse yours.

So it was back to business as usual; that is to say, insanity in the guise of education, soon enough.

The art teacher started calling Kenny "Holyfield" after the famous boxer whose ear was unceremoniously chewed off by Mike Tyson, and the nickname stuck. Kenny liked the attention, I was glad he was back to normal, and life went on.

———————◦((◦))◦———————

Two weeks later, on a whim, my best friend, Bobby Ellis, and I went to Brendan Byrne Arena in New Jersey to see the rock group Rush. We bought tickets at the door so they sucked, of course. We figured we would be sitting up in the clouds but we didn't care – we went to every live show we could in those days. Standing in line to get our tickets checked, Mr. Vango walked up to us. I forgot that he worked for the security firm that worked concerts, shows, and such. He checked where we were sitting, and whispered in my ear.

"I'll see you later"

I told Bobby the story about the ear fiasco and he joked that he didn't want to sit with me.

"That gentleman is gonna come all the way up here and shoot your ass," he laughed,

"and nobody'll know because it's gonna be so loud and we're up her in the stratosphere!"

That made me think a little too much. Truth be told, I don't even remember the opening act, as I was going over possible scenarios (all bad) in my head. Right before Rush started, Mr. Vango appeared beside us.

These are the guys." He said to the very official man next to him

A very tense moment passed before the very official looking man handed us laminates and told us that he hoped we enjoyed the show.

"Follow me, gentlemen," Vango smiled.

We did.

Right down to the *5th row front center* of the stage.

We were VIPs!

If I'm lyin' I'm dyin'.

As the thundering bass of "Tom Sawyer" made my legs vibrate Bobby yelled into my ear:

"This guy that moved us, you cut his kid's ear off?!?"

"Yeah," I screamed back, "but it was a complete accident and they understand."

"Fuck that shit," Bobby yelled back, "break his leg next time, maybe we'll get

backstage!"

I just turned and looked at him and mouthed the words "Not funny."

He laughed and screamed over the music: "The fuck it ain't! It's hilarious!"

And you know what? In hindsight, he's right.

Jesus tells me I'm full of shit.

There I was, in the middle of [what I though was] a pretty profound lesson on the ability of today's teenagers to multitask when Jesus burst in and announced:

"The world is just as fucked up as it always was, we just *know* it now because of the internet and shit!"

"I'll buy that," I agreed, "but what, exactly, led to this revelation Jesus?"

"I was taking a smash (1), and I always think good when I'm on the toilet."

"You think **well** on the toilet, and you've got toilet paper on your shoe."

Lest you think I would correct the icon of Christianity, or let him speak such improper English, I feel that I should clarify: Jesus, in this case, wasn't the Lamb of God (pronounced like you were asked, as a group, to do something unpleasant. "Who has to pick up the dog shit? *Jeez, us?*)

Instead, this was Jesus, pronounced like you were calling on the head of the Greek Gods

(Hey, Zeus! Wanna play dodge ball?)

"Damn!" Jesus (pronounced Hey Zeus) Marquez Rosales observed, puling off the clingy toilet paper, "but I'm right, right? The

1   "smash" - taking a dump; defecating; going poopie, #2, putting the kids in the pool, *etc.*

world is super fucked up but it always was, just the Romans and shit didn't have cell phones and cable so they didn't know how fucked up the people in Africa were."

"I think there's some merit in that argument, now let's try it with 100% less profanity and in full sentences."

"Aw damn"

"Not a sentence."

"No, I mean aw damn, I forgot to tell you that the toilet is overflowing."

The sudden awareness of dampness around my feet gave me the slightest impression that Jesus might just be telling the truth, albeit 5 minutes too late. The chorus of obscene euphemisms for "jeepers, that smells offensive" that suddenly thundered from the dirty dozen students in my class confirmed my worst fears.

"I think it was full of shit."

"Thank you Jesus."

Here's something they don't cover in your secondary ed. courses in college (2):

How to remain your composure while keeping 12 special ed. teenage males under control while plunging a toilet that is overflowing with the contents of a Puerto Rican's weekend eating habits. (fajitas on Sunday, it would appear.) Should you ever be faced with such a situation, here's what worked like a charm for me. *(P.S. Don't be naïve future teachers. You will be asked to do things that were never covered in your precious textbooks, trust me on this.)*

So anyway, the first thing I did was to convince the disgusted horde that since *I* was going to do the *really* nasty work, the least they could do was help.

2   While I have not, in fact, attended every university, I am reasonably sure of this.

Much laughter ensued.

———◎———

Then I pointed out that I had enough money to buy the willing volunteers lunch should we have the entire mess cleaned within fifteen minutes.

Much running for cleaning supplies and rubber gloves ensued.

———◎———

Food…say it with me…Motivatus Maximus.

After I convinced the school nurse that there really was no *medical* emergency (can't blame her, really, twelve large males run into her office and swipe the rubber gloves…)

Some 14 minutes and change later, after using a dustpan for a purpose for which it was never intended, and a practical lesson on the importance of "double bagging" the aforementioned dozen denizens of Mr. Step's class used up all the available antibacterial soap in the aforementioned nurse's office. All that was left to do was contact the maintenance guy about possibly wet-vaccing the carpet between the volcano-like lavatory and my classroom. I assumed that, since my boys and I did the unspeakable work, he wouldn't mind at all cleaning up a 5'x4' piece of carpet at some point during the day. Know what they say happens when you assume? You make an "ass" out of "u" and "me."

Cute.

Unfortunately, true as well.

It should be noted that the maintenance guy at Moorzakunt Academy, whose name rhymes with Falbert, was a very little man with a very big inferiority complex. For some reason, he didn't like me; despite the fact that (at least regarding my room) I did his fucking job. One thing all the principals I ever worked for must admit, I keep my yard clean, and I insist that my students do the same. Anybody who ever suffered under me for a full school year was borderline OCD by he time he/she finished.

———— ((•)) ————

Back to Falbert the maintenance facist. He pissed and moaned that "the toilet should never have been that full, blah, blah, blah"

"No shit," sneered Tyree, without a trace of irony.

That was all maintenance dude needed.

"Forget this. I'm not one of these kids"

I was, for once, speechless.

"I'm not one of these kids. You can't talk to me like that. You *won't* talk to me like that."

"Step didn't say nuthin', " Tyree defended (God bless him) "I said that."

While I was deeply touched by he defense of my honor, I sensed that a *challenge* of sorts, had just been issued by this very small older gentlemen whose load I did my very best to lighten. My students sensed it too, and they are, metaphorically speaking sharks around blood when hostility is in the air.

Maintenance guy: "He (yours truly) knows what I mean."

Yours truly: "Men, we have clearly disturbed Mr. _____ Let's let him get back to work. I'm sure he's very busy."

Quick summary of reactions:

- *My kids* looked at me with "WTF?!" written all over their faces (understandable)

- *I* maintained a look of calm innocence on my face (Oscar worthy)
- *Maintenance guy* strutted away with a "guess I told him" smirk on his face (delusional)
- *Jesus* looked absolutely thrilled that everyone forgot he blew up the toilet (again, understandable.)

———————•《0》•———————

After being barraged with questions all along the theme of "why didn't you rip that motherfucker's arm off?" I quieted my buzzing hornets and explained that violence never solved anything, and that the only way to demonstrate real power was to show compassion. I'm not sure if that's exactly what I said but I gave thousands of those speeches in my teaching lifetime and they were all moving and beautiful. Occasionally, they were actually listened to.

True to my word, I treated my mini maintenance mob to lunch; actually I gave them each two bucks and told them they could put that toward their totals. I'm generous, folks, but I'm still a teacher (read: not rich.)

After our post potty pandemonium feast, we resumed our lesson on how modern students possess an evolved type of multitask learning unlike the previous generation. The day went by fairly quickly, and (despite the faint odor of fajita feces from the rug) smoothly.

The End.

———————•《0》•———————

Yeah, right.

Let me tell you something about me and something about

"emotionally disturbed" kids that any friend of mine or any special ed. teacher could tell you.

Me, I'm not into public displays of toughness. I was raised by a father who taught me that the true measure of a man is what he did when nobody was looking. That being said, me and maintenance midget had a very meaningful conversation, in private, when I stepped into his office and asked him, in so many words, if there was any unfinished business between us. I don't remember exactly what I said but I was involved in thousands of those talks in my teaching lifetime and they were all moving and beautiful.

———— ◉ ————

Now, about my beloved "emotionally disturbed" kids. First of all, I have yet to meet a teenager that isn't emotionally disturbed by some definition. However, those that are classified as such are a handful to teach, but once they care about you, they're as loyal as Doberman pinschers on crack and twice as dangerous; and they're *smart.*

Smart enough to take the previously double bagged remnants of a lavatory conundrum out of a dumpster, locate the pick up truck driven by a cantankerous maintenance man, get the truck open, (3) and...

I'll let you create your own visual. As for me, I get choked up just thinking about it.

I do love those boys.

---

3   hey, 1/3 of them were Puerto Rican, probably took 'em all of 30 seconds

Fuck France

This chapter ought to kill any chance I have of selling my book in Europe. Alas, such are the ramifications of refusing to omit funny shit from one's book.

When the terrorist attacks happened on 9/11, I happened to be in front of a room filled with young men who didn't scare very easily. That changed real fucking quick when my buddy Gabriel Okay came into my room the *second* time. The first time Gabe came in, he announced, in his often-imitated Nigerian accent:

"Step, a plane crashed into one of de twin towahs, can you believe dat?"

"Damn," I retorted, "the pilot had to have had a heart attack or something, to be flying

that low in a major metropolitan area."

Gabe left, and I went back to teaching whatever I was teaching. Then he came back, with a look on his face that told the whole story before he even opened his mouth.

"Step, anudda plane crashed into the udda twin towah; both of dem have collapsed."

When the doctor told me and my wife that my first son, Cain, had died, I heard it for the first time – a loud silence. This was another one. Looks were exchanged, minds raced, and kinetic energy started to build as the reality of just exactly what was going on started to settle on the inhabitants of my classroom like the dust settled on those souls unfortunate enough to be a ground zero on that day.

I was bombarded with several panicked variations of "Step… what the *fuck* is goin' on?"

Not to be overly dramatic, but any teacher that was in front of a class at that moment, or any similar, potential life changing, moment knows the pressure of knowing what you say might actually be the difference between chaos erupting and self preservation by way of compliance.

My first instinct was to hop in the truck and race to get my own kids out of day care and meet up with their mother. One of my former martial arts instructors was involved with the SEALs, so I have pretty good contingency plan in place if and when the shit ever really hits the fan. However, when I looked at my students, I saw them (for the first time) as other people's kids.

And they were scared.

The gang initiations, the shootings, the drug dealing, car stealing, all of the stuff you would think is scary, are things that don't scare my guys, because they *know* about them, they *understand* them, and they *choose* to be part of them. This was different.

They didn't understand this, and the only thing they *did* know was that they weren't in control. So I thought, and acted, like a father instead of a teacher. (1)

"The first thing you all need to know is that you're safe. I will not let anything bad happen to you. I know a lot of people and I know a lot of things not related to being a teacher and believe me, you're as safe as any people in the U.S. right now. (2) If I had to

---

1   That particular strategy has become my mantra as a teacher, and I highly recommend it to anyone that wants to survive in this business.

2   Not totally true, but the composure of my class was a bit more important than the truth at that particular moment.

make an honest guess, I would say that we just got attacked on our home soil, and that more attacks will probably be reported. Let's get Gabe's class in here, we'll bring the TV in, and I'll make some phone calls before we decide what to do."

———— ((◉)) ————

They seemed satisfied with that, and we watched, together, the events of that day unfold.

———— ((◉)) ————

Fast forward to post "Shock and Awe," and the first thing I'm teaching every day is what's going on in the world. I drew a very detailed map on the whiteboard, and every morning I got up early and wrote (over the area) exactly what was going on in that area; at least, what was reported on/in the various new stations/publications. It took a shitload of work, and the closest I came to homicide at work was when Josh pushed Trumaine into the board and erased both Koreas and half of North America. Nonetheless, it kept the guys informed, and it kept them *calm* as a result. Most of them said they went home and told their families what they heard, and they felt better knowing, too. The biggest problem I had those days were other kids cutting other classes to come listen to the "daily state of the world report in Step's class."

There are worse problems to have.

———— ((◉)) ————

So every morning me, a very large cup of coffee, and several newspapers and magazines would get together in good ol' room 4 for some updating of the map, so that when my tentative teenage terrors tiptoed into town I'd be ready to get them up to speed on the previous day's events on the war in Iraq.

S.N.B.F.S. (Side Note Before we get back to Funny Shit) Although my "O- fficial" teaching degree is in secondary ed. English, I have found that when I do current events with my classes, they are, almost always, riveted to the subject matter – provided I go over it first and "translate" it into terms they can digest and remember. I always tell my kids the same boring story, which I now impart to you:

When I was in high school, I was a pretty smart kid, in the academic sense (dumb as a box of rocks in other ways, but that's another story;) however, for all my vaunted intellect, I couldn't carry on a five second conversation with any adults about what was going on in the world. I knew trigonometry, Latin, and European history, but I didn't know shit about the laws passed, decisions made, wars fought, or people elected "in my best interest." I decided then that when I taught, I would perform with stunning efficiency so that I could gain enough autonomy to sneak some really cool, and useful shit into my lessons under the guise of Literature with a capital "L."

Fucking worked, too. One thing my students will tell you - they might have to re-read Moby Dick to remember all the symbolism and allegory, but they ain't afraid to watch CNN or read TIME magazine, and they can hold their own in the "informed decision making" department. (3)

Shit – started rambling again didn't I? Sorry 'bout that. Back to

---

3   For those of you reading this amazing novel under a rock, who think that having a plethora of contemporary teenagers that read anything beyond *Game Informer* and watch anything beyond *American Idol* is nothing to crow about, I envy your residence in nirvana; just keep your eyes on Cooper and Brittany – they have pre-marital sex and heroin in the suburbs, too.

my "fun with war and profane patriotism" anecdote:

> So I would point to the area we were discussing, like Saudi Arabia, and tell the guys what was going on there related to the current state of the world at war. One of the interesting things that came from my daily briefings was the first time I got to France. Billy, (whose grandfather served in WWII) mumbled 'fuck France."
>
> Me: "Beg pardon?"
>
> Billy: "Fuck France."
>
> Me (inquisitive) "Care to elaborate?"
>
> Billy (confused) "Huh?"
>
> Me (simmering) "Care to explain wwwhhhyyyyy you feel so profanely anti-French."
>
> Billy (suddenly talkative) "Oh, [insert 15 minute dissertation, courtesy of Billy's grandfather, on how the French government have bad mouthed the U.S. and refused to help us since the Revolutionary war.]"
>
> Me (convinced) "Works for me. Fuck France."

Yeah, yeah…I can hear you now: he's teaching intolerance! He's reinforcing ignorance! He's a Polish Jew that hates on the French!

Well I hear the rest of you, too: this book is great! This stuff is hilarious! I can't wait to buy your next book!

Guess which group of outcasts I'm listening to.

"Fuck France!" would be the resounding cheer, every time my intrepid finger would come to rest upon said European territory, and we would move on to a plethora of other places, both friend and foe alike.

Truth be told, I was teaching teenage boys, so I had to rein them in – declaring certain copycat expressions: "Iraq is wack!" (no, Semaj.) "Fuck Iran, too!" (very original, Kenny.) "North Korea can suck my big black dickizzle!" (take your meds, Isaiah.)

Actually, the whole "Fuck France" thing would've faded into obscurity in a week or two, replaced by some new inappropriatism, had it not been for the fact that I got **_formally observed_** during one of my "Step's world news report" lessons.

Uh oh.

For those of you not affiliated with the teaching profession, a formal observation involves one of your supervisors or administrators coming into your class, watching you, looking at your stuff, taking notes, and assessing how woefully inadequate you are as an educator. Usually, they give you a few days notice, so most observations are a fucking dog-and-pony show where shitty teachers give a command performance, while the aforementioned administrators look on in awe as the students wonder "who is _this_ motherfucker and why doesn't he come to work every day?!"

My policy has always been — my door is always open, what you see is what you get. Just don't judge me on one moment in time, unless you're prepared to be judged as such in return. When you're a cocky asshole such as I, you better be ready when somebody walks in that open door.

Especially when that person happens to be Lester Mannheim, the head of the board of directors for Moorzakunt Academy.

Uh oh.

Lester Mannheim was, if I may indulge in a moment of reflection, a pretty "plugged in" guy for a man in his late seventies. In fact, it was his decision to pop in on teachers now and again, so he could see for himself what was going on in the trenches of M.A.

Pretty noble, considering I saw Lester's office at the central administrative building: air conditioning, super premium leather desk chairs, etc…I sure as hell wouldn't leave that to come into my room – kind of like Hermes going into Hades to rescue Persephone. (4)

All that aside, Lester emerged at my door, walker in hands, animated and disoriented, khakis pulled up to just below his chest, coffee stains on his powder blue polo shirt, and [much to the delight of my students] bright orange, tiger striped, Nike shox running shoes.

"They some bangin' kicks old head! (5)" exhorted one Fedor Cruz.

"Thank you, thank you young man" Lester replied. "O.K. if I sit at your desk Step?"

"Mi Casa Su Casa Dr. Mannheim."

"Eh?"

I smiled. "Sure thing Doc."

"Oh, good." He grunted, settling in behind my desk. "What are we learning about today, boys?"

We all looked at each other. "World events. You know, the war and stuff."

Lester rubbed his hands, "Oughta be interesting."

"That's *one* way of putting it." I thought

While Dr. Mannheim shuffled papers, rifled through my desk, and looked around the room, I got back to business. "Right. We left off in Afghanistan where, last night, several insurgents – what's an insurgent? Good job Tyree, several insurgents blah blah blah …"

Then we got to France.

⸻ ((◉)) ⸻

As my finger moved toward the land of great cheese and the Arc de Triomphe, one voice in my head said "just move past it, just

4   Students! That's an *allusion.* Can you dig it? I knew that you could!
5   Those, my elder comrade, are very impressive sneakers!

move past it, nobody'll know." But the other voice, the one that always gets me into trouble but usually results in letters that start with *"you're the best teacher I ever had..."* sneered into my ear, "What you see is what you get, right? You gonna compromise who you are? What will these kids think of you if you do that just because he's in the room?"

Fucking voices. They never take my financial security into consideration.

"Today, in France..."

Billy, who was waiting for this moment, looked at me for a fraction of a second, as did Josh, Marcus, Tyree, and the rest of the political posse, looking for a sign, something to tell them it was alright to engage in business as usual. Billy couldn't wait.

"Fuck...France?" he more inquired than stated.

"Fuck France." chimed the rest of the choir.

That woke Lester up. Literally. It seems that the warmth of the room, his advanced age, the comfort of my desk chair, and my supremely anesthetizing voice had Dr. Mannheim slipping blissfully into Nappyville, USA. Alas, the resounding chant of "Fuck France" roused him but good.

"Whassat your say?" he inquired, the way you ask your mom what she said after she wakes you up on Saturday to do chores.

The moment of truth.

"Well doc, we decided that the government of France is a bit unfair in their view of..."

"Oh, hell yeah." Lester interrupted me, "chicken shit bastards, ask for our help all da time, then when you need 'em, ppphhhtt (farting noise.) Whazzat you said about 'em?'

I was speechless.

My boys were not.

"We say 'Fuck France!'" my class exclaimed, a bit too loud for my taste.

"Yeah, o.k., yeah, fuck'em. France, that is; unless they come to their senses," Lester laughed, " but I wouldn't hold my breath waiting for that, know what I mean?" he laughed as he nudged Josh on the arm with his notebook.

My guys were hysterical.

"That is some good shit, old head!" (6)

" You a funny dude."(7)

" You was in World War I right?" (8)

"Where'd you get them kicks?" (9)

So Lester entertained questions from the knuckleheads for about an hour, until his bladder couldn't take it anymore, and he excused himself, shaking all the guys' hands and telling me how much he enjoyed himself before being escorted to his car by twelve kids that would have normally mugged him.

I received my evaluation a few days later. Dr. Mann praised me for my ability to engage a normally difficult population while guiding discussion related to difficult and potentially volatile subject matter. "Furthermore," he added, "Mr. Stepnowski should be commended for his integrity and ability to incorporate elaborate visual aids into his presentation." He concluded with various commendations and criticized my "lack of display of student achievement" in my decoration of the classroom. (He must have missed those hundred or so tests, quizzes, and projects lining the hallway when he came

6   Your words are very entertaining, oh peer of mine.

7   You, my friend, are quite humorous.

8   I didn't pay attention in American history; furthermore, you appear to be about a hundred years old to me.

9   Where, pray tell, could I purchase a pair of those bright orange, tiger-striped, Nike Shox?

in.) All in all, a five star formal observation.

There's a lesson in there somewhere, but I'll be damned if I know what it is.

Oh well, fuck lessons.
And fuck formal observations,
and…
well, you know.

Intermezzo - What you say, and what we hear

What you *say*	and what we *hear*
1. "This is stupid"	"I am stupid, or (at the very least) too lazy to try to learn this."
2. "This is gay"	"I am confused about my own sexuality so I make inappropriate adjectival references to any work I find frustrating." ALSO, SEE #1
3. "This shit is boring"	"My low attention span, nurtured by years of apathetic teachers, non-involved parents, and low personal expectations, keep me from understanding this. ALSO, SEE #1
4. "I ain't doing this."	"I CAN'T do this."

or (alternative version)

"Not realizing that I am playing right into the hands of the people who are

very heavily invested in my ignorance,
I am willingly throwing away my
education so the aforementioned
people can control, imprison, and/or
kill me with impunity."
ALSO, SEE #1

5. "I don't care."

"Of *course* I care, or I wouldn't even
have *come* to class; alas, I have to *act*
like I don't care because it's not
acceptable in my circle of "friends"
(none of whom really give a crap
about me) to be intelligent.
ALSO, SEE #1

"Please tell this stupid motherf***er that you have two livers."

Danny Coyle: autograph collector, autograph forger, and autograph seller.

Danny Coyle: entrepreneur, perpetual "D" student, aficionado of all things greasy and fattening. Danny Coyle: patron saint of bad decisions and gastric bypass.

Danny was, despite his spherical form, a hustler. He would find out where every sports star, celebrity, and beautiful person du jour would be habitating during their stay in Philadelphia or New Jersey, and then he would stalk and "apprehend" them with a precision and certainty that would have made any bounty hunter proud.

Once they were in his chubby, cherubic presence, the celebrity captive would sign *anything* (shirts, jerseys, shoes, hats, you name it) *multiple* times, to free themselves from the incessant, sycophantic, ranting of this maladjusted meatball. Several very prominent professional wrestlers (even you Hulkster) folded like origami in the grip of my man Dan.

Once he had the potentially lucrative John Hancocks in his grubby little fingers, he would speed home, get on his self-created, and heavily visited, E-bay site and sell the shit faster than it took the blindsided celebrities to sign it. In retrospect, if young Mr. Coyle had applied the same effort and enthusiasm to his studies that he did to his "autograph business," he'd have been a fat Albert Einstein. In his own words:

"Step, Why should I care about geometry when I'm makin' a couple hundred bucks a weekend doin' this?"

"Because you never know when somebody will report you to the better business bureau." I replied, with just a hint of malice in my voice.

"I'm legit! Ain't nothing wrong with my business!" he laughed, eliciting laughter and high fives all around from the rest of the urban youth, many of whom had paid hard earned drug dealing money for dirty socks with Scottie Pippen's name scrawled on them, among other treasures.

"What about those *other*, less ...*authentic* signatures?" I gambled

It sounded like somebody hit a "mute" button, and what appeared to be instant perspiration sprung forth from Danny boy.

Bingo.

"We'll talk later?" I purred

Suffice it to say that my guess [that perhaps young Mr. Coyle had taken the liberty of practicing his penmanship in the name of profit] proved accurate. Long story short, Danny started to focus much more on school and less on hunting down celebrities.

Save your sarcasm, I got him off a wayward path and focused on school. Oh, and I got an awesome autographed poster of Stone Cold Steve Austin for my gym, which I was assured, under threat of dismemberment, was authentic.

Now that Dan the man was focusing the majority of his "efforts" on school, you would think that he'd be the epitome of common sense and work ethic, right?

What's that? You *dis*agree? You *don't* think that a kid who sold semi-legitimate signatures could be trusted?

Wow, you're pretty smart. You should be a teacher.

So there he was, the picture corpulent concentration during one of my famous Biology tests. I say "famous" because something memorable happened every time I gave one. Once I caught David Solaris trying to cheat by keeping his book open on the floor. Problem – it was his **History** book.

Question: What is photosynthesis?
Answer: The place where the Confederate soldiers surrendered.
(Say it with me folks, S-p-e-c-i-a-l E-d)

Another time Isaiah Bryant couldn't remember the parts he needed to label on the male reproductive system, so he went into the bathroom to "cheat." Upon realizing that there was no "hidden information" lurking in his tighty whiteys, he panicked at the loss of time and re-entered the classroom, you guessed it, hanging out. Ladies and gentlemen, I simply cannot make this shit up.

So back to Danny and this month's biology test. He was so obviously looking at Donnie Amato's paper, that Oedipus could have seen him *after* he plucked his own eyes out (Oedipus the King, kids, important book – go read it.) The fact that Danny was cheating was bad. The fact that he was being obvious was very bad. The fact that he was cheating off of the only kid in class with a grade lower than his was fucking stupid with a capital STU, and I was about to tell him so when his hand shot into the air, and Danny Coyle: poster boy for sound bites, asked of me:

"Will you please tell this stupid motherfucker that you have two livers?!"

And I answered him.

Yes I did, I answered him. Loudly.

"FIRST of all, you fat fucking twit, how do you know what answer

Donnie has on his test?"

"My bad," he responded, looking truly bewildered, "I saw you watching me

so I though you was cool with it."

For a moment, I was speechless. Then that moment passed.

"No I'm not *ookaaaay* with it, you moron. One, you're cheating. Two you're TALKING. Three, you're cheating off Amato, the WORST FREAKIN' BIOLOGY STUDENT IN THE WHOLE CLASS!!"

"He's right, you know." Chimed in Donnie Amato.

Speechless. Again. But just for a moment.

"aMAto.....I growled."

"Sorry"

"Back to you Coyle. In response to your *question...*"

At this point it should be noted that I was positively hissing with anger, and the uproarious laughter in the classroom that had accompanied the our animated dialogue had died down considerably, albeit not completely.

"In response to your *question...*no, you most certainly do not have two livers."

Danny looked deflated. "Oh...really?"

"Yes."

Oh...damn." He pondered the situation. "That means that I'm..."

"The stupid motherfucker."

"Yeah....damn. I'm gonna have to study more."

"More?"

"Or just, you know, study...at all."

The class resumed testing. No shit. Education at Moorzakunt was like a medical M.A.S.H unit. Save 'em for today so we can try again tomorrow. I was just resuming my work on a handout for the class when Danny Coyle: captain of the don't when to quit brigade, spoke up:

"Do girls got two livers?"

"NO!"

More laughter and chaos.

I stood up, hammered down on my desk in a way that would have made Thor proud, and demanded that everybody – how did I put it? "Get the fuck back to work before I get medieval on your assess!" (1)

Back to quiet.

Back to the test for them.

Back to the worksheet for me, until...

"How about turtles? *Turtles* got two livers for sure, right?"

Speechless.

---

1   That, my astute reader, is an allusion to the movie Pulp Fiction. You knew I
      was talking about the movie even though I didn't *say* the actual title. Spread the
      wealth, go teach someone else what allusion is (as soon as you're done reading
      this book and recommending it to a friend or twelve.)

From prom chairman to adopted black child in less than 24 hours.

Rashheed (yes, the double "h" was on the birth certificate) Carter, one of my all time favorite students was, if you'll pardon my over indulgence in simile, nice as pie, poor as dirt, funny as hell, and dumb like a fox. We shall come back to one of my most memorable encounters with Rashheed in but a moment, but first you need to know about the one, and only, prom ever enjoyed by the denizens of Moorzakunt Academy - and how the gentle hearted but simple minded author of this chapter came to organize it

It all started innocently enough.(1) I skipped a staff meeting. It was my fourth year at M.A., and I was, in my own deluded reality, a hot shit teacher whose "outside-the-box" methodology made staff meetings and such trivial things beneath me. (2) So, as I was driving home on that brisk October afternoon, I was blissfully unaware that my arrogance was about to lead to one of the most frightening assignments of my entire teaching career.

"If we're going to have a prom, somebody has to organize it," observed Ms. Apple

"I nominate Step!" laughed Mr. Child,

"You can't nominate Step," chuckled Mr. Long, "he's not here to defend himself."

---

1   ASTUTE READER NOTE: Any anecdote beginning with these 5 words is sure to lead to Armageddon.

2   I know, I know, I'm thinking the same thing…what an asshole.

———«(◐)»———

Apparently, the logic of that phrase hung silently in the air for the better part of a minute, and I was subsequently summoned to the principal's office on Monday morning.

———«(◐)»———

"You're prom chairman, Step," announced Mr. Long, "the vote was unanimous."

I learned a valuable lesson that day that has served me well throughout my teaching career. If a group of more than ten teachers agree on ANYTHING, the thing in question is either utopian or apocalyptic in nature.

"You're shitting me," I protested. "I don't know a freakin' thing about proms. I didn't even go to my own proms! And how am I supposed to organize a formal dance for the mutants that go to this place?!"

Mr. Long smiled, "Ask Child, *he* nominated you. Now get going, the prom is in four weeks, so you've got a lot of work to do. I can't wait to here what you're theme is going to be."

I heard him laughing in his office as I walked down the hall.

Note to self "A": Never miss another staff meeting.
Note to self "B": Kill Mr. Child, slowly, at first opportunity.

———«(◐)»———

As it turns out, I was a pretty good prom organizer. I understood the fundamental concept that the prom wasn't about *me*. So I spent a week or so collecting reconnaissance from the student body about what they wanted. I threw out the fucking stupid answers, threw out the uninspired shit, and narrowed it down to what could be done within budget and time constraints, understanding that I would have to bust my ass in the meantime.

As I sit and think about it, that sounds that a pretty good business model for just about any project.

We decided on a patriotic theme, and with the help of the Mary Lou Bomb, art teacher extraordinaire, some very enthusiastic students, my then-girlfriend-now-wife, and a **very** small contingency of teachers willing to help, the gym was transformed into a red white and blue panorama of patriotism. My friend Ricky volunteered his services as DJ, I got local businesses to spring for food and drinks, and Mr. Long contributed out of pocket expenses for additional decorations and such. (A fact that was kept secret until this publication.) The final piece of the promenade puzzle was a huge (think 50'x 25') American Flag that a hardware store in my old neighborhood used to display on the side of the building every Veteran's Day; the owner's name was Mr. Simms, and I thank him for trusting a punk kid with what became the "wow!" element of Moorzakunt Academy's 1992 prom.

Before we cue up the 80's music, dance poorly, and drink lukewarm punch, let's get to know Rashheed Carter. Rashheed wasn't like most of the kids in my class. He wasn't violent, he called everybody "ma'am" or "sir," and he was a black kid with freckles that loved to skateboard and read plays. Come to think of it, Rashheed wasn't like most kids, period.

<hr />

From his name to his mannerisms, he was a wonderful, unique, kid. When I kept my classroom bathroom clean by putting towels, hand soap, and pictures of Maxim girls on the walls and charging a quarter to use it, Rashheed was there every day with 50 cents and a smile. When Ms. Long shut down my bathroom operation, Rashheed dropped to his knees in the hallway and pounded the ground like Charlton Heston in the final scene of *Planet of the Apes*. His intentionally ironic theatrics were lost on the vice principal, and the teachers who snitched on me – but not on me. In fact, 'Shheeds' ability to laugh at himself, while simultaneously offending the sensibilities of hypocritical people, led to the following amusing anecdote:

Rashheed wanted, more than anything in the whole wide world, to dance with Cheryl Dollmyer at the prom. Cheryl was a wonderful, innocent sweet sixteen with a legitimate learning disability and the personality of a 9 year old. She was indicative of the majority of our student body at the time, before we became overpopulated with wanna-be thugs, violent offenders, and males with 90% behavioral issues and 10% learning problems.

———————

Whoops. Almost got off topic there. Next time that happens, just push me off my soap box and tell me to get back to the story, o.k.? Thanks.

———————

So Rashheed wanted to dance with Cheryl, a fact not lost on Cheryl, who though that Rash was the sweetest kid ever. Cheryl's "boyfriend," Ronald Prankowizz, was well aware of this as well. (Note: Ronald was not, in fact, Cheryl's boyfriend. He was just an emotionally disturbed kid that though he needed to "protect" Cheryl from anything with a penis other than himself.)

Ron, who looked like a very pale, very tall, very skinny, version of Harry Potter was nuts enough to threaten yours truly with "hot death" for "getting too close" to Cheryl after I patted her on the shoulder and congratulated her on winning a spelling bee.

Nice kid, but nuttier than a Christmas fruitcake.

The problem: Rashheed's grandmother (and legal guardian) could afford to neither buy Rash anything remotely resembling formal wear nor drive him back to school for the prom, as she was also guardian to Rashheed's two [much] younger cousins.

To summarize: poor kid just wants to dance with his secret crush, psycho kid doesn't want poor kid anywhere near her, object of affection blissfully unaware of drama and willing to dance, but lingering shadow of inner city poverty looms heavy.

Enter:

SuperStep! vanquisher of all things that are just plain wrong.

———>((•))<———

I volunteered to take Rashheed home with me, get him ready for prom, and drop him off at grandmom's after the big dance. Grandma agreed (I know, unbelievable, right? This woman trusting her boy to some strange white man with one abbreviated name,) but she did; she insisted, however, that she would get a ride to the school and pick him up when it was over. You never argue with grandma; thus was an agreement reached.

By the way, I told Rashheed, (and Cheryl) about all this within earshot of Ronald Prankowizz *very much on purpose*, so if you think I'm going straight to heaven for my altruism – think again.

FRANK STEPNOWSKI

So I take my man Rashheed home to my apartment in Fishtown after our half day of school. Fishtown was not what you would call "culturally diverse" when I lived there. Nor were my neighbors what you would call "racially sensitive." Most of 'em didn't like me to begin with, so I could just imagine the litany of "what is he doing bringing this nigger kid into the neighborhood?" going on behind closed doors.

Just seeing all the doors shut and blinds peek open as Rash skateboarded down the street to my apartment gave me an idea.

A wonderfully, Grinchy, idea.

"Hey Rash, want to fuck with my racist neighbors?"

A few minutes later, Rash was practicing his skateboard tricks outside, grinding the curb, kick flipping with youthful exuberance while the nosy neighbors began peeking from their house in greater numbers, unaware that I was watching them form my perch, wondering "don't any of these people work?" When I though our audience had reached it's fullest potential, I exploded out of the front door, whip (courtesy of an old Indiana Jones Halloween costume in hand.)

"Boy, didn't I tell you to wash them dishes?" I howled

Rash, for his part, played his part so well that I nearly lost it in mid performance. He dropped the skateboard and covered up like a previously abused child.

"I's sorry mistah Step, I reckoned I could practice a bit fuhst."

"I'll practice on your ass if you don't get in that house and do them dishes!"

"Yessir, Yessir, I is truly sorry sir," as he clutched his board and bounded into the house.

"It is getting impossible to hire good negroes these days!" I exclaimed as I slammed the door.

When we got inside, we moved the dishes around loudly as we

laughed 'till tears came out of our eyes. (3) Dawn Marie, my then-girlfriend-now-mother-of-my-four-children, having insisted that she make lunch for me and Rashheed, showed up and Rash came inside – giving my asshole neighbors plenty of time to burn up the phone lines. "Miss Dawn," as he kept calling her, had other motives (as I well knew, sneaky bitch that she is.) During lunch, she mentally sized up Mr. Carter, and returned about an hour and a half later with dress pants, a shirt, and a tie that fit him perfectly.

As God is my witness, I don't know how you women do it.

Dawn told him that Cheryl would never be able to resist him now. Rash, with tears in his eyes, said he would pay her back as soon as he could. Dawn threatened to rip his arms off if he ever suggested such a thing again.

"Yes Miss Dawn, thank you."

"You're welcome, hon."

NOTE: If I could get a nickel back on every dollar "Miss Dawn" spent on my students in my lifetime, I could have printed this book on golden leaf paper.

"How much did that all cost?" I inquired.

"Shut up and let Rashheed get a shower while I show you what *you're* wearing."

"Yes, Miss Dawn."

—————●((●))●—————

---

3   Yeah, yeah, I can hear some of you from here. "It's easy for you to laugh about slavery, you were never a slave, etc. etc." Yeah, well neither were you so shut the fuck up. If, by some twist of fate, you *were* enslaved at a point in your life, I assume you now possess enough respect for just being alive so as to be able to laugh at life's absurdities, and I thank you.

About an hour later, Dawn looked great, and so did Rashheed and I, both learning simultaneously that when a woman wants to dress you, you're best not to argue. We hopped in the car and I realized, too late, that Rash had on skateboard sneakers.

"You didn't think of shoes." I reminded Dawn

"Yes I did," she replied, "but those look comfortable, and they're part of his identity."

"Yeah, but…"

I got one of those "do *you* want to get laid on prom night?" looks

"Yes, Miss Dawn."

———— ((◉)) ————

Judging from Rashheed's chuckle, I think he knew what just happened, so I threatened to whip his ass again. He responded immediately, and in character:

"Yessir, Mr. Step sir, I reckon I'll stop laughin' at you now."

Rash and I started pissing ourselves again, while Dawn just shook her head.

———— ((◉)) ————

I could give you all the details about the prom, but only two things matter to this story.

Rashheed danced, several times, with Cheryl, who kissed him on the cheek and told him he was "so nice." I don't believe Rash has since washed that cheek. (Ronald was…oh, shall we say, "prohibited"… from interrupting by several of my more menacing students, all of whom couldn't wait to help Rashheed "put his thing down.")

Mr. Child got projectile diarrhea from a rather "modified" cup of prom punch. Revenge, indeed, is a dish best served cold. On ice, actually.

———«(◊)»———

Prom night drew to a close, and Mr. Long and Mr. Kopp (my mentor, more on him later) both accosted me with satisfied smiles.

"For somebody who didn't want this job, you did nice work," Long reassured me.

Kopp added" look at the looks on those kids' faces, how can you not feel good about that?"

I acquiesced, but in truth, the smile on Rashheed's face after he danced with Cheryl made the whole thing worthwhile.

"I'm glad Child volunteered me," I admitted

"Yeah, where is Child?" asked my mentors.

The potential of that question, combined with the insidious smile on my face, hung silently in the air for about 10 seconds.

"You're going to Hell, Step," they concurred.

No way, Jose', I'm heaven approved. Just ask Rashheed's grandma.

———«(◊)»———

When I walked Rash outside to meet up with his grandmom, I was surprised to be photographed and hugged, in that order, immediately upon exiting the school.

"Look at my young man!" she gushed, "so handsome."

I sat on the grass in my suit and played ninja turtles with Rashheed's younger "siblings" while pictures were taken from every angle; when the grandmaparazzi was done, she ordered all of the kids, and her adult niece, into the niece's car, leaving me standing there with grass stains on the ass of my suit and Raphael and Donatello in opposite hands.

"You are a good man. You made Rashheed very happy," she professed, with tears in her eyes but a dignity I aspire to achieve someday before I die, "you must know that I consider you a son from this day forward."

Sometimes, albeit rarely, I know when to keep my mouth shut, nod, and accept the weight of the moment. She kissed me on the cheek, squeezed the Raphael hand, and got into the car. I handed the little boy the ninja turtles and told Rashheed I'd see him on Monday. When I turned around, Dawn was standing with her arms folded, *totally* digging me. How could she not?

I just got adopted by grandma.

Sometimes, I know when to keep my mouth shut, nod, and accept the weight of the moment.

Sometimes I don't.

—◉—

"You are SO lovin' me right now."

She rolled her eyes.

"You get to go home with me tonight, but only because grandma loves you."

Somewhere, in a less than aromatic lavatory, Mr. Child (as he would later admit) was wishing for me to go to Hell.

Maybe, but not if grandma has anything to say about it.

WTF NJD

I fully expect to get an Email from every teacher that reads this chapter saying, "I can top that!" To which I say: I know! I Know! That's what I'm trying to tell everybody! Teaching is a whole hell of a lot more than writing up pretty lesson plans and talking in front of a bunch of kids all day. Sometimes, albeit rarely in some cases but frequently in others, the teaching profession takes a wrong turn at the corner of *How it's Supposed to Be Boulevard* and *Didn't See That Coming Avenue* and things get…well, freaky.

The first time I had a WTF NJD (<u>W</u>hat <u>T</u>he <u>F</u>uck, this was <u>N</u>ot in my <u>J</u>ob <u>D</u>escription) moment, I wasn't even a full time teacher yet. I had completed my student teaching and my practicum training and, waiting on a full time position somewhere, ANYwhere, I was putting in time as a substitute teacher. If anybody out there can think of a more thankless job than substitute teacher in the public school system, speak now or forever hold your peace.

———◦((◦))◦———

You there, the lady in Chicago…nope, you're wrong.

How about you? No, you, the guy in the red flannel shirt in Wisconsin…no, that's good, but no.

Mike Rowe? Love your show! Dirty? Yes. Thankless? No.

In the back there, the guy with the artificial tan and the little dog…are you serious? No.

———«●»———

As I said, I was still…what?

Fine. The pretty brunette in the scrubs from Lady Lake, Florida…o.k., *MAY*be nurses have a more thankless job, but you gotta admit, it's close.

———«●»———

Okay, I'll take the rest of your submissions for "jobs that are more thankless than substitute teachers" later. They must be typed, submitted in triplicate, and in proper MLA format, and they must be submitted between the hours of 1:00 am and 2:00 am on February 28th. In the meantime, here are some stories that are most definitely in keeping with the WTF NJD theme.

WTF NJD Part 1 – Looking out at Lunch.

I was still a substitute teacher and I was lucky enough to see an eyeball get knocked out of its socket. Yep, hanging by a thread of optic nerve or something <u>out of the socket</u>. I'm on cafeteria duty, two kids arguing over a tray in the line, kid #1 throws a punch, misses, kid #2 lands a devastating right to the temple and POP! goes the eyeball. I'm holding a tray under the protruding peeper, trying not to hurl on the kid's high top Pumas, calming him as best I could until more qualified help arrived, and I'm thinking "everything I've been through in my life and this is the grossest fucking injury I've ever seen and I'm not even a real teacher yet!"

WTF NJD Part 2 – Can you Hear me Now?

Pepito Jalapeno' had a headache. No, he didn't. Pepito Jalapeno' thought he had a headache, what he had was a big roach in his ear. I'll say that again in case you didn't hear me, HE HAD A BIG HONKIN' ROACH **IN HIS EAR**!!!!

Ask me how I know.

Thanks. I'll tell you how I know.

I know because I walked in on our ultra fucking dedicated school nurse, forceps in hand, whilst she was extracting said *periplaneta Americana* from Pepito's right ear.

"Oh, good," she says, "hold this flashlight for me."

Like it's the most normal thing in the world. Oh, sure, sure, let me just hold this here flashlight while you pull, slowly, this titanic cucaracha from my man's ear. I'll just hold this light steady and watch and not scream like a little girl at the sheer horror of the scene before me. Oh, look, it's still ALIVE! Very cool, very cool. That everything? Yes? No, thank *you,* Ms. Vermicelli, I'll try not to be traumatized for the rest of my life.

WTF NJD Part 3 – Hot Hot Heat.

"Where the heck is Matilda? Matilda! Matiiiilllldaaaaa!"

Such was today's quest for my buddy Donnie Jagger: behavior management specialist, accomplished weightlifter, Rolling Stones fanatic, and all around nice guy.

"Lost Matilda again?" Realizing the stupidity of my question too late.

"Nah, bud," Donnie retaliated, "I love the name, can't get enough of it, so I thought I'd wander the halls yelling it out."

Duly chastised, I offered to help look for the missing Matilda, as I was on my one (40 minute) break of the day while my guys went to gym. I was a bit shocked that "Big M." was doing so well at Moorzakunt hide and seek. Finding a 5'10", 300 pound plus black girl with a tendency to scream and flail violently wasn't exactly "Where's Waldo?"

"Kinda *hard* to lose Matilda, ain't it, bro?"

I think Donnie might have strangled me at that moment, had Steve McFlurry not called from somewhere down the hall:

"You better come here, bud! I'm not sure how we're gonna handle this."

Don and Steve had *seen* and *done* it ALL in their tour of duty as behavior management personnel at Moorzakunt Academy, so if Steve was at a loss…I couldn't wait to see the problem.

Or so I thought.

As soon as I saw Steve laughing and shaking his head outside the open door of the front hallway bathroom, I should've opted out of Mission Matlida. Up until I looked into that bathroom, I thought seeing that roach get pulled out of Pepito's ear was going to be the worst visual image on my hard drive.

Or so I thought.

Matilda was a bit chilly, it being mid-November and all, so she found herself a nice warm spot to curl up – on the floor of the tiny bathroom, right next to the baseboard heater. There she was, curled up as best she could around the porcelain potty, rocking and repeating in clipped language, "hot hot heat, hot hot heat, hot hot…"

Oh, almost forgot, she was naked.

Stop laughing, it was *so* not funny. I have retinal scars to this day.

Before you plus-sized ladies start sending me hate mail know this, I loooove the big girls, o.k.? My wife is six foot plus with more curves than the Tour de France, and I liked Anna Nicole better **before** Trim Spa, so my visceral reaction to Matilda had a lot more to do with the fact that she was:

- on a dirty bathroom floor
- naked, with very little personal hygiene (talking about a severely brain damaged young lady here)
- wrapped around a toilet that hadn't been flushed since last usage (most likely *by* Matilda)
- without a doubt, going to resist us wildly when we tried to get her up and out.

Matilda, God bless her, did not disappoint, and the sight of three big, tough guys trying to get her up and into the nurse's office in some sort of decent manner without grabbing the wrong thing or getting hit, spit on, or bitten, was (I'm sure) a sight to behold. At least my guys thought so; they caught the extraction part of Mission Matilda as they were leaving the gym to return to my class. Getting Big M. into that office with my idiots cheering her, laughing at us, and blocking the hallway was like a goddamned UFC fight gone horribly, horribly wrong. I probably would've killed one of them if I had not been acutely aware that it was going to make an amusing anecdote for my book someday.

It should be noted that, for about 3 months after that, every time we had to restrain a kid, Steve would do a dead-on impersonation, chanting "hot hot heat" which made the restraint much harder but always confused the restrainee as he/she wondered why we were laughing our asses off.

WTF NJD Part 4 – Fender gives me the finger

Diarra Fender was one of those kids that I could write a separate book about just based on his exploits. Diarra was, in plain English, a crack baby with an endless list of things "wrong" with him. He wasn't a bad kid, per se, but his complete and total lack of social awareness made him a walking train wreck. Diarra looked like one of those toy monkeys that clangs the cymbals together and smiles and gyrates; he would flinch at ANY movement (guess why) and I don't think he stayed in any foster home or placement for more than a few weeks. He would have to be told almost continually to take his hand out of his pants.

A hyper-sexual, brain damaged, trash talker who would talk shit then flinch and curl up in the fetal position the minute anyone even turned toward him…what a mess. They always kept D.F. from being one of my students because they were worried that my guys would kill him, but that just goes to show you how much the talking heads pay attention – the REAL thugs know the difference between a threat and a charity case, and my guys did more to help D than any of the phony-ass counselors or administrators.

This is not to say that my man didn't give me a plethora of potential stories. Let's see…he took a dump in his backpack and carried it around for a whole period waiting to "dispose of it." He ruined Mr. Springsteen's Cinco de Mayo party by helping himself to big portions of both refried beans and plantains using his *hands* and *feet*. He offered "favors" to a student (use your imagination) for 50 cents so he could buy a bag of chips, and repeated that offer several times during his tenure with us. One thing you have to give him, he didn't want to burden other people with his problems, which is probably why Ms. Indahizzle came screaming into my room when she found him eating his own head lice. All this and more, but since only one Diarra Fender incident happened completely under my watch, and since it fits perfectly into this chapter of "stuff you don't think you'll deal with as a teacher," I offer it here:

Mr. Springsteen was out sick, his substitute had walked out – literally, walked out, quit, after 20 minutes with his class, swear to God. So I was asked to watch both classes. I know, right? Could this be a *bit* more illegal? Sure, I'll watch TWO classes of special ed. kids simultaneously. No problem! They're right across the hall from one another, after all.

I was making the phone call to the gym knowing that Mr. Wang or Mr. Donovan would be happy to come down and keep an eye on Andy's class when I heard the scream.

I almost dropped the phone. The scream was so loud that Donovan heard it from his end and sprinted to my room; sounded like somebody cut the big toe off of a rabid chimpanzee.

Close enough.

Young Mr. Fender, for no apparent reason, kept sticking his hand in the doorjamb, giggling and shaking every time he pulled it out. The guys in Andy's class, not wanting anything to happen while he was out sick (say what you want about them, our guys are loyal) kept pulling him away and forcing him to sit down.

Problem? They're special ed. themselves, so they get tired very quickly of dealing with such nonsense.

Bigger problem? I was on the phone securing coverage of the room.

Godzilla coming into Tokyo sized problem? D. had his hand in the jamb when Billy Aushwinger made his dramatic [late] entrance by slamming the door open at full speed.

———————————

Heard the scream, caught the last glimpse of D. running down the hall, saw the blood everywhere, watched two students throw up and several others freak out, noticed the finger on the floor in the hallway, listened to a few teachers scream and freak out.

All this in about 10 seconds.

What would you do?

What? They didn't' cover this in your education classes?

I must have missed that day, too.

———————————

Necessary sentimental flashback: When I was in 8th grade, my left index finger got cut off. (Accident involving a temperamental Catholic school window.) To this day, I can count to ten thanks to the level-headed tact of another 8th grader, Mikey Pilatis, (*sorry if I messed up the spelling, Mike – if you ever read this book, Email me and I'll refund the price. Least I can do, right?*) who scooped my pointer off the 2nd floor ledge and into a shoe box and, well, the rest is another story.

That moment flashed into my mind and me, being a big believer in "what goes around comes around," figured I had to repay the debt. Eye for an eye, finger for a finger, so I grabbed the detached digit (knowing full well what plethora of blood-borne diseases Diarra might have), flew down the hall (knowing full well that time was critical if D. was ever gonna use that finger again), wrestled him into the nurse's office and held him down so the nurse could work her mojo (knowing full well that Missy was a one-woman M.A.S.H. unit) until the ambulance arrived.

D.F. got his finger back, and I got a few more gray hairs.

WTF NJD Part 5 – I saved the best for lasst*

*   Yeah, I know. I spelled lasst with a double ss, so the word "ass" is in there. Now then, given the nature of this chapter, and knowing that the word "ass" is integral to this particular *piece de resistance,* it kind of makes you wonder whether or not you really want to turn the page, doesn't it?

I knew I could count on you, you sick bastards.

I figured in a world where Chuck Palahniuk books are best sellers, I could rely on the deviant impulses of my fellow reptiles.

Oh well, you asked for it.

Jonathan Bomber should have been, from a high school geometry standpoint, a square. At roughly 5'7" and roughly 400 lbs.

(give or take one normal Jonathan meal or one normal Jonathan shit,) he was as tall as he was wide. I'll spare you all the "more chins than a Chinese phone book" jokes, I'll forego the old "when Jon sat around the house he really sat *around* the house" lines, and I won't waste your time with tired insults like "when Jon got on the scale it said 'one at a time, please'." No, I'll simply say that, with his coffee-colored complexion and body mass index, Jonathan Bomber looked like Clifford the Big Red Dog took a soft poop and then dressed it in a greasy gray XXXXXL sweat suit.

I'll give you a minute to let that visual sink in.

———————

Still having trouble? Hey, I'm here to help…

Jonathan also had a lower lip that looked like everything that got sucked <u>out</u> of *The Real Housewives of Orange* County (1) got pushed <u>in</u> there.

Need more?

Jonathan gave off the aroma of a kid that didn't bathe often and, when he did, often failed to get in the myriad folds and wrinkles of his landscape. In fact, he once told me that he found an old Nutter Butter cookie in one of his "folds" one time.(2)

Need more?

No, I thought not.

———————

---

1   Not that there's anything wrong with liposuction! I love you ladies, and you're all hot! Please don't sue me, you're already rich and I'm just a teacher. Wait, what am I worried about? You don't read books. Damn! There I go again! Sorry! I didn't mean that!

2   I may have forgotten the actual cookie, (might've been an Oreo or Chips Ahoy!) but the story is 100% true.

So there I was, on a beautiful June afternoon, talking to my buddy Gabriel Okay: teacher of the impoverished, computer genius, future president of Nigeria, and the worst hockey player on Earth. Our classes were eating lunch and, having taken over the recently retired Mr. Springsteen's room, Gabe and his young bucks were right across the hall from me and the wolf pack. In the middle of our chat, I noticed Jonathan take out his lunch box. I noticed this because his lunch box was an Igloo cooler, one of the BIG ones. Gabe noticed me noticing Jon and laughed, in that beautiful Nigerian accent of his,

"Oh, dees ees evary day wit Jon. De stuff he pulls outta dat box, whoo! eets deesgusting."

Great. Now I'm curious.

"Ahm telling you, you gonna lose your apeetite watching dat."

Boy, he wasn't kidding.

Jon's first course was a very large Tupperware container of what appeared to be spare ribs.

Ever put ribs or something like that in the fridge over night and the fat congeals with the BBQ sauce to make this semi-solid, fatty, gel? Well Jon tore into the ice-cold ribs, fatty junk and all.

"What the..."

"I TOLD you eet was deesgusting. Wait and see some mah, et gets *worse*, believe me."

"There is no fucking way it could get..."

Mid-way though his attack on the gelatin encased cold meat and sauce, Jon started (with his other hand) on his second course, one half of a WaWa hoagie that was *at least* a day old. (Don't judge me! Anybody who's ever lived alone on a tight budget knows damn well what a refurbished hoagie/sub looks like.) The sight of the congealed fat and day old mayonnaise working it's way down Jon's jowls almost turned me vegetarian on the spot.

"He's got maw, I'm telling you, dees happens all de time. When I try to tell heem about how it is bad faw heem he says "fuck you, you Kunta Kinte muthafucka, go back to Afreeca!'"

"And you say?"

"I tell heem I am from *Nigeria* and dat I hope he explodes on de bus on de way home."

＝＝＝((◉))＝＝＝

By the time I tore myself away from the freak show, Jon was washing down a half gallon of mostly melted rainbow sherbert with…

waaaait for it…

A two-liter bottle of *Diet* Ginger Ale.

The last thing I heard leaving the class was Gabe's hysterical laughter,

"Diet soda! Dat's great! Hees watching his figga did week!"

As I walked back in my class Danny, no slouch in the lunch department himself, inquired "What're you laughin' about?" in between bites of his usual WaWa Italian hoagie, extra meat extra mayo.

"Jonathan Bomber's eating lunch and…"

"THAT nigga got PROBlems!" announced Terrell, interrupting me.

"True dat" laughed Tyree, "that boy make Danny look like Kobe Bryant."

"HaHaHa…Hey!"

"Chill out Danny," I comforted him, "you can't begin to hang with what I just witnessed." When I got to the part about the congealed fat, most of my guys lost it:

"Damn!"

"Aw HELL no! That's trifling!"

"I *told* you that nigga got problems."

"What happens when that boy freaks out? Who takes him to the time out room?"

When the last word of that question came out of Chris Trucker's mouth, silence fell upon us for a fraction of a second. You see, Chris had a very strange tendency to talk about stuff right before it happened, a tendency that earned him the nickname "Negrodamus." Well Negrodamus jinxed the shit out of me *this* time, folks.

Not even a week later, the sounds of "forced obesity extraction" filled the hall.

When a teacher couldn't take a kid anymore, or there was a fight, or a kid broke something, or threatened somebody else [and meant it,] somebody called the Beta Room, the office where the behavior management team hung out, then the guys would come to the room and remove the perpetrator(s) from the room, taking them to the Beta Room for quiet reflection, therapeutic discussion, and behavioral analysis.

Well, at least that's what was *supposed* to happen.

The problem with having a behavior management team (glorified bouncers) in a school for severely emotionally disturbed students (crazy kids,) and less than motivated teachers (lazy fucks) is that the phone never stops ringing Usually, by the time Don, Steve, Marc, Greg, Anthony, Eddie, etc. got to a problem they, and their supervisors, [Joe Kopp, Bobby Chopper, or Chris Dockery] were fried, frustrated, and fed up.

Imagine how they felt when they saw Jonathan splayed out on the floor in the hall.

Don and Steve were coming in the door at the far end of the hallway when I got to the door of my room. By now my guys were accustomed to these sorts of interruptions and occupied themselves or finished their work while I helped; often, they would volunteer to help. (Special ed. my ass, my guys were better workers than half of the staff.)

Leading the way was the new director, Christine Dockery, certified hottie, good friend, talented power forward, accomplished shot drinker, spoiler of nieces and nephews, and older sister of teacher Traci "best ass in the business" Dockery.

Big Dock insisted, in her best keep-it-professional voice: "Jonathan, you will now get up and walk with me to the Beta Room, or I will have Mr. Jagger and Mr. McFlurry carry you there."

———————

I couldn't resist.

"*First* of all, Dock, you *know* how aroused I get when you talk all professional like that; second, Donnie's the strongest guy I know, but he can't deadlift *near* enough to get that piece of shit off the floor."

Jonathan was offended. "Fuck you Step, I'm, I'm g-g-gonna lay here and ain't sh-sh-it you gonna do."

(Did I mention Jonathan stuttered when he was mad or scared? Well he did.)

I was amused and, from the smirk on Dock's face, encouraged to play my role in this "good cop bad cop scenario. But first, a bit of humor…

"Gabe, grab an arm!" I implored

"Ho no!" he screeched. "Dey don't pay me enough fow DAT! Dat peece of sheet can lay deah all day."

———————

Dona, Steve, Chris and I were in hysterics, as were my guys. Jarren added to the hilarity:

"Only Gabe can call you a peece of sheet and make it sound nice."

Now EVERYbody was in hysterics, Eric took it to the next level:

"Can you imagine if Gabe and Jonathan had a baby? I can't eat dee-dee-dees sh-sh-sheet! Oh wait, I *can* eat dat! I eat *every* t-t-ting!"

You had to be there. It was fucking hysterical.

Everybody was laughing and doing impersonations

Except Jonathan,

"Fu-fu-fuck you niggas, I'ma I'ma stay here and shit my pants. Wha-what now?"

Playtime was now officially over.

<hr />

I slipped fluidly into the role that my students affectionately referred to as "The Punisher." From the Marvel comic books (and later movies,) the hard-assed, ultra-violent, alpha male. A walking death threat, with the weaponry to back it up – in this case, a classroom in very near proximity filled with a dozen very dangerous inner city youth looking to let off some misplaced anxiety in the form of physical abuse.

"Listen very carefully, fat ass," I growled, "because I'm going to say this only once. You threaten *me, ME*?!?

"I d-d-didn't fretten…"

"Shut…the…fuck…UP. Can you count to three, fat ass? I'm gonna count to three, then I'm gonna open this door and let my boys show you what happens to fat peeces of sheet *(very hard to keep a straight face at this point)* that don't listen to me. One, two…"

Problem: the probability of Jonathan getting to his feet in three seconds was about the same as peace in the Middle East by tomorrow.

Bigger problem: The more he flailed and floundered, the more animated my guys became, as evidenced by their shouts, threats, and posturing.

Economic stimulus package sized problem: Jonathan exerted himself a great deal scrambling to his hands and knees and bear crawling a few feet, and when a very overweight, hyper-anxious kid that just ate a very large, fatty meal…

———— ((•)) ————

Sweet Jesus, no.

Oh Lord, yes.

Earlier in the year, I thought seeing that roach get pulled out of Pepito's ear was going to be the worst visual image burned into my memory bank, then Matilda erased that with her naked on the dirty bathroom floor performance; but this, *this* was a whole new nightmare. *This* was the numero uno "What the Fuck that is NOT in my Job Description" moment.

Most of the eruption was contained by the adult diaper that Jonathan had to wear.

Key word: most.

It seems our boy had a bit of an incontinence problem, go figure. The sumo sized diaper made it's tragic appearance as Jon's quintuple X sweatpants made their way South as he bobbed and weaved to get upright. Before any of us had a chance to make a pithy comment about the aforementioned fashion accessory, Mount St. Jonathan erupted.

Some of it actually hit Stevie on the shoe, a blue and silver Asics running sneak that, I believe, was burned shortly after the incident.

Donnie (God bless him) kept himself just composed enough to fire off a one-liner in the face of this projectile diarrheatic horror.

"Looks like Krakatoa, bud. Kinda like ASS-CRACKatoa."

I am laughing myself to tears as I sit and remember this, but I was not, if memory serves, laughing at the time. You see, our belligerent Buddha with the Hershey squirts still needed to be taken to the time out room for some chocolate-covered down time, and I had promised to get him there. I tried the obvious approach first, facing my class, in full "Punisher" mode:

"Alright gentlemen…"

They weren't having it, and I was greeted with a dozen slightly different versions of "Aw Hell no, you gonna have to whoop my ass 'cause I ain't going' NEAR that shit."

Can't blame them for that.

The professional approach then?

"Well it's going to take a team effort to.."

They weren't having it, either, and I was greeted with Chris Dockery's nicely rounded backside walking toward the door, followed by the much less appetizing asses of Don and Steve.

Can't blame then for that.

"Hey Gabe…"

"HO! Your CA-razy! That sheet is de most deesgusting… ach!" and he slammed his door

That left me, the shitty brown Buddha with the fat lip, and a whole lotta nobody.

———— ‹‹◉›› ————

I eventually got the situation resolved, no thanks to the chicken shit motherfuckers (yes, I'm talking to ALL of you) that left me alone with the *"round mound of can't keep it down,"* but it was, to put it mildly, tricky . In fact, if Hercules were alive I'm sure he would have equated getting Jon, in some sort of semi-hygienic form, to the time out room was the equivalent of one of his labors; *at least* as hard as cleaning the Augean stables. It involved some heart-to-heart conversation, some threatening, a bit of bribing, (a box of double stuff Oreos I think,) about thirty dollars worth of cleaning supplies, and a beach towel that I had in my truck that was only used *once* after that incident. I got *"Mr. multiple chin that couldn't keep it in"* where he was supposed to go, but it wasn't easy.

And it sure wasn't in my job description.

P.S.- now the truth can be told.

Hey Donnie, remember that towel I gave you to wipe off your face after the big water gun fight at the end-of-the-year party? ASS-CRACKatoa, baby!

Orthodontic Softball and the Tears of a Clown.

Marcus McHuffy was one of those kids. Just smart enough to be arrogant, just dumb enough to be ignorant, just screwed over enough in life to have a huge chip on his shoulder, and just mature enough to be salvageable. You don't know anybody like that do you?

You do?

How did you handle them?

———•((◦))•———

Hmmm...that's pretty interesting, I'm definitely going to try that next time. In the meantime, let me tell you one of my most memorable Mount Saint Marcus stories.

———•((◦))•———

Marcus McHuffy was one of those kids. He came to me from Ms. Tombs classroom, so he knew the school, and he was pretty aware of me and my boys. O.K., that's an understatement, Marcus knew exactly who I was and he knew a few of my boys very well due to the fact that they had fought more than once. You see, when he was in Ms. Tombs' class, he always thought he was "too big" for them so he teased and fought with his classmates and teacher constantly; yet, when confronted by any of my cherubs, he immediately announced his inferiority complex by talking shit to them. That, and his cocky comments in my direction painted a fairly large target on his ass.

Marcus looked a bit like the entertainer Christopher "Ludacris" Bridges, if Ludacris was younger and had a fairly large target on his ass. He was intelligent despite having been dismissed by everybody in his life except for his grandfather and an impossibly cute social worker whose name I really wish I remembered. The problem with Mr. McHuffy was that his self-loathing almost always manifested itself in an inflated ego and hollow self-promotion. You don't know anybody like that do you?

You do?

How did you handle them?

Me, too! In fact, when I tried to redirect Marcus' misplaced energy into a positive direction, namely sports, he got his entire top row of teeth severed from his gum line in a bloody horror show, but I'm getting ahead of myself...

"Who the hell would play softball against us?" I gently inquired.

"Lotsa schools like ours have teams that must be looking for games!" exclaimed Edward Zarmenian, the gym teacher of record during my time with Marcus.

Ed Z., proud dad, UPS bigwig, part-time DJ, and possessor of the greatest hook shot since Kareem Abdul Jabbar, though it would be great idea if we took our little operation of marching the "best" 15-20 kids to the field across from Moorzakunt on Friday afternoons to play what remotely resembled softball, and tried to "boost our kids' self-esteem and give them something to work for" by setting up games against other alternative schools with real softball teams.

"Hey," Ed envisioned, "it will boost our kids' self-esteem and give them something to work for!"

I exclaimed, for the first of many times, "you have GOT to be kidding me!"

Don't hate me for being cynical. I had been trained by years of having great intentions catch fire and burn me like well-intentioned napalm, and I knew goddamned well that the self-esteems in question, many of which were evolving from academic caterpillars into beautiful academic butterflies in my classroom, were going to get stomped like the San Jose Sharks in the first round of the NHL playoffs.

(Quick joke: what do the Sharks and the Titanic have in common? They both look great 'till they hit the ice. Whoo! that's a good one)

I did not want any part of Ed's insane plan that was destined to take a tremendous amount of work only to end poorly, with ungrateful kids, insane coaches, and broken butterflies, and I told him so in the following manner:

"Sure, I'll help, dude. If you make the phone calls and secure the field, I'll help coach the team and organize the tryouts."

What?!? Did I just say that? ("Yes, you did," says the little angel on my right shoulder)

Why the fuck do I say these things?!?! ('cause you're an asshole, says the devil on my left)

"Yeah, I might be an asshole, but at least I'm willing to put my ass on the line for these kids so they have something to look forward to! Whaddya got to say to *that*?"

"Who the fuck are you taking to?" asked Ed.

Internal dialogue notwithstanding, I helped Mr. Zarmenian organize out first ever softball game against Saint Gabriel's Home for Wayward Assholes (1) It took close to two months to make this a reality, with Mr. Z demonstrating the patience of a saint every time he was confronted by another limp dick administrator with yet another piece of paper saying we needed this waiver or that insurance or this approval or seventeen copies of that mission statement, et cetera et cetera ad nauseam. Every time we thought we were done, another note and another round of "you have GOT to be kidding me!"

Leviathan piles of waivers and write offs and permission slips and pay offs were finally waded through and, knee deep in bureaucracy, Ed Zarmenian, Johnny Wang, the late Joe Kopp, Marc Rosencrantz, and yours truly took 18 of the finest softball players Moorzakunt Academy had to offer across the street and onto the diamond for the first game of our inaugural season. Marcus McHuffy led us onto the field for the first inning. Having endured more shit than *any* group of adults should suffer from one Ludacris-looking-ball of free-floating anxiety, we decided

- not to strangle Marcus with the laces from his glove
- not to allow several members of the team to beat Marcus with their bats
- to make him our starting pitcher

It would, after all, boost his self-esteem and give him something to work for; besides, all the other kids would learn from this. Marcus really came around, learned respect, and became a team player, so he was gonna get the glory. Perfect storybook ending, right?

We took the field first.

Warm ups were over, Ed was making a batting lineup, Kopp

1   Not the real name of the school we played, but you probably guessed that, smarty-pants.

was on the bench with the rest of the team, Wang was umping first base, Rosencrantz and a teacher from St. Gabe's were going to call balls and strikes, and I was standing behind Marcus, just behind the pitcher's mound. The St. Gabe's teachers were spread out accordingly and, at long last, after two months of arduous work and seemingly insurmountable obstacles, we were going to play some softball!

I remember thinking "this is beautiful," as Marcus pitched his first pitch (ball one) on that beautiful April afternoon.

I remember thinking "you have GOT to be kidding me!" when Marcus pitched his second pitch, and the batter hit a screaming line drive right into Marcus' face.

Blood literally exploded out of double M's mouth and onto pitcher's mound and when his semi-conscious face was lifted, his teeth seemed to be floating in a waterfall of blood. Later, at the hospital, we would find out that his entire top row of teeth were floating freely, having been severed from the gum line.

We would learn some other things at the hospital as well.

I threw Marcus on my shoulder and sprinted for home, (not smart but well intentioned.) Ed walkie-talkied the school and had Steve McFlurry grab the school nurse, haul ass over to the field in his truck and grab Marcus (smart and well intentioned.) Joe Kopp called Marcus' group home and told them to get a representative to the hospital that he knew Marcus would be rushed to once the ambulance he called for arrived. (Very smart and very well intentioned.)

Steve was pulling out of the Moorzakunt driveway as I was running up, I had just finished getting him *in* the back seat as the ambulance pulled up - "you have GOT to be kidding me!" - and then helped him *out* and Missy got in the ambulance with him.

Missy, consummate professional, flaming red head, scrub stylist, and bestest school nurse ever, managed to keep the toothless terror calm on what I'm sure was an arduous ride to _____ Memorial. Once they got there, they rushed Marcus right into emergency and fixed him right up.

I wish.

Once they got to the hospital Marcus, who by now was nearly unconscious, was asked questions about his insurance.

I'll say that again, in caps, so as to enhance the ironic insanity. Marcus, who at this point looked like Freddie Kreuger and Jason Voorhees had gone 2 out of 3 falls in his mouth, WAS ASKED QUESTIONS ABOUT HIS INSURANCE!! Seems they wouldn't even give him a towel or a Tylenol without the legal signature of a member of the group home where Marcus resided.

I was later told that Missy, the normally bubbly and oh-so proper nurse, engaged in a streak of profanity that would have made Scarface proud.

Didn't work. The cold hearted pricks at _____ Memorial made Marcus sit there, in excruciating pain, bleeding all over himself and slipping in and out of consciousness, while the clueless pricks from his group home took their good old time getting to the hospital, over *one hour* later.

I'm getting homicidal impulses just recalling this, so I'll keep it short.

Eventually, Marcus' "guardians" jumped through the appropriate legal hoops and his broken jaw and the dental maelstrom in his mouth were properly given proper attention.

Marcus McHuffy, to his infinite credit, blamed nobody but himself for what he called [through a wired shut jaw] "a puhfect stike on da secnd pish a da game."

I, gentle reader, was not so mature, and had to be physically restrained when I got my shot at the jerk-offs from the group home.

Mr. Zarmenian, once again, showed the patience of Job when the talking heads tried to put the permanent "Out of Business" sign on the softball season because of one unfortunate incident. He went on to coach a pretty good team of kids and, believe it or not, boosted their self-esteem and gave them, and others, something to work for. (In your FACE, cynical English teacher!) Eventually, we even raised enough money to get cheesy softball jerseys.

Missy resumed her duties as the nicest school nurse on the planet, although when she was asked to recount this incident, I noticed her hair turn a slightly more sinister shade of red.

Marcus' grandfather and impossibly cute social worker went to war with the group home and petitioned, successfully, to have Marcus turned over to his grandpop for legal guardianship. At the ripe old age of 80-something I have no doubt that he provided better care than the residential home that I really wish I could mention by name right here but won't.

Instead, I'll let Marcus have the last word.

———⟫(⟪)⟫———

Graduation at M.A. was a small operation, usually 7-12 kids at the most, with their families, (maybe 75 people total) held in a gymnasium, with a looooow budget ceremony followed by pictures and snacks. It was very intimate and sometimes very humorous; and since most of these kids were the first of their family to graduate from anything, it was low on calories, but big on taste. When the Moorzakunt Academy graduation of 199somethingorother was approaching, our administration decided that it would be "just great" if one of the students could speak at the graduation ceremony. I crossed my fingers and prayed.

"I think it would be just great if Marcus McHuffy spoke,' gushed Audrey Applesauce.

⸺⸺≼((◐))≽⸺⸺

Thank you God.
All praise to Allah.
Hail Zeus.

I tried to contain my polytheistic enthusiasm but I was unanimous in my support of Marcus being the "student speaker" for the graduation ceremony…because Marcus was one of those kids. Our young hero of the extreme dental makeover had become an erudite public speaker, mature young man and seizer of opportunity.

"They gonna let *me* talk?"

"Oh, yes." I positively giggled.

"Man, they know I'ma keep it real, right?"

"Marcus," I pleaded, "if you ever had a shred of love for me anywhere in your soul, promise them a nice, vanilla, by the numbers "valedictorian" speech…"

"Then get up there and drop the real knowledge on them when they can't do nothing to stop me."

"Precissssely." I hissed, in true *"boy the apple on that tree looks tasty"* fashion

You gonna help me write it?"

"The fake one?"

"Yeah, Step, the fake one. I think I can handle the 'angry urban black kid' one."

He actually made the little quote marks in the air and gave me that little smirk that let me know he thought my question was stupid. I don't think…I mean…okay, I promised myself I wouldn't cry…

I don't think I've ever been more proud. (sniff)

———⸱⫯⸱———

Marcus and I shared several hours over the next week or so writing the safest, blandest, most politically correct graduation speech of all time. This was the "Air Supply" (2) of speeches, and we laughed so hard at some points, and shared so much personal insight of each other, that I can easily say that writing that speech with Marcus was one of my fondest teaching memories.

Upon completion, with graduation looming, I started to get worried that double M would rage against the machine a bit too much and reduce himself to a monosyllabic thug in front of some of the people who believed he was just that all along. I warned him against just that, and he assured me that he wouldn't give the "haters" the satisfaction.

———⸱⫯⸱———

The big night arrived and Marcus McHuffy only had two people in the folding chair audience for him – his grandpop and the impossibly cute social worker who I worked closely with over the years to get Marcus to this moment and whose name I wish I remembered so I could give her credit here. A few of my other favorite guys were graduating as well so this was a potentially emotional night for me. I was resolved, as always, to remain in "Punisher" mode: nod appreciatively, accept compliments with humility, and smile politely for pictures, slipping away quietly at ceremony's end.

---

2   80's soft rock group known for their ultra-soft, painfully safe music. I actually have their 1988 Greatest Hits on my iPod wedged, ironically, between AC/DC and Alice Cooper, the latter of which belongs in the Rock N' Roll Hall of Fame like, now.

I wish.

I don't remember the exact speech but I do remember it was beautiful, surgical, and the perfect balance of sweet and sour. He criticized the educational system that failed him early on in life, the family that abandoned him, and the group home that treated him like a number. He chastised the teachers who didn't teach, and the students who didn't care, and he closed by offering thanks and love to "the only three people that really gave a shit about him."

I was more surprised by the number *three* then I was about the fact that he said "shit" in front of the principal, CEO, and collective administration.

"Pop-pop, Ms. _____, (the impossibly cute social worker) and Mr. Step. Y'all are the reason I'm here. I'm going to Rowan University and I'm going to make you proud."

I.C.S.W. hugged me and, though tears, said "we did it Step, *he* did it."

Mr. McHuffy shook my hand and nodded his regal head, telling me he was proud of Marcus, and that he was very thankful that we didn't give up on him.

I cried,
a little,
during the hug.

Piss off. I'm not made of stone.

Epilogue:

Last time I talked to Mr. McHuffy, he was maintaining a "B" average at Rowan University, making him one of only four kids (during my 15+ years at M.A.) to go to post-secondary education, and the ONLY one to attend a University.

Listening to him talk about how he was adding "street cred" to the audio-visual club by being the only Afro-American kid involved allowed me to sleep soundly knowing that I had sent yet another young cynic into the world, armed with just enough intelligence to be dangerous, and just enough of a chip on his shoulder to take that dangerous intelligence and scare all of the right people.

Beacause Marcus McHuffy is still one of those kids.

Excuse me, one of those ***men.***

An epiphany in a cage leads to a nap on a desk.

WARNING: This chapter involves dirty dancing, flagrant flirting, tipsy team teaching and many other alliterative violations of good conduct that no teacher worth his/her weight in Motley Crue CDs would ever engage in.

DISCLAIMER: If you think less of those involved, it wasn't really them.

CAVEAT: Except my part, I did it all, and I looked good doing it.

Well, now that we got *that* shit out of the way...

I remember it like it was yesterday.

O.K., that's not entirely true. I remember as much of that evening as I was able to piece together once my mind recovered from what was surely the death of many a brain cell. (Curse you, Jell-O shots, you gelatinously innocent looking agents of chaos!) It was the day before the day before Spring Break, and all of the teachers, aides, and counselors of Moorzakunt Academy were going to go out and blow off some steam.

Two things you ought to know here: one, when teachers blow off steam, it's not like when a lot of other professions go out for happy hour. Teachers, particularly those who deal with a more, shall we say, challenging demographic, blow off steam the way Mount Vesuvius blew off steam on AD 79, which leads me to my next point. Two, I've never seen a group of professionals (and I've been in the bar business in one capacity or another for over two decades) that feel more entitled to engage in "feel good" behavior once they're turned loose. Translation: if you're main squeeze is a teacher, hold on tight when the tequila shots start workin' their magic, and if you're single and stressed, you're odds are better than they would EVER be in Vegas. Comprende'?

No surprise, then, that within a few hours, the DJ knew us all by name, the bartenders were drinking *with* us, and there was more horizontal planning going on than twenty simultaneous games of *Battleship*. Thank God my future brother in law, Frankie Omen, the gym teachers, Kevin and Aaron, and I had all agreed to go back to my house, where Dawn was going to be ready with greasy food, Excedrin, lots of water, and beds ready.

Praise Allah that we had contingency plans set up for the next day, as we were going to have to teach the future criminals of the world, on the day before a holiday, on three hours sleep and with massive hangovers; and thank Vishnu that Aaron had agreed to be the designated driver.

Come to think of it, where is Aaron?

———⸬———

"Yeaahhhhh babyyyyy, get it in ya!" howled Aaron, as Cindy inhaled a shot of something brown from his belly button as he lay on the bar.

Uh oh.

"Good fing Frankie's our desi...desi...good fing Frankie's

drivin ush home," whispered Kevin, ever so eloquently, in my ear, complete with spit.

Double Uh oh.

On cue, Frankie O. led the charge into a large cage that was stage left of the DJ booth, with his shirt off and hat on backwards, if memory serves.

Super-powered Uh oh.

It was time to start power drinking water and coffee.

Right after I got in that cage, baby.

———— ((O)) ————

About three minutes later, it looked like *Coyote Ugly, Soul Train,* and *Saved by the Bell* Collided in a cage. There was so much dancing, singing, and rubbing going on that, combined with the amount of alcohol in our system, I honestly thought we might all combust. Moments like that need but a teensy push to become memorable for life, and our DJ knew it. I don't think anybody that was in that cage that night will forget when the opening line emanated from the speakers…

We don't need no education…

Oh no he DIDn't

———— ((O)) ————

As you may have guessed, most teachers know that particular Pink Floyd song by heart, and we demonstrated our memorization skills by singing along, LOUDLY. By the time we hit mid song, we all had arms around each other, drowning out the DJ with screams of *"Hey teachers, leave those kids alone!"* It was magical, and Frankie Omen, no doubt enlightened by the sheer magnitude of the love in the cage, made a poignant observation about the profession:

"You don't get this shit with the 9 to 5 people!"

Well said coach, well said.

——————◆——————

Of course, the night had to end at some point, and I'm not going to glamorize the ride home, which involved turning away a few young lasses, public urination, throwing up in my truck, several punches to the nuts, and (believe it or not) a discussion about the merits of socialism in a primitive society.

I will instead, remind you that we all had to teach the most difficult kids in the entire school system in a few hours.

Go ahead, put the book down now, I dare you.

——————◆——————

No way, right? I know, I know, *I lived it* and I can't wait to read this shit!

——————◆——————

The following morning came entirely too early. Mother nature shone her flashlight of interrogation into our sleepy eyes.

Then she waterboarded us.

"Dude…" Aaron murmured, "how much did we fuckin' drink last night?"

"Enough to make my breath smell like your ass," chided Kevin.

"I'd like to know" Frankie inquired through the hazy wall of sleep, "how you know what his ass smells like."

"Will you all," I demanded, with as much empathy as a man with a migraine could muster this morning,(1) "shut…the…fuck… up!"

————)((•)) ————

After a spirited debate about greasy food is good for a hangover (Frankie and I made our point between bites of sausage and egg McMuffins) and how food made hangovers worse (Aaron and Kevin argued feverishly as they gulped water in sync,) we set out to teach the youth of America. Only this time, *we* would be the ones not in our right minds.

Irony with a capital I, wouldn't you say?

During the nearly half-hour drive to Moorzakunt Academy, the fearsome foursome became acutely aware we were in no shape to properly perform at our fullest. Suddenly, like a swallow touching down with feathered wings on the shores of San Juan Capistrano, it came to us:

Team teaching!

It would be easy for Aaron and Kevin, being co-gym teachers. For the two Franks, however, we would have to engage in some cross-curricular, History-meets-Language Arts sort of shenanigans. Necessity is, after all, the mother of invention.

"You two mothafuckas is drunk!"

"For real, you two look like ass of a baboon that been sittin' on a hot rock!"

_____Such was the insightful commentary offered from the student

1   man, migraine, muster, morning…alliteration is always appropriate, agreed?

population of M.A., having first laid eyes on Mr. Caper and Mr. Basil. Fortunately, our intrepid gym instructors were ready for such stinging accusations.

"No, we were late night deep sea fishing and it rained, so we are feeling a little under the weather at this time. Otherwise, we are just fine."

From what I understand, there was a moment of stunned silence before 24 potential "guard the pin" players proved that they weren't nearly as ignorant as their paperwork would suggest,

"GET the fuck outta HERE, Caper! You are both SHITfaced, and that's all we gotta say!"

Apparently, the rest of the day in the M.A. gym involved a whooooole lotta "independent play," and some well disguised napping behind that day's copy of the Philadelphia Daily News.

Meanwhile, in my room (I had recently been given a room in the main building, as the trailer was condemned) things were getting a bit more creative.

———◆———

"I have often seen cinema as the bridge that connects the textual world of the author and the historical fact of….uh, hist"

"THANK you, Mr. Damian," I interrupted, "for that informative albeit less than erudite explanation of what lay ahead of us today in our pursuit of educational advancement."

A moment of silence (much like what was happening in the gym around that time) greeted my monologue, so I got right down to it.

"It's the day before a holiday, and we're gonna combine classes and watch a movie today."

We received a standing ovation.

Without the standing, and without the ovation.

OK, the kids were really happy and they made a lot of noise.

We decided that *A Man Called Horse* would be the perfect synergy of historical coolness and literary panache'. That, and the fact that it was 114 minutes long, made it (when combined with lunch and gym periods) almost a whole day of low impact fun.

———— ((●)) ————

Frankie Omen requested that he be awake during the scene when Richard Harris, as John Morgan, gets hung from the hooks in a coming of age moment. Since that was around the middle of the movie, that meant I got first ride on the nappy time express.

Now you would think that a 260 lb. Man sleeping on a desk while another man of near equal girth sat at said desk, pretending to read The Daily News, while a combined class of around 22 emotionally disturbed students watched a Native American rite of passage story (munching on popcorn generously provided by the aforementioned girthy guys) would be a sight unique enough to warrant suspicion.

You would think that, unless you've read the other chapters up to this point, in which case you're fully aware of what a circus Moorzakunt Academy could be on occasion. In fact, *most* people wouldn't have batted an eyelash.

You do know where I'm going with this, right?

———— ((●)) ————

Enter Hope Pringles, administrator, who, in a stunning display of both professionalism and restraint, abstained from alcohol the night before. The ironically named Hope decided to make the rounds (i.e. ball busting) and see what the people who did indulge the night before (i.e. EVERYone) were doing to improve the education of their students.

Having just come from the dodge ball bonanza in the gym and "freedom of expression" day in the Art Room (bravo Mary Lou!) Ms. Pringles was on the warpath, and the sight of yours truly curled up like a kid awaiting the Polar Express (on a desk not made to accommodate me) combined with our munching movie mob, made her less than happy.

It occurs to me that I'm using a lot of parentheses (to express side thoughts) in this chapter, so I thought I would use them to express the subtext of the interaction that occurred between Ms. Pringles, Mr. Damian, and I:

"What is he doing on the desk?" (Wake that fat fuck up and get him working.)

"Oh, he's got food poisoning but he didn't want to abandon the kids, so we agreed to combine classes and do some cross curricular work involving Native American customs. (I realize that what I'm saying is total bullshit and that you know that but it's the best I can do under the circumstances.)

"You two are a disgrace to the teaching profession.' (You two are a disgrace to the teaching profession.)

Before Frankie was forced to endure any more of this indignity at my expense, I forced him to endure another, more olfactory-oriented indignity. To put it simply, I unleashed a silent but deadly fart that accomplished a twofold purpose:

It nearly burned off Frankie's developing unibrow

It caused Ms. Pringles to immediately evacuate the premises, leaving us in movie watching comfort.

There will be a few things I regret when I have to face death someday, but that fart will not be one of them. (2)

I got up, let Mr. Omen have his shift in dreamland, and proceeded to teach a stellar lesson on how the colonists used subterfuge and doublespeak to obtain land and more from the Native Americans, followed by a follow up speech to the kids on how a holiday from school does not automatically condone irresponsible behavior on their point.

Thank you, Mr. Omen.

Smell me *now*, Ms. Pringles.

---

2   I recently spent some time with Frankie, who is now my brother-in-law, and he assured me that my well timed flatulence is something that he most certainly *does* regret.

Four bodily functions in seven pages

There's a line in the Warren Zevon song *Play It All Night Long* that goes:

"There ain't much to country livin'

sweat, piss, jizz and blood."

With all due respect to that late Mr. Zevon, and he was a tragically heroic genius, teachers have been known to encounter some extraneous bodily functions in our line of duty (or is it doody?) So, to preface the four short anecdotes that you're about to read, hopefully with an empty stomach, I offer my own little tune:

"There ain't much to teachin' special ed.,

shit, piss, jizz, and puke." (Can't you just hear the steel guitar twangin' in the background?)

No?

Alas, only the chosen hear the music hidden in the bodily waste of the students of America.

Mari Mari quite contrary, how does your garden grow?

Marisol Olycheet was a young lady that the Maryannes – Short and O'Connor (you remember them from the chapter about Stanley's giant redwood) dealt with exclusively. Marisol was a charming young lady most of the time; however, thanks to some severe brain damage and some "interesting" home life, she could be a real handful when she got upset. The story I'm going to tell you, boys and girls, involves Marisol's first week at Moorzakunt Academy. Apparently, Marisol's family was into the idea of environmental friendliness long before Al Gore started making movies. The Olycheet family were so interested in recycling, in fact, that Marisol would not go to the bathroom unless she did it in a tin coffee can.

I'll say that again. Or better yet, you read it again.

Yes, she would not go to the bathroom in the lavatory. Her family collected the, um, fertilizer, for their garden, where they grew what produce they could, being strapped for cash. Mar was so accustomed to forwarding her feces to the Folger's can that she panicked at the prospect of pooping in the potty.(1)

Anybody who has taught children with severe learning disabilities knows that what I say is true. Very often, these kids that come from families that don't speak English (and haven't accustomed themselves to family behavior that you and I might deem "normal") are treated like oddities and/or burdens. I have encountered far too many families that treated their "special needs" children like people from the dark ages treated men and women with mental disorders; specifically, that they're "crazy," and should be locked away or dismissed.

Painful, but all too true, and that's why the two Maryannes had to deal with several hours of screaming, kicking, biting, and other pleasantries until Dawn Creeger, a wonderful woman with a heart of gold, saw fit to run to the market and purchase a can of coffee.

The teachers drank the coffee and Marisol, well…

the daisies around "B" building *were* particularly lovely that Spring.

---

1   If you don't recognize all the alliteration in that statement by now, I have failed you – and I apologize profusely

Catfish defies the laws of physics with a golden shower

Charlie Punter, affectionately known as "catfish" for reasons I don't know and never asked (Charlie was at M.A. when I got there,) was an odd young man to say the least. He looked like a little old man waddling from place to place, mumbling to himself and laughing at whatever private joke was being told in his head. Make no mistake about it, there was a party in Charlie's mind, and you were not invited. Catfish had one defining characteristic, though; he managed to piss himself just about every day. In the dead of winter, he would warm himself and, in the sweltering days of summer, he would add to the humidity.

Now on one particular day, I was in the middle of a stunning lecture on the allegorical nature of George Orwell's *Animal Farm* when our man Catfish pushed open my door, announced, to no one in particular,

"I ain't goin. I'm gonna play checkers, and I ain't goin!"

Of course, my room was filled with 13 or 14 teenagers with attention deficit issues (among other things,) and they thought that Charlie's random outburst was just about the funniest thing they'd ever seen, and let young Mr. Punter know that they supported him

"Yeah C-dawg! You tell 'em!"

"You ain't gotta go nowhere you don't wanna go!"

Charlie smiled, adjusted his glasses, told a class full of black kids "I don't like black kids," and waddled away.

Now you would think that my Afro-American armada, after such a comment, would have jumped on Charlie faster than white on rice on a polar bear in a snowstorm. However, my guys...

Come in closer, so I can whisper.

Closer.

My guys were more mature than most "responsible adults;" you see, they hear words, but understand motives, and they knew that when a mentally handicapped kid insults you, you chalk it up to "crazy" and feel bad for the kid rather than use his insult as an excuse to inappropriately vent your own anxiety

Charlie continued unmolested down the hall until I caught up with him.

You didn't really think I was going to let him "not go" someplace he was clearly supposed to go, did you? I don't care what's wrong with the kid, rules is rules. Turns out Catfish was being sent to the "time out" room for threatening to take a shit in the middle of the class.

If only we knew just how much foreshadowing was involved in that threat.

Greg Johnstone, "time out" room expert, sat Charlie in the corner and told him to sit still and be quiet.

The sitting part? Check.

The quiet part? Check.

The pissing so hard that it came out of his sweatpants in an arc? Check.

I'll say that again. Or better yet, you read it again.

Catfish, after announcing that he had to pee, did so. With such velocity that, after the stain on his gray sweatpants announced that he wasn't kidding, a stream came forth and turned him into a seated learning-disabled cupid statue.

It happened.

I was there.

I am not at all embarrassed to admit that, some weeks later, several of the male staff of Moorzakunt Academy, after more than a few Miller High Lifes, attempted to recreate the profound peeing prowess of Mr. Punter. None of us succeeded. (2)

---

2   I meant none of *them* succeeded. Nobody that you allow to teach *your* children would engage in such chicanery

1-900-are-you-fucking-kidding-me?

I'm sorry to *start* the chapter with profanity, but you'll understand why in a few minutes.

Jerry Lampanelli, no relation to the woman from the comedy roasts (mainly because I changed his last name) was, like the kids say, a piece of work. Our fearless leader, Mr. Long, was helping Jerry, as he had come to inherit a little bit of money, and he had no real family to help him manage it. When I say a little bit of money I mean just enough to sustain an 18-year-old kid and when I say no real family I mean nobody was close enough to this kid to give a shit about him.

Heartwarming, right?

So Long would appropriate money to Jerry, taught him how to budget, etc. Talk about above and beyond the call of duty for the principal of a school. I had Jerry my second year at M.A. and I remember him as being quiet, polite, but otherwise undistinguished. Fortunately for me, I never got to se the private, personal hygiene side of Jerry Lampanelli that would ultimately prove to be his legacy. Jerry was given a chance to live in the "apartment" above the computer room, in exchange for his keeping an eye on the campus after hours. Seemed righteous enough, teach the kid some responsibility and let him earn his keep.

I string you along all the time, so I'm going to give you the payoff quick on this one.

Ready?

Mr. Long received a phone bill at the end of the month.

$1,600.00

All from calls made to 1-900 numbers after 8 p.m.

Translation: Jerry was calling phone sex lines and beating the bishop at an impossibly frequent pace.

Still don't get it? Okay, during the time Jerry was supposed to be guarding the campus, he was on the phone with hundreds of middle aged, financially savvy housewives claiming to be young horny housewives, and creating enough friction to heat the apartment in the winter.

No? Still? Okay, when Jerry moved in three weeks prior, it was an *apartment*. Now, it was a *cave*, complete with stalactites on the floor and ceiling.

<hr />

After Long told us about the masturbatory madness, he asked me and Don to be there when he confronted Jerry. We needed a few minutes to exchange jokes, laugh hysterically and marvel at Lampanelli's pud pulling prowess. (Yeah, I said it!)

Satisfied but far from subdued, we called Jerry into the office, and the charges (literally and figuratively) were laid at Jerry's feet, which probably had remnants of last night's fantasy marathon on them.

Know what Jerry said?

"It wasn't me."

I know, right? Are you fucking kidding me?! I was a bit taken aback by this brazen display of denial, and I let Jerry know it.

"Are you fucking kidding me?! Dude, you're the only one on campus when these calls were made. Man up, and take the hit."

"Bud," Donnie added, "if you would have donated that sperm instead of wasting it, you could have bought a house.

I wasn't ready for that, and it took everything in me not to totally lose it. Mr. Long was not as amused, but I could see him biting the insides of his gums to keep from laughing.

Jerry, for his part, denied any knowledge of the making love alone marathon.

———— ◦《◉》◦ ————

Jerry left the campus under a cloud of controversy, and Long had to hunt him down and rectify the money situation. Jerry was ready to abandon his "inheritance," and Long actually tracked him down to give him the balance.

You're a better man than me, Long. I would have paid the titanic phone bill, then used the money to hire those biohazard guys from *Monsters, Inc.* to clean up that sperm saturated apartment.

Lisa loses her lunch on everybody's favorite English teacher.

Ah, Lisa Corpulente'. Where do I begin? Lisa was 5'8", 275-pound avalanche of too much drama, poorly applied make up and sexual inappropriateness. If Tammy Faye Baker, Jabba the Hutt, and Lolita merged, Lisa would result, come forth, and make you uncomfortable.

Lisa was on the new swing set, swinging her heart out. Unbeknownst to Lisa, John Fuzzyellow, our intrepid maintenance man, had yet to anchor the swing set into the mulch covered Earth. Which is probably why he put those big-ass signs that said

STILL UNDER CONTRUCTION - DO NOT TOUCH !

on either side of the swing set.

Oops, forgot to mention, Lisa was dyslexic as well, so she probably read those signs as

HEY! FAT GIRL, COME SWING ON YOUR OWN

PRIVATE FUN AREA! (3)

I was fortunate enough to be covering gym activities on that particular Friday, and had just emerged from "F" building with the 22 best behaved juvenile delinquents of the week, all set for 90 minutes of touch football and trash talking taken to an art for. Mr. Rosencrantz and I froze in our tracks, as did the rest of our posse', when we laid eyes on Lisa, swinging enthusiastically.

Blissfully unaware of the fact that the swing set was joining her.

Adrian, bless his heart, tried to warn her. I believe it went something like:

"Bitch, you gonna rip that shit outta the ground!"

I honestly think he was more concerned with losing the swing set than he was looking forward to the inevitable disaster. Either way, it was too late to save Miss Corpulente'.

Sing with me, America:

Ring around the swing set, can't believe it hasn't flipped yet
A wrenching noise, some laughing boys
All fall down!

Alas, my inner sense of karma kicked in and I sprinted, along with Mr. Rosencrantz, to help Lisa, who was now on her ass in the mulch. Unfortunately, it was one of those "time stands still" moments as we saw the top of the swing set, the length of steel that held all of the swings, descending in slow motion toward the stunned kabuki face of our dazed damsel in distress.

Batman and Robincrantz arrived too late, as the "clunk" indicated.

---

3   Let the hate mail from plus sized women begin. (5)
5   Unless, of course, you've been reading closely; in which case, you know that the big gals are mine all mine. You listening, Queen Latifah?

It was sad, in retrospect. Lisa looked like a big doll, sitting on her butt, glassy-eyed, and then she got whomped just as she was coming out of her daze. The thunderous laughter behind us didn't help matters, either.

When Lisa announced, through slurred speech, that she felt sick and needed to get to the nurse, *but couldn't walk*, Mr. Rosenberg disappeared faster than funding for education after Election Day.

Thanks, Marc.

Dick.

I carried Lisa to the nurse's office, much to the delight of the throng of potential touch football players, and intrigued staff members in attendance.

Ever seen *The World's Strongest Man* contests on ESPN, when guys have to carry very uncooperative cars over unpleasant distances, while people hoot in the background.

Yeah, something like that.

Of course, once I got her there, I unapologetically professed how awesome I was for helping Lisa, how empathetic I was, blah blah blah. It was enough to make you sick.

He said, ironically.

Lisa, who had managed to sway to her feet while I rhapsodized on about myself, announced to the world that she might have been concussed.

She announced that by vomiting.

A lot.

All over my head.

I forgot this, but one of my former co-workers reminded me that I looked down, smiled, and proclaimed: "I distinctly remember saying that I *didn't* want the creamed corn."

There *must* be a lesson in there somewhere, but I missed it whilst I was picking Lisa's ham and cheese hoagie and sour cream and onion chips out of my flowing raven locks.

Intermezzo - what you think vs. what I know.

Hey students! Know what happens when you ASSUME? That's right! You make an ASS out of U and ME. Actually, you make an as out of U and I laugh about it with my friends, but you get the point. I have learned, over the years, that students (particularly teenage students) assume a LOT. Here, students, for the first time ever, a collection of what you think vs. what I know.

- You THINK that you're "getting over on me" by refusing to do class work, homework, etc. because you THINK that you'll be able to pick the job you want, live the life you want, and do it all your way because the politicians and parents have made it impossible for me to fail you, kick you out of class, or slap some sense into you. Alas, I KNOW that in a declining economy, all of the jobs that you *could* have kept (minus a high school diploma) go overseas or to illegal aliens who are *glad* to have them; furthermore, I KNOW that you're fragile little egos will shatter like a cheap window when you emerge into the "unprotected" world beyond the classroom, where you *can* be fired, evicted, incarcerated, and/or eradicated.

- You THINK that it's perfectly acceptable to disrespect men, women, the elderly, and anyone else that you can get away with, because you THINK that it's funny and that doing so puts you in control; however, I KNOW that *fear is the parent of cruelty*, and that you're trying to create enough laughter to drown out the crying inside of you because of how ignorant you are, how fucked up your life is, and how little control you have over anything.

- ∎

And while we're on that subject...

- You THINK that because most teachers are significantly older than you and forced to wear formal clothes to work that you can try to intimidate and/or threaten them; however, I KNOW that being a parent, paying your own bills, getting up for work every day, perhaps even serving in the military, working out with the desperation that comes with getting older, and growing up in a time when you actually had to *work* and *wait* for things toughens you up, and they (if they wouldn't lose their job for doing it) would beat your little punk ass within an inch of your thus far non-productive life.

- You THINK that being smart, asking questions, and being excited about learning makes you a dork, a geek, weak, lame, whatever. You THINK that laughing while you perpetuate your ignorance and stupidity makes you cool and that the people who cheer you on and do the same are your friends. I KNOW that you and the rest of the pinhead posse will be *working for* the same "smart kids" that you tease – they will <u>control your life</u>, <u>decide your income</u>, and <u>pass laws that you and your dumb ass family have to follow</u>.

On a related note…

- You THINK that you're going to play your sport at the professional level. I KNOW the statistics regarding how many scholastic athletes make it to the professional ranks and they're too harsh for you to handle. Go score your touchdown, dunk over someone, dribble the soccer ball between his legs, throw a no hitter, whatever; but you better work that shit between your ears too, trust me. Know my favorite cheer? I heard it first from the Princeton fans when another in team in football was dominating them. Goes like this: "That's Alright, That's O.K., You're Gonna Work for Us Someday!"

And finally…

- You THINK you're never going to grow up and become the guy or girl that tells this stuff to the next generation of dumb ass kids coming up. I KNOW that you will.

A Feast of Fools: Some Major Players in My Rise to Mediocrity

"The idiots are taking over"

-NOFX (The idiots are taking over.)

I need to call a Kopp.

"I think something is fundamentally wrong with me."
That's what I told Joe Kopp, (real name, awesome isn't it?) the school psychologist at Moorzakunt Academy, while slowly banging my head (literally) onto his genuine artificial walnut desk. Before I continue our conversation, I must digress…

Joseph Kopp, who died long before the world stopped desperately needing him, was the closest thing to a mentor I ever had in this crazy business. When an inquisitive student confronted me last year and asked, "Step, who taught *you* how to teach?" Joe's face was the first one that sprung into my head; followed, as always, by warm memories of our experiences together and the wisdom he imparted [somehow] through my thick skull and the warmth he shared with my cold heart. Anything decent I ever did as a teacher found it's genesis in the teachings of my academic sensei, and my respect for him grows more profound as my experiences in the profession multiply.

Thanks, Joe, for putting up with my neurotic, hyper-controversial ass, and for seeing that there was a quasi-decent teacher in there somewhere. You'd be proud of me, I'm still cutting through the bullshit and teaching kids what's important.

…and pissing off all the right people in the process.

———((●))———

"Joe, (bang)I think (bang)something (bang)is fundamentally wrong(bang) with(bang) me!

"Stop! You're puttin' a dent in the corner where I put the papers I pretend to read! What's the matter this time?"

"Everybody that comes to this shit hole (bang) teaches here for a short time and gets the fuck(bang) outta (bang) dodge, moves on to something better, or totally different (bang). The ones that stay only stay here 'cause they can't (bang) find (bang) anything (bang) better."

"So?"

I looked up, with a pained expression and a red forehead. "What do you mean SO?"

"So what? Maybe you're *meant* to teach these kids. Maybe something's keeping you here because they need you. Maybe you're the only one that can reach them. Maybe one of these kids is destined to have the child that will have the child that will change the world, and destiny dictates that he be here when you're here and you'll keep him from doing something stupid and making it to the time when he'll start the whole thing in motion, ever think of that?"

———((●))———

Joe, it should be noted, had a William Faulkner-ish ability to weave run-on sentences.

———((●))———

"No, I never really considered that I might be *meant* to do this."

"Unselfishly help the impoverished. Educate the less fortunate. Empower the weak. Not the worst legacy a man could have, Frankie."

———⸭———

Joe, it should be noted, had a Mahatma Ghandi-ish ability to make you feel enabled.

———⸭———

"Thanks, boss. I was starting to think I was mentally irregular or something because I *like* teaching here. I thought I was kidding myself and that maybe I was afraid to try and teach real kids."

"Ain't nothing real-er than what we deal with every day, Frankie. Think about it. If we do our job, nothing happens. No drama, no violence, no heartache. A good day is an uneventful day, and you keep it pretty calm in the eye of the storm, my friend."

"Thanks Joe," I acknowledged, getting up to leave, "one question, though."

"Anything for you, Buddha." He responded, arms wide open, with that *"I -just -dropped -some -serious knowledge -on -this -kid -and -fixed -him* smile.

"If I'm such a great teacher, why do these kids keep getting' in trouble?"

He laughed like I just asked God why water is wet.

"Frankie, Frankie, Frankie…they're **here** because they're fucked up, remember?"

———⟫⟪⟫⟪———

Joe, it should be noted, had a George Patton-ish ability to cut though the bullshit.

———⟫⟪⟫⟪———

I could write a book just honoring Joe and the impact he had on me, but I'll let him rest in peace. Suffice it to say, there would be no "Step" if a man with otherworldly passion and patience hadn't generously given his valuable time to a conflicted agent of chaos.

Thanks, Joe. I love you buddy.

A few Mr. Long stories made short.

Richard Long is, probably more than anyone else, responsible for the stain on the educational landscape that is Frank Stepnowski. He hired me for my first teaching gig, taught me the ways of the business, and helped me through many trials, most of which were self-imposed. I was brash, impulsive, arrogant and inexperienced, and many people would have cut me loose and disavowed any professional connection to me; but Mr. Long never lost sight of the fact that I was trying really hard to be a great teacher, and I always found a way to smash through any limitations that prevented me from doing so. If Joe Kopp was my guru, the wise sage on top of the mountain, Mr. Long was the big brother that was confident enough to praise me when I set the world on fire, stern enough to rub my face in it when I shit on the rug, and caring enough to not dwell on either. Everyone should be so lucky to have a boss like that.

I have been told by too many parents, guardians, students and supervisors to count what a credit I am to the profession. You can all thank Richie Long for that, for the reasons mentioned above, and so much more.

NOTE: I've also been called everything from the antichrist (true story!) to a stain on the teaching profession. None of

that is Mr. Long's fault, so blame me alone if you feel as such.

Oh, and you can kiss my ass, by the way.

Now that we've got that out of the way, here are a few short Mr. Long stories:

Hang him High

"I just got a phone call from Ed Gunn, the computer teacher."

"Mr. Long, I can explain."

"You can't choke kids with phone cords, Step."

"He punched me in the face, Rich! Did Gunn tell you *that?*"

"Don't kill Mr. Gunn, he was actually laughing when he told me about it. Christ knows, Thorn had it coming...."

"That's what I'm saying, when I..."

"HOWever , that doesn't excuse your behavior. I'm going to have a sit down with you and Thorn, once he gets out of the nurse's office"

"Will there be a phone in the room?" (I couldn't resist.)

"Why? You want to call unemployment?"

Ouch.

The truth of the matter is that Charles Thorn did, indeed, have it coming. Appropriately named, he was a thorn in the side of every teacher forced to endure him. (So, of course, he ultimately wound up in my class. See how that works? You keep the kids in line, you get the worst of the worst. No good deed goes unpunished.) I had managed to keep Charles and his unique combination of intellect and arrogance at an even keel. He would continually remind me that he was one of, if not *the*, smartest kids at Moorzakunt Academy. I reminded *him* that that was roughly the equivalent of having the biggest dick in second grade. Whoopee for you, Thorn.

I had been battling with CT for a few weeks prior to the phone "incident." Most of the guys in the class were ready to kill him as well, mainly because he never stopped talking about how he was "getting over" on his grandmother, who was raising him. Most of the kids in the room were being raised by their grandparents, so Grandmas were iconic people, and not to be fucked with.

I received a call to my little half of the trailer one day from Grandma Thorn, she was just checking in, since "Charles never tells me anything about school." Lucky for me, unlucky for Chuck, he was being a real douchebag when grandma called, so I took the opportunity to let her know that "Charles was being a bit of a handful these days." It should be noted that the phone hung on the wall near the door, so (being that it was nice out,) I stretched the phone cord to the landing outside the door so I could speak somewhat privately. I waved to Mr. Eddie Gunn, the computer teacher, who was out on his steps taking a nip from his omnipresent flask. I was in the middle of talking to grandma:

Well, ma'am, truth be told, Charles has been a bit of a handful lately, and…"

CRACK!

Thorn suckered me, hard, in the jaw. He stood with his fists clenched, his best ferocious look on his face, and spat:

"You don't get to talk about me unless I *tell* you …"

———

You can probably figure out the rest, but he never got it out. Before the guys were out of their seats, I had grabbed him by the hair, and looped the phone cord around his neck once or twice, careful to have kept my hand in the loops I could control the amount of pressure. As I "strangled" him, I continued to talk to grandmom, who (thank god) was hard of hearing and still talking about Charles' "smart aleck attitude."

"Actually, I have Charles right here," I said, voice filled with cheer as I squeezed until his eyes pleaded for mercy. "No, he doesn't want to come to the phone, he can't really talk at the moment."

Ed Gunn stared in awed silence, flask dangling from his hand.

I actually "waved" to him and smiled. Then I said goodbye to grandmom and gave Mr. Thorn my undivided attention.

Guess what?

Thorn had a roll of quarters in his hand when he punched me. (I know, who the hell carries a roll of quarters around??)

He also had a switchblade in his pocket. Lucky for him he didn't cut me with that, especially since…

He was higher than the Space Shuttle. (Blood tests from the nurse's office, and HE ADMITTED TO IT.)

————)(O)(————

Of course, Mr. Long knew that long before the tests came back. Funny I didn't notice how much Thorn smelled like weed when he was punching me in the face, but now that we were in the office, it was unmistakable. Long let Thorn know the penalties for being under the influence, possessing a weapon, and assaulting a teacher. Thorn never got to mention that I was unfazed by the punch or that he hadn't been *proven* to be high [yet,] and by the end of the meeting, he was apologizing to me and thanking me for not pushing the issue any further.

Just so you know, I only had one problem with Charles Thorn after that. He came to the prom I organized at M.A. in on of those *Dumb and Dumber* frilly powder blue tuxedoes; unfortunately, he came high as well.

He was hitting on my fiancé, and trying to cop a feel when I reminded him that one does not require a phone cord to effectively strangle someone. Dawn just thought it was funny, and I guess, in hindsight, she was right; because Charles Thorn became (several years after graduating from M.A., at great expense to him, Char*lene* Thorn.)

Does this mean I should feel guilty for hitting a girl?

At any rate, Mr. Long saved me on that one,

and it wouldn't be the last time.

Book 'em Longo

Maybe the greatest single contribution that R. Long made to my teaching career was his ability to overlook minutiae in favor of seeing the bigger picture. When you're actually trying to teach the kids I taught, you've got to break free from convention, and you simply can't do that without administrative support.

I can hear you out there, shaking your heads, my fellow teachers, and I feel your pain. Let me explain to the rest of the world what I mean.

Most of my classes consisted of 12-14 hardcore special ed. kids, although my classes these days have 24-27 "regular" ed. kids or a combination of regular and special ed. See how confusing that shit gets, and I haven't even *scratched the surface* of sub-categories and special needs, etc.

I solved that problem very early in my career with some good old-fashioned common sense. Listening?

I only care if they're learning or not.

Good job, Step, there goes you're chance of staying employed in the teaching field. You need to individualize instruction, read the IEPs, follow the curriculum, yadda yadda yadda.

I'm well aware of that, folks. My attention to detail is *legendary*, and I know what specialized instruction every one of my students require, but I know something that trumps all of that shit 100% of the time. Listening?

If the kids know you don't care, everything you do is an exercise in futility.

Caring, of course, means deviating from the curriculum and talking about things in class that don't relate directly to 11th grade English, 10th grade History, 3rd grade Mathematics, whatever. When my guys were scared after 911, we *talked* about it. When we were in a school where incarceration and gang affiliation were part of students' daily life, I researched that stuff and we had discussions so they were *correctly informed* about the potential consequences of their actions.

<hr>

On lighter notes, I did Shakespeare with my guys just because everybody else said it was impossible, and when they said they wanted to learn biology (are you fucking kidding me, you don't know basic Earth science?!?) I hit the books and re-learned biology so I could teach it to them. Of course, many teachers would say "I'm not going to spend all that time learning new material, or re-learning old material, I'm sticking to what I do every year because that's what I get paid for."

That's why you suck.

I can hear the rest of you clamoring out there, "I wish to high heaven I could do that stuff, but the bosses want us to stick to the curriculum, and we have to keep the test scores up!

I know, guys, I really do. I also know how lucky I was to have Mr. Long as my boss during my embryonic stage as a teacher. He let me do whatever I thought was right to teach the [allegedly] unteachable – and we had some fucking <u>amazing</u> results during our years together, and a whole lot more successes than failures.

I believe there might be a lesson hidden in there somewhere.

How did Long cover my ass and help me show the kids I was attentive to their needs? Let me count the ways…well, he never questioned what I was working on in class. If I was teaching about the cancer cells because one of the kids' moms was suffering and they all wanted to know more about it, so be it. If I wanted to do a novel with the class because I knew it would hold their interest, he would split the cost with me and we'd buy a class set, not bothering to worry about the occasional curse word or violent act in the text. (By the way, we were reading *I Am Legend, Holes,* and *V for Vendetta* YEARS before they were made into movies, ain't that right guys?)

Last but certainly not least, I can remember, on more than one occasion, finding boxes of copybooks, folders, workbooks, etc. on my desk. Nothing attached, just "Step" written on the box. Somebody understood that for kids to truly feel like students, they needed to have materials of their own.

Thanks again, R.L.

FRANK STEPNOWSKI

I thought Tourette was a French pastry

Okay, I think I was pretty clear that when I started at Moorzakunt Academy I was not certified in special education. So it stood to reason that I didn't know what Tourette's syndrome was. Therefore, it stands to reason that when Luigi Rigatoni (not his real last name, could you tell?) kept telling me to "go fuck myself " under his breath, I was mildly annoyed.

Actually, Mr. Rigatoni's commentary was far more diverse than "go fuck yourself," as I will elaborate upon in this brief but entertaining anecdote.

"This is Luigi," announced Mr. Long, "he'll be in your class for a few weeks."

"Thank for all the info, Long." I thought to myself; but the truth is that this particular scenario happened often enough that we both knew the drill:

Kid gets placed at M.A. based on the mountain of paperwork that accompanied him/her.

Kid is informally re-evaluated (read: yanked out of the class in a panic) after threatening to kill someone, giving the teacher a heart attack, assaulting someone, etc.

Kid is put in my room [regardless of age, academic level, diagnoses, etc.] until formal re-revaluation is scheduled.

My little cherubs and I do our best to prevent further outbursts from our part time tenant, and

I do my best to inflict some education upon them in the meantime.

"Welcome, Luigi," I mused, "have a seat until your brother Mario gets here."

Luigi, for his part, looked like a ball of kinetic energy ready to explode. With pale skin, burnt orange hair, freckles, and enough facial tics to power a small generator, he didn't *look* like a Luigi Rigatoni, if you know what I mean. My musings on the non-Italian nature of his outward appearance were cut short by what I *thought* was a very muffled reference to me as a "cocksucker" as Luigi found his way to a seat in the back.

"Excuse me? Did you say something?" I inquired, menacingly.

"Nah, nah, I'm goin' to sit hear, awright?"

"Sure," I responded, narrowing my eyes in suspicion, joined by the accusing looks of Damon, Hillard, and Hector, all of whom heard the "cocksucker" reference.

"What?" Luigi asked, hands out, big smile on his face. Then, very quietly,

"fuckin' assholes."

Do I need to tell you the reaction of a class full of emotionally unstable but fiercely loyal inner city kids to a hyper kinetic white boy that just insulted them [and their teacher] in a span of thirty seconds?

No? Good. That'll save some time.

———•((•))•———

After I regained control of the room and pulled the wolves off of Mr. Rigatoni, who had the nerve to act offended (!) I resumed my lesson. I don't remember what I was teaching that day so, for the sake of poetic license, let's say I was refuting the notion that Athens was the most "civilized" of the Greek city States, because they refused to educate their women, like the allegedly "barbaric" Spartans.

"So, you see, the Spartans were actually…"

"Ass fucker."

I shot Luigi a very fast look that said *you can't possibly be that stupid to talk more shit after I just saved your life, can you?* He smiled and gave me another one of his patented *"What? Why you lookin' at me?"* gestures.

I resumed my informative lecture, fully aware that the guys had ALL heard Luigi, and were primed to explode like a bunch of thermobaric warheads (1)

"…pro education. In addition, the Spartans promoted the idea of unity by…"

"cwazy cocksuckers."

"Alright THAT does it!" urged Rodney, who was seated right in front of Luigi, and therefore got to him just before the rest of the cwazy cocksuckers.

Fast-forward several minutes. I have regained order, AGAIN, and we have Luigi surrounded. His face is twitching like Shakira's hips on Red Bull but he's actually *laughing to himself* in the face of certain doom.

"Luigi," I petition, "is there a reason why you keep cursing us out? Have I done something to offend you in any way? Is there something we can do to help you?"

Needles to say, I was interrupted by a tsunami of suggestions from my guys about "what they could do" for Luigi and other, more direct, implications. Luigi, in typical character, just laughed to himself and professed that he didn't know what we were talking about, leading one Anthony Jackson to put forth the following astute observation:

"That little fucker's crazy."

With the very real possibility that Luigi was certifiably insane, or had a death wish, ringing in my ears, I whisked him out of harm's

---

1   Nasty little weapon of mass destruction. Look it up!

way and right down to Mr. Long's office for further clarification as to the nature of Luigi's emotional and/or academic status.

"Oh that little fucker's crazy." Noted the esteemed Mr. Long, as we sat in his office, with Anthony keeping watch on Luigi in the next room.

"I mean, he has Tourette's of course, but he's crazy as a bedbug." Long laughed, "Mary Lou Bomb (art teacher) has already broken three brooms over him this year because he keep calling her "cwazy old bitch" every ten seconds."

"Hold up," I urged, "what the fuck is Tourette's? Sounds like a French pastry or something!"

"Oh, that's right," Long observed, "I keep forgetting, because you're so good with the kids, that you're not special ed. certified."

"Thanks, I think. Now what the fuck is Tourette's?"

<hr />

What followed was a brief but nonetheless informative and accurate explanation of Tourette's syndrome, which explained why Luigi couldn't keep himself from referring to me and my Stepchildren in such colorful terms."

I should point out here that I probably could have earned a certification in special education after a few years of these kind of meetings in Mr. Long's office. I would bring the kid in, he would explain the situation, and I would take the kid back to class and explain, in detail, what I had just learned to the class who would, in turn, understand the kid better (often relating in some way) and therefore tolerate him/her much better.

I KNOW there's a lesson in there somewhere. You got it right?

Good job.

You cwazy cocksuckers.

———⊃《◉》⊂———

Wow. I just re-read that last paragraph, and there's so much valuable information in there that I'm going to end this chapter right here. Seriously, folks, if you want a quick synopsis of my teaching style for your records, there it is.

Admit that you don't know everything.

Ask hard questions, ask them to the people you know will provide the best answers.

Accept the answers, even if they aren't the ones you wanted.

Take what you've learned and teach others. Reduction of ignorance is always appropriate to any educational scenario.

Learn about your students, then accept them, flaws and all.

Reap the rewards; specifically, your students will accept you, flaws and all.

How did I get so smart?

Thanks, Mr. Long.

Kevin Caper - Special Ed. Choreographer.

Many of my funniest recollections from the earliest years involve Kevin Caper, a hyper-energetic red head that was one of the fastest, and funniest, human beings I was ever fortunate enough to share an alcoholic stupor with.

Biggest mistake I ever made was telling Cape that I was writing a book someday. That crazy –ass white boy called me twice a week at least to show me "some shit for your book." One of my all time favorites was when he trained his *very* special gym class (read: autistic, learning disabled, severely retarded, etc.) to dance, sing, and play make believe instruments (tennis rackets, wiffle ball bats) while Cape sang the theme song to *The Fat Albert Show*. I'd walk into the gym, and there would be asshole Caper strutting his stuff, singing "Kev's gonna show you a thing or twooooooo, Na, Na, Na gonna have a good time!" while Aria, an autistic girl with a heart of gold and the appetite of a small third world country would shout out "Hey Hey Hey!" as the rest of the out to lunch bunch gestured wildly and laughed uncontrollably.

I had no choice but to shake my head and laugh, "you're going to Hell, Mr. Caper, but you'll be in my book some day."

Cape would look at me like I insulted his mother. "What? These guys LOVE this shit! Watch this! O.K. guys, Michael Jackson time!"

The guys and gals sprinted to return their "instruments" and lined up like they were getting ready to start the finale' of *A Chorus Line*. The anticipation on their faces was something to behold. Cape emerged from the back office with a boom box bigger than the one Radio Raheem carried in Spike Lee's *Do The Right Thing*. With a push of the play button, Michael Jackson's *Thriller* blared across the gym. Robert, a severely retarded young man that never spoke unless he was in gym class with Cape or art class with Ms. Bomb, announce that "it was on!" and Cape and his gym class started doing the zombie dances from the *Thriller* video. Now for the good part – they did them WELL.

If I'm lying may God strike me dead.

———————

O.K., a very small lightning bolt struck my computer after that last statement, so God evidently feels that I must CLARIFY my previous statement. The young men and women of Mr. Caper's class *performed the dance sequences from the Thriller video more accurately, and with 100% more synchronicity than you would ever expect a group of special education students to muster; and they enjoyed the hell out of themselves doing it, too.* If I'm lying, or over exaggerating in any way, may God strike me dead.

I said, may God strike me dead.

———————

Alright, now that we got THAT straight, I can tell you that my initial apprehension that Kev was exploiting kids with disabilities to get into a book I was sure would never be completed was quickly replaced with a deep sense of appreciation and respect when I saw the joy on the faces of the kids whenever whacko Mr. Caper had them practice one of their numbers or skits. Cape had to go to North Carolina for a wedding one time, and when I tell you those kids lost their fucking MINDS for three days, I am not kidding. I helped covered his classes on the first of the three days he was out and if one of those kids asked me one more time "When Mr. Caper coming back? He coming back, right? When? When he coming back?" I think I might have abused them myself.

Ah, but Mr. Caper wasn't just our resident special ed. choreographer! No, no, gentle reader, he was also a master (MASTER!) of practical advice, so key for young, influential minds. Minds like that of young Robert Forrest.

Cape and I were shooting the shit in what passed for a gym office at Moorzakunt Academy: basically a phone booth stuffed with jump ropes, Frisbees, and every type of ball known to man. In the middle of our conversation, the aforementioned Mr. Foster burst in.

"Hey, Mister Caper, I gotta talk to you. Oh, hey, Step, sorry – was you talkin'? Sorry. Anyway, I gotta ask you something. Mr. Caper, that is – not you Step. So, can I ask you something? It don't matter if Step is here, but I gotta ask you something."

I love teenagers, especially crazy ones; they carry on both sides of the conversation for you.

So Caper, adopting his best exaggerated "I'm here for my students" posture, swings his chair around, shoots me a quick "watch this awesomeness" look, and opens his arms, letting Robert know he was ready to pass on the wisdom of the elders.

"Well, I'm touching myself. A LOT."

The smile on my face could have illuminated the inside of a black hole, as I raised my eyebrows and shot Caper a quick "let's hear your advice for *this* one, asshole" look.

Cape, true to form, landed on his feet like a cat. He asked Robert what he meant by "a LOT," as the wheels turned frantically in that red head of his, no doubt postulating some kind of advice that would be both practical and inoffensive.

Mind you, I wasn't going to make this easy for him, as I continued to make faces and gestures (use your imagination) behind Robert's back, all with the intent of napalming Mr. Caper's otherwise cool-as-the-other-side-of-the-pillow exterior. Both of us, however, were rendered temporarily speechless when Robert responded that he was "pleasuring himself" seven or eight, maybe nine times a day. (1)

I exchanged a "WTF" look with Kev before he turned into Robin Williams in *Good Will Hunting:* (For added fun, try to picture in your mind the faces and gestures I was making while Dr. Caper spouted this shit. For even more fun, let's count the number of times mister masturbation expert says "it's perfectly natural.)

"That's perfectly natural, [One!] Robert. All young men have sexual impulses at this age, and it's perfectly natural [Two!] to explore them, My biggest concern is that you're missing out on a lot of other stuff while you're....um....exploring."

"That's what I'm worried about," Robert gushed, "and when I told my mommy she said I should talk to my gym teacher about it."

Cape was stunned to silence for a fraction of a second, then:

"Oooookay, that makes sense. So anyway, why don't you, when you feel, you know,"

"Like I want to stroke my penis?"

"Yeah. Then. When you feel like you want to do that, and it is perfectly natural, [Three!] take that energy and put it into something more productive, like…

---

1   I hear you people. I'm thinking the same thing. First the $1600 phone sex bill from Jerry, now this. Is there Viagra in the water supply around here or what?

Cape looked around frantically for a sign, which was granted to him by Saint Spalding, the patron saint of the roundball.

"like shoot hoops!" Cape exhalted. "Yes! When you get the urge to…"

"Stroke my penis!" Robert shouted, a bit too animated if you ask me.

"Yeah! When you get that urge, go out and shoot some hoops until the energy wears off. I'm not saying you shouldn't help yourself once or twice a day (god forbid) because it's perfectly natural, [Four!] but…"

"But I can get better at ballin' and still stroke my…"

"Yes!" Cape and I both responded, neither of us wanting to hear that phrase again, especially with the spark in Robert's eyes when he said it.

"Thank you, Mr. Caper. Thank you. I will shoot hoops, and I'll get better. Thank you. Thanks, Step. You didn't really help, but thanks anyway. I'll see you, Mr. Caper!"

With that, Robert bounded out of the "office," leaving Kevin Caper in a state of smug accomplishment. He smirked at me and repeated

"Yeah, Step. You didn't really help, but thanks anyway."

I couldn't resist.

"Well, you are the gym teacher, so ***it's perfectly natural*** that you should be the expert."

I dodged the basketball launched at me and escaped, unscathed.

———»«O»«———

For you *Sesame Street* fans in the audience, that was Five! Five it's perfectly naturals, Ah Ah Ahhhhhh!

Epilogue:

You're going to love this

I get a phone call in my classroom a few days later. Lamont answered and looked at the phone funny, then he covered the receiver and said:

"I think it's Caper, but he don't sound right."

I flew out of the room and down to the gym office. When I realized that Cape was out of breath from laughing, I told the rest of my guys (who bounded right behind me at the prospect of trouble) to go back to class and that I would be back in a minute.

"What the fuck, Cape?" I demanded.

He composed himself and told me that he had just received a phone call from Robert Forrest's mother.

"She just wanted to thank me for being such an inspiration to Robert. She has to literally pull him off the basketball court down the street from their house. He spends so much time there anymore, he's going to play in the NBA someday!"

After much laughter and back slapping, we recovered and pondered what we could accomplish in life if we took every "perfectly natural" impulse and applied it to another course of action.

Oh, I don't know…maybe write, edit, format, publish, and promote a 300-page book in six months?

I'm just saying.
And it's perfectly natural.

Don and Steve - Court Jesters in the Twilight Zone.

Donnie Jagger and Steve McFlurry.
What a pair of assholes.

I'm kidding, but I know they would *love* that introduction, because they're assholes.

So where do I begin with these two? In appearance, they couldn't be more different, Donnie was about 5'8', with an upper body chiseled from years of heavy work in the gym, Steve was about 6'3', with an upper body honed from years of riding a lawnmower and drinking Miller High Life and watching NASCAR. However, regarding sense of humor, you will never find two individuals more symbiotically linked. Complete nut jobs the two of them, but funnier than a nudist in a cactus patch.

Let's start with the hallway.

Don and Steve were infamous for the creative "soundtracks" they created to accompany various personalities that worked at Moorzakunt Academy. Their *modus operandi* was to wait until the target was down the hall, or engaged in conversation, and they would pop their heads out from the recessed areas in the hall where the class bathrooms were. Once their smiling faces popped out like the Whack-A-Mole game, the chorus would start; many was the time that I got caught talking to someone with a soundtrack when those two assholes started. Trying to keep a straight face was pretty close to impossible, eSPECially when they intensified their act knowing you were fighting to keep it cool.

My personal favorite was when Lynn du Soliel, a particularly nasty administrator, used to stalk the halls. Lynn had a tendency to wear very colorful outfits with baggy sleeves and/or pants; the boys rewarded her clown-like choice of wardrobe with a circus-oriented theme. It took an act of Herculean willpower to not break up if you were at your door while Lynn prowled the hall (looking to bust balls), when behind her two heads would pop out and announce

"UNDER THE BIG TOP!! (followed by circus music and juggling motions with hands)

dant dant daaanna dyant tan danna, dump dump danna dyant dant daaanna!…"

Lynn would, every time, spin around and glare only to find empty hallway and, if she was really frisky, locked bathrooms. Students were more than happy to help by coming out of the bathroom, having hid in there with either of the two knuckleheads and emerging while Don or Steve hid behind the door. The kids were always ready to help when funny was on the menu.

Now Donnie will tell you that *his* favorite was tormenting Freud Settlethis, a psychologist that would strut the halls, leather attaché' in hand, looking for lost souls to save and teachers to belittle. It should be noted that Dr. Freud changed his tune after working with our little angels for a year – guess being told repeatedly to *"go fuck yourself, you old-ass communist lookin' mothefucker"* has an affect on you.

The good doctor, with his serious beard and serious clothes and serious face bore a striking resemblance to the old Dr. Van Helsing characters from the early Dracula movies, so his "soundtrack" was a bit on the nostalgic side. When Dr. Settlethis would try

WHY ARE ALL THE GOOD TEACHERS CRAZY?

reprimanding a kid or chastising a teacher, or even do something with good intention, the Whack-A-Mole heads would pop out *and…*

"Creature of the NIIIIGHT

I cast you OOOUUT! (followed by cheesy horror movie music and bat wings flapping)

Ooooooo WEEEEEEE oooooo , dink dink dink DINK dum dum dum DUM!…"

Dr, Van Helsing was a bit slower on the trigger than Ms. Du Soliel, so by the time he turned and investigated, the chaos chorus would be long gone.

Unless, of course, Freud happened to be talking to me.

Because Steve, Don and I were such good buddies, I earned their special attention.

Lucky me.

If I was taking to the good doctor, Don and Steve would do a little number from The Exorcist. Loved the movie. Scared the shit out of me. Still does; but I'll be *damned* if I could hold it together while those two idiots shouted "THE POWER OF CHRIST COMPELLS YOU!

THE *POWER* OF CHRIST COMPE*LS* YOU!!!" while you're face to face with Dr. Settlethis.

I eventually got to know Dr. Freud pretty well and, as I said, he came around to our way of thinking (that is to say, a bit more practical and empathetic, a bit less idealistic and elitist) and I found him to be an engaging, witty guy; although he did confess to "hating those two ignoramuses that seemed to do nothing but hide in the halls and torment folks."

245

(Somewhere, Don and Steve are pumping their fists after reading that)

A classic quickie that Stevie came up with to rattle substitute teachers was the old soundtrack from the T.V. show <u>George of the Jungle</u>. Some new sub would be walking down the hall, trying to be professional but scared shitless when, from behind them, without warning...

"BUM! BUM! BUMBUM BA DUMDUM!

Substitute jumps, (startled, of course,) and turns. Empty hallway.

They continue walking...

Watch out for that TREEEEEE!"

Sub is really startled now, not expecting this twice. Waits a minute, takes a few steps, looks back, takes a few more cautious steps. All clear (or so they think) they begin walking again...

"WEH-E-ELLLLLL!!!! GEORGE GEORGE GEORGE of the JUNGLE!!!"

Rookie is now totally flustered and/or annoyed, stopping cold. Knowing this, one of the boys, usually Donnie, emerges from his hiding spot, walks right up to the newbie's face and yells, with a dramatic hand flourish:

"FRIEND TO YOU AND ME!"

Sub seeks out principal's office and resigns.

Oh well, you know what I always say:

If you can't handle G.O.T.J., you ain't ready for S.E.D.

There were many more "soundtracks," but it's high time I paid appropriate homage to the glimmer twins' now legendary response to the practical jokes pulled on them. The boys fucked with me incessantly, doing everything possible to take me off my game; however, I was, in truth, what your parents would call "the instigator." That means I was the little bastard that fucked with people until they felt the homicidal urge to retaliate.

I would do little stuff just to let the boys know I loved them, like when Steve used to clean the school (after school hours) for extra cash; I would lay in wait until he was in a room vacuuming and, once he turned off the vacuum to move desks, I would unplug the cord in the hallway and practice all the new knots I learned from the book on nautical knots I purchased. Then **he** would practice all the new curse words he learned trying to un-knot the cord.

I also thoroughly enjoyed replacing Steve's "hidden" VHS tape collection, one at a time, with National Geographic specials. I used to chuckle to myself thinking of Steve, getting comfortable, everything in place, popping in [what he thought was] a pre-set scene of his favorite porno, only to be greeted with *"…here we see the Galapagos iguana in it's natural habitat."*

Steve loved me. To this day he gets a mini erection whenever you mention iguanas.

Finally, and probably most infantile in nature, was my tendency to hit Steve in the balls when he least expected it. To be honest, I didn't start it — that was a torment that several of the guys on the behavior management team had started among themselves, *I* just *perfected* it. My retractable key chain came in particularly helpful for long-range nut-knocking, although a well placed backhand worked for close quarters combat. My favorite weapon of testicular destruction was when I *allowed* Steve to catch me with the vacuum cord in my hand, ready to knot it up. Then, when he ran up to me in triumph, I whacked him in the twig and berries with the plug end of the cord, then walked away laughing while he was doubled over in the hall.

Now Donnie took a bit more creativity to properly enrage, as he was more creative in his torment of me; thus, he was less prone to response when I reciprocated. You might have guessed by now that Donnie was a borderline obsessive fan of *The Rolling Stones*, and one of his prize possessions was his denim jacket with the classic Stones tongue embroidered on the back. It was a beautiful, expensive jacket, and a sacrosanct item to my buddy.

So when I offered to help cover the Beta Room so Don could go potty, then buttoned up the jacket on Preston, one of the "B building" kids who had *soiled* himself in a major way...

Let's just say that Steve almost asphyxiated laughing as a very short, VERY angry Italian chased a very large, VERY ashamed Polish Jew around the campus like some Bizzaro version of the National Geographic specials that Steve loved so much.

———————◎———————

Now you might think, in reading this book, that I spent my whole day engaging in shenanigans and horseplay, but if you combine everything in this book and multiply it by the square root of infinity, it doesn't come close to the 15 YEARS that I spent actually working for and with my students at good old M. Academy, so I did spend a LOT of time in the classroom teaching. Furthermore, when I was doing my job, I was a control freak about getting what I wanted done *when* I wanted it done and *how* I wanted it done,

…and that gave Don and Steve an idea. A wonderfully grinchy idea.

⸺◦⸺

I came into work on the day after "the retaliation" ready to give a science test that we had spent the entire week reviewing for. If you know anything about the kind of kids I taught, you know that they are creatures of habit, and they do NOT like having their schedules tampered with. If we're supposed to have a test today, on Science, during 1st period, you had best have a Science test, 1st period, today, unless you wanted a wholesale meltdown on your hands. So it was with great trepidation that I noticed that the desk drawer where the test materials were located was stuck.

"Hmmm…" I thought, "must've jammed it" and I commenced pulling, hard, on the drawer, trying my best to remain nonchalant while doing so, and pausing every time one of my fidgety students looked my was.

"Hmmm…" I thought, "maybe I can open the drawer underneath it and wedge it open" and I opened the bottom left drawer.

I said I opened the bottom left drawer.

I *said* - mph – that I OPENed - rrrrgh – the bottom – mmmmph – right - CRACK (oops) DRAWER!

Shit.

⸺◦⸺

One of the tribe, an intrepid young man name of Hillard Beneathya, couldn't help but notice me yanking on my desk drawers like Steve yanking on himself during an iguana special, complete with grunting noises and minimal results.

"What's up with your desk , Step?"

"Damn if I know, Hill."

By now the rest of the tribe were interested as to why a guy that could bench press a small Volvo couldn't open a simple desk drawer.

"Didja try 'em all?" asked young Hillard

I answered by pulling on each and every of the seven drawers, only to find them closed tighter than Hannah Montana at a slumber party. (1) To you, the reader, it would seem obvious what had happened to the innocent victim that was my desk.

Alas, you are smarter than I, dear reader. I never suspected a thing, until I ripped the front off the "test" drawer off in a frustrated rage.

"Wow," observed Hillard and Chad, "that's a LOT of screws."

———◉———

While my guys took their science test in as much silence as they were capable, I monitored them and simultaneously counted the amount of screws Don and Steve had used to put the "Home Depot lockdown" on my desk.

"Three hundred and one…Dave, put the cheat sheet away, three hundred and two, three hundred and…no, Danny, you don't have two livers, three hundred and three…Semaj you might want to close that science book under your desk. Yes, *that* one. Three hundred and four…"

One science test and THREE HUNDRED and TWENTY SEVEN SCREWS later, I sat in front of what used to be my desk

1   Don't hate me, Miley. I love your show; and I'm pretty sure my 10-year-old son Frankie is in love with you.

while my guys went to "music" or "art." (It was still early in the year and the elective teachers hadn't yet requested that my guys be banned from electives.) I knew that Jagger and McFlurry were lurking nearby, waiting to hear the wailing and cursing that were no doubt going to come forth from my room.

I kept it cool, in part because I didn't want to give them the satisfaction, in part out of silent respect for the sheer magnitude and brilliance of the prank itself; I mean, three *hundred* and twenty seven screws?!? That's just spectacular.

Hillard, who loved hands-on projects, mechanical work, etc. begged for the chance to disassemble my desk and repair it from the ground up. He did, and I rewarded him for it.

Don and Steve were impressed at how well I took it, and I found myself roaring with laughter as they recounted how *they* roared with laughter while doing the deed.

"Don't you have to get home, bud?"

"Nah, it's only 5:30, and I think I can fit a few more screws here at the bottom."

"What're we up to?"

"I don't know, I figured we'd just use up whatever's in the can."

(insert uproarious laughter.)

Like I said…assholes.

Soundtracks and screw-jobs aside, Donnie Jagger and Steve McFlurry were also an accomplished welcoming committee for the new teachers that arrived at Moorzakunt Academy with dreams of changing the world. One can only imagine how they would be introduced over the loudspeaker:

"At a combined weight of over 475 pounds (pounds pounds pounds)

From the fighting city of PHIL a DEL phia (phia phia phia)

The ASShole (asshole asshole asshole) twins…
Donnie Jagger and Steve Mc Fluuuuuuuurrrrrrrrryyyyyyy…"

———— ‹‹◖›› ————

Which brings us to Meredith, the poor young girl that was hired to be the "counseling"(2) secretary.

She answered her very first "official" phone call, only to be greeted by Don, who was doing his impersonation of Janet Rosenberg, the alpha-secretary that ran the front desk like a well-oiled machine for the entire Mr. Long era. In an exaggerated version of Janet's signature Jewish whine, (think *Golden Girls* meets *The Nanny*) Don started into her:

"Hon, I need one bagel, toasted lightly, it's gotta be lightly or I can't eat it, with lox, is your lox fresh? If not, some thinly sliced gefelte fish, "

"Ma'am, I think you've got the wrong…"

"Ah ah ah DON'T interrupt me boobalah, I lose the train of thought! Now, a need a hot water with lemon, and a Jewish hoagie, that's an Italian except I ain't paying for it, with extra jackomeen (3)…"

Click

Mr. Long had to beg Don and Steve to relax before we lost *another* secretary on her first day.

Don and Steve used Janet Rosenberg's voice like they owned

2   You'll notice I always put "quotes" around the word counseling; mainly because, with the exception of two people (hi Candy! Hi Howard!) every 'counselor' we had during my fifteen years at M.A. was a fucking clown who didn't *counsel* anybody, they just talked at the kids the handed them whatever the company line was. What? You've got them at *your* school, too? You don't say!

3   "jackomeen" was Don's pet name for mayonnaise and/or sperm; he named it after former New York Rangers goalie Eddie Giacomin. Don hated mayo, and he hated Eddie Giacomin; sperm, I can't say for sure. (4)

4   I know, I worked with some weird motherfuckers

the rights to it, so you would think that they would cut her some slack in the torment department.

You would think that.

The asshole twins had the unique advantage of not needing to stay in the good graces of the secretary, as they never needed to use the main phone, the copier, etc; hence, their vocal assertion that Mrs. Rosenberg looked like Zira, the female chimpanzee doctor from the original <u>Planet of the Apes</u> movie. They would hang around the corner from the front desk, like two young scamps from a Mark Twain novel, and yell, in their best *Janet Rosenberg doing Zira the Chimpanzee doctor* voice:

"Wheeeere's Tay-lor?"

or perhaps

"I'd like to kiss you but you're so damned ugly!"

or perchance

"The gorillas have gone into the forbidden zone!"

By the time Janet became annoyed enough to get up and chase the annoying insects bussing around her desk, they were long gone, running down the hall to torment whatever substitute wandered into their path:

"BUM! BUM! BUMBUM BA DUMDUM!
"FRIEND TO YOU AND ME!"

Sat it with me folks, assholes.

But they're still my boys. Don was actually the man who took me to the hospital on the day when I was told that my late son Cain was diagnosed. He was the rock I needed when everything that really mattered to me shattered.

I love you like a brother, Don, and always will.

———⊂«◐»⊃———

Steve, you beer-drinkin', couch –fuckin', paint' deliverin, NASCAR-watchin', iguana masturbatin', John Deere ridin', maniac …you're still an asshole.

You've Got (Basket)Balls, Andrew Springsteen.

To put it mildly, basketball was a way of life at Moorzakunt Academy. I'm pretty sure that when Doctor Friedrich Moorzakunt was creating his dissertation on child development, he never dreamed that three pointers, hard fouls in the paint, and trash talking elevated to an art form would take center stage at a school bearing his regal sobriquet.

Such is life.

As such, when it comes to stories of hoops hilarity, I've got a million of 'em, and most of them involve my dear friend, Andy Springsteen.

Athletico anecdoto numero uno – "Nice bracelet"

As you might imagine, setting up basketball games with other schools was not the easiest thing to do. Faced with the prospect of a game against a group of inner city street thugs with criminal records and a very vague sense of right and wrong proved unattractive to most coaches and players. When my buddy Andy Springsteen (no relation to that singer fellow) tried to arrange games for our Bad News Bears Basketball bunch, he was greeted with everything from laughter to hang ups to, in one regrettable case, commentary on both his sanity and sexuality. Andy, however, in addition to being twice the teacher (and ten times the basketball player) I am, is a persistent little bastard. Must be a point guard thing.

"I got us a game!" Andy bubbled

"A game of what?" I inquired

"Basketball! I got us a game, two Thursdays from now, at Red Briar Academy."

"Andy, my man." I countered, in the same tone of voice a person uses when they try to talk their friend off the ledge of a building

"Yeah?"

"I love ya brother, but we don't have a basketball team."

Andy smiled. "We work with these guys all the time, they all play basketball 24/7, and we have those old uniforms that were donated. We get Jarren, Chris, Ben, Adam, and a few of the others, we'll be fine."

I'd like to take a moment right now to thank whatever divine forces have filled my life with people like Andrew Springsteen; smaller than me, smarter than me, and filled with a sense of optimism and adventure that overruled my cynicism and conservatism. Andy, and those like him, have enriched my life immeasurably.

At the time of this story, however, I was still my old self.

"You, my friend, are out of your fucking mind."

"Come on," he cajoled, smiling that smile that made it impossible to say no, "you know it'll be fun. At the very least, potential for total chaos, and you love that, you *know* you do."

I stared at him with my best "the*re-is-no-way-I'm-going-along-with-this*" look.

He didn't buy it for a second.

"Come on coach Step, let's schedule our first practice!"

Of course, our guys were delighted.

Damn you, Andy Springsteen.

The boys were as hyped as I'd ever seen them about anything.

Even with the "ghetto ass" uniforms we gave them, the "wack ass" gym we had to practice in, and the "bitch ass" team we were scheduled to play, the young men of M.A.'s first ever basketball team were paying attention (for the most part) to Andrew as he taught them the fundamentals of "real" basketball; and they didn't bitch (too much) when I put them through the first conditioning drills of their miserable lives. This is not to say we didn't have problems.

Problem #1 We had less than two weeks to practice.
Problem #2 We could only practice during the guys' gym classes.
Problem #3 Most of the best players were in trouble all of the time (just like in Division 1 schools!)
Problem #4 We sucked. Hard.
Problem #5 Red Briar Academy, despite the fancy name, was an alternative school for kids just like ours, maybe worse; and we were going into *their* house.

Solution #1 Drill the basics, work on foul shots (because, God knows, there was gonna be a LOT of fouling.)
Solution #2 Combine gym classes so we could double our practice time. (Thank you, John and Patty for being understanding gym teachers.)
Solution #3 The people who ran the school were willing to overlook suspensions, punishments, etc. as long as Andy and I kept the "bad ones" at practice. (just like in Division 1 school!)
Solution #4 They didn't know they sucked hard and, in hindsight, Andrew's optimism was starting to rub off on the little bastards, (and the big one, too.)

Solution #5 After being shot at, jumped into gangs, being expelled from schools, arrested, and living in juvenile facilities, going into another "bad" school to play basketball seemed like a trip to the amusement park. I mean, how bad could it be?

How bad could it be?
Famous last words.

The game was…how shall I put this? Difficult to watch, painful to coach but,(I will now admit some 15 years later,) fun to be a part of. I don't know who the two referees were, but they ensured themselves a ticket to whatever heaven awaits by trying to maintain order that day. A lot of fouls, a lot of trash talking, and a three point victory for the Moorzakunt Dragons. I was prepared to retire undefeated after that auspicious debut, but coach Springsteen was having none of that talk.

The most memorable part of the game, for me, happened before the opening tip. As I meditated silently, arms folded, my best *you-embarrass-me-and-I'll-dismember-you* look on my face, I noticed something.

Six, SIX of the starting ten players on the floor had house arrest bracelets on their ankles!

Making no attempt at all to hide them, 6/10 of our basketball players were sporting (on top of their knee high Scooby Doo socks and $100 Nikes, proof that they had committed crime worthy of GPS monitoring within the last few weeks.

This was not going to pass without photographic evidence.

I called for the opening tip to be halted (sometimes it pays to be the biggest guy in the room) and commandeered a camera. I made the players squeeze in the shot and immortalized the moment.

The good news – once I pointed out *why* I was taking the

picture, players on both sides, that had previously been glaring at one another, started exchanging stories about what they did to get in trouble; unfortunately, high fives and laughs turned into flagrant fouls and bad crossover dribbles the minute the game started.

The bad news – the photo, which I would have LOVED to include in this chapter, is nowhere to be found. Hey guys, if you're out there reading this and one of you has the picture, send it to me so I can put it in the next book, or give it to Oprah.

Hoopus storius hilarious II – Over the fence or under it.

Two years into Andy's "fun little idea" to start a basketball team we, the Moorzakunt Dragons, were the consensus number two team in our league. A league that grew to consist of eight to ten other schools that (like us) harbored criminals in training. I say eight to ten because at any given moment, one or two schools might have to opt out of a game because they didn't have enough players. Reasons for forfeit ranged from suspension to expulsion, incarceration to death.

No, I am not kidding; and many of you that teach "at risk" kids are nodding and laughing to yourself thinking, "sad, but true."

You can't help but ask yourself, "number *two* team? Who's number one?"

That would be Willcrosse, the alternative school located, ironically, just down the street from us. Willcrosse was bigger, better financed, and had a student population about ten times the size of ours; therefore they were athletically superior to our tiny academic island in every conceivable way. They were our nemesis, our antagonist, the thorns in our special ed.side.

And, boy, did they know it. I can't tell you how many fights started on public transportation because the Wilcrosse guys started

FRANK STEPNOWSKI

talking trash about their dominance in both basketball and softball. (Yeah, we were stupid enough to start that, too.) Back when I first started my teaching career at Moorzakunt Academy my mentor, Joe Kopp, had a basketball team and, even then, Wilcrosse was the enemy.

Joe, who had moved on to become discipline director of another high school, had just passed away on April 1st, and Andy and I were absofuckinglutely determined (to honor him) by beating Wilcrosse in our final game of the year. We were playing for the "championship" *in their gym* in 10 days. Not nearly enough time. However, if there was ever a time when we were the "good guys," when we had any sliver of divine justice on our side, this had to be it. I shit you not, people, when I tell you that – if the devil exists – I owe him my soul thanks to a Faustian bargain involving our victory.

Obviously, if my soul is the property of Satan (some would argue it always was) we won the game. You, my friend, know by now that the end result is not nearly as important as the journey to get there; nor is it as funny as the *reaction* to our win, which involved a sprint for our lives and a very uncooperative fence.

But I'm getting ahead of myself.

The day arrived and we walked our intrepid players down the street, through the gates, and up the long driveway into the bowels of the beast. (1) Andy and I were joined on this venture by Pete Mercury (2), due to some school regulation about *staff per student ratio involving any off-campus activity* bullshit. At any rate, it was nice to have Pete with us, as the potential for unpleasantry was off the charts at this point.

1   Students, did you catch the prepositional phrases and personification? You did? I'm so proud of you!
2   Pete [real first name] Mercury ['cause he was built like a planet; that is to say, positively spherical.]

Andy gave voice to what I was feeling.

"I feel like Sam and Frodo going through the Black gates into Mordor in *Lord of the Rings*"

"Nice literary allusion," I chuckled, "I was thinking more *Escape From New York*."

There were students hanging out of windows, throwing shit at us. Insults and threats rained down in waves, and a huge painted banner awaited us at the top of the hill, just above the door to the gymnasium. I can't tell you exactly what it said because it was a rhyme involving the real name of our school, but the last line was WE GONNA WOOP YOU JUST LIKE BFORE

"You want my red marker so you can correct that?" Andrew asked

His irony, and sense of calm in the eye of the storm, broke me and Pete up, and we must have looked like asylum escapees, laughing our asses off as we walked through the gauntlet of student (and staff!) intimidation. Our guys, it should be noted, showed no fear at all, and were stone faced and silent walking up the driveway and into the gym.

That made them more mature than me.

Just before I entered the gym, I turned, smiled, and saluted all the members of the Wilcrosse welcoming committee with an over-exaggerated double middle finger salute.

Say what you will, I know how to make friends.

Andy and Pete left the pre-game speech to me this time, knowing how close I was to Joe Kopp, and the significance of this game. I though it best to keep it simple.

"First off, none of you will be harmed in any way for playing your best today, I personally guarantee that. Second, you know that if you win today, you're the champs. Might be the first time in your life you could say you were the best at *anything*.

Think about that. Finally, you all knew Mr. Kopp. He never beat Wilcrosse. *We* never beat Wilcrosse. Until today. Now get out there, beat their ass, and let's get the fuck out of this shithole. Mr. Kopp on three - "One, two three, KOPP!"

"Nice" smirked Andrew

"Stuff it, Mr. Happy. They threw shit at us. No more Mr. Nice guy."

Pete chimed in, "When, exactly, were you ever Mr. nice guy? I missed that day."

I lost it "You fucker have *got* to stop making me laugh when I'm trying to be serious."

We took the court like a bunch of wolverines on crack
We were down 12 points in the first three minutes.
We were losing by 23 at the half.
We were, to put it mildly, taking some shit from the crowd.

I should point out that NONE of the students of Moorzakunt Academy accepted the offer to go and root their team on. Can't say I blame them. To make matters worse, the staff at Wilcrosse seemed to seize the momentary opportunity to boost *their* student population's self esteem by encouraging the verbal assault on us. Can't say as I blame them. Our guys, facing an insurmountable lead at the half, were not happy with our coaching. Can't say as I blame them.

<hr>

"We can't win playing like this." Observed one Jarren Weltson
"No shit, Sherlock, I countered."
Jarren fired back at me, loudly, with hate in his eyes and profanity

on his tongue, about how, if we just let them play "streetball" they could win this thing and make Mr. Kopp proud.

The rest of the guys, Andy and Pete included, stood silent (and in awe) while I let a student talk to me in such an insubordinate "tone."

After a VERY loud few seconds of silence, I said quietly, "You're right."

10 basketball players nodded, two coaches looked at me like they were proud of me for getting it right.

I simmered. "You're right, Jarren, I and LOVE the anger in your eyes right now. Now use it. Get your team together, go out there, and do what you have to do.

He did.

They did.

We won.

The play that drove the final nail in the coffin was a thing of beauty. After a furious onslaught that closed the deficit to 3 points at the start of the fourth quarter, the Wilcrosse boys were reeling, our guys smelled blood, and the hard fouling began in earnest. A sloppy, mean spirited final twelve minutes left the game tied and my heart in need of repair. Coach Andrew, of course, was in great spirits.

"This is like one of those after school specials," he giggled, "we have to win, right?"

I would have strangled him if I hadn't been suffering from cardiac arrest.

"I'm gonna need a few hoagies and a beer after this,' moaned Pete

"A *few* hoagies and *a* beer," chuckled Andrew.

"Will you two SHUT THE FUCK UP?!" I wailed

Andy put his arm around me, smiled at me the way the old master does to the young [stupid] pupil in all those kung fu movies.

"We're gonna win. We *have* to. Relax."

God bless you, Andrew Springsteen.

He would, years later after many Yuengling Lagers, admit that he was pretty sure we would lose.

God damn you, Andrew Springsteen.

The game was tied with 30 seconds left, and the coaches stopped bantering long enough to watch a fast break gone horribly wrong. Chris grabbed a rebound off a missed Wilcrosse lay up, fired it to Jarred, who flew down the line and shot a pass, at the last second, right into the waiting hands of...

Stretch Armstrong.

Stretch Armstrong was the nickname of the tallest (go figure) and best player on the Wilcrosse Patriots basketball team. The real Stretch Armstrong was the name of a popular toy from the 70's.

The real Stretch Armstrong was white, flabby, and fun for all ages.

This Stretch Armstrong was none of the above.

He seized the pass and flew, uncontested, toward the game winning dunk at our end of the floor.

Well, **al**most uncontested.

Joey Tibideaux never made it down with the rest of the team for the fast break. Not surprising Joey, whose complexion resembled a damp piece of lined paper, and whose claim to fame was being able to sneak cigarettes better than any kid on campus, was both slow and, at this point, winded.

Small, white, poorly conditioned, and non-athletic.

I must remember to ask Andy why he was in the game at that point.

———————◦《◉》◦———————

So there is Joe standing between the foul line and the top of the key, with Stretch bearing down on him like a black locomotive with 2% body fat. Game over for us, right?

Wrong.

The "S" train may have had 2% bodyfat, but he had 1% brain power and 99% ego.

Thank you Joe, Kopp, wherever you are; and thank you Lucifer, my soul is forfeit.

Stretch, not content to just dribble around Joe and lay in the winning two points, wanted to "posterize" the little white kid by dunking over him. Irony of all ironies, we used to joke with Joe that, with his "speed," he should just stand still during practice and work on taking charges.

———————◦《◉》◦———————

Stretch charged.

Joey took it. Ouch.

Foul. Two shots for Joey, with 5 seconds left.

THAT call took a lot of balls, and if you were the referee that made it, and this book found its way into your hands — you made a group of young men very happy, made two men very satisfied, honored the memory of one man, and ensured the eternal damnation of another. Mad props to you, my friend, you have my proper respect, sir, *proper* respect.

Joey, still recovering from having a pair of sweaty balls hover on his forehead before the black kid they were attached to crashed down on top of him, wobbled to the free throw line with the chance to ice the game.

I was still recovering from the elation of the foul call.

Andy was smiling and winking at me like he knew it all along.

Pete was thinking what deli was nearby.

Joey stepped to the line, dribbled three times, spun the ball once, bent his knees, whispered a prayer,

and missed both shots.

The second miss, however, hung on the rim long enough for Stretch and company to overshoot the rebound, leaving Adam Naromi poised to grab it, and tip in the winning basket as time expired.

Then all hell broke loose.

I was worried that Satan had, indeed, come to collect my soul as promised if we won the game. Just kidding, but it sounded good. The truth of the matter is that, as elated as we were (all 13 of us,) the opposition (hundreds of them) were just as pissed.

A strange thing happened then. Collectively, at the same moment, everybody associated with the game realized the same thing. A *team* from a school for fucked up kids just beat another *group* of fucked up kids, at a *school* for fucked up kids. It was Friday, nearly time for dismissal, and there was NO WAY for the small amount of adults present to A: maintain control. B: identify every face involved C: correctly punish the perpetrators if, say, a huge fight were to break out, with 99 percent of the damage aimed at the disposable heroes from that little school down the street.

I am brave to a fault, folks, but I ain't stupid, and neither were the rest of the guys on the team. We hauled ass out of there, leaving clipboards, water bottles, extra balls, and anything else that might slow down ten speedy teenagers, two athletic teachers in their late 20s, and Pete.

We were at the bottom of the hill before you could say Usain Bolt, and we realized halfway down that the FENCES WERE SHUT AND LOCKED because the last of the busses had pulled in to Wilcrosse while we were playing and the animals must be kept in their cage until dismissal time.

So, like any kids that have ever run from the cops (me and Andy included) we hit the fence like we were auditioning for American Gladiators. We could hear the malicious inner city mob coming up behind us at warp speed as we scaled the fence, dropped down on the other side, and prepared for a quick sprint back to home base for much celebration and storytelling.

Until we remembered Pete.

Remember that scene in Indiana Jones when Indy comes over the hill, and mere seconds later, an angry tribe of headhunter comes over the hill in hot pursuit?

Yeah, something like that.

⚬

Andrew and I still piss ourselves thinking about that sight. Pete, power waddling down the hill, sweat on brow, and short arms flailing like a chubby Tyrannosaurus Rex with Parkinson's disease, with the cast of the movie *The Warriors* behind him.

I'm laughing out loud just thinking about it now.

Fortunately, our team of basketball misfits were all accomplished "escape" artists, and they must all of had at least one "plus sized" friend who couldn't make it over the fence. They began pulling on the bottom of the fence like they had rehearsed it. Springsteen and I overcame our sense of awe fast enough to help and, with the harsh sound of creaking aluminum our soundtrack, we got the fence curled up just enough for planetary Pete to stop, drop, and roll to safety. In true South Philly form, he got up adjusted himself so that everything was in place, smoothed back what little hair was left, and addressed the oncoming mob.

(insert heavy Italian accent here) "Lucky for youz they got me outta there,'cuz I got something *for* ya - ya fookin' bunch a...

Not that we didn't want to hear the rest, but we grabbed Pete by the arm, jaunted across the street, and were halfway home by the time the staff of Wilcrosse got around to collecting their student body uprising before they got over the fence of doom.

Epilogue:

Mark Lillistein, the CEO of the company that financed and oversaw Moorzakunt Academy, received a bill for the damage to the peripheral fence of the Wilcrosse school. He told them, politely, to suck his yarmulke. Good job, Mr. Lillistein.

As for us, we took the team to the Chinese buffet on Monday to celebrate. Permission granted and bill paid by Mr. Lillistein– good on ya, mate! Andrew Springsteen became the most beloved coach to ever claim the title at M.A. Pete got his hoagies and beer, and a shit load of General Tso's chicken come to think of it.

And me? I had my moment, just me and Joe.

We did it sensei, we did it for you. Now I gotta go before Pete eats all the lo mein.

Knowing Joe, he was shaking his head and laughing with us the whole time.

Funny Basketball Story #3 – The Call of the Wild.

Patty Grouper, one of our many gym teachers during my extended tour of duty at M.A., was hot for me in a big way.

Not really, but I know that she just read that and yelled "what?!?!" out loud, which is part of the fun of writing a book. Hey Pat, gotcha. (3)

So there I was, shooting the shit with Ms. Grouper in an unusually empty gymnasium. Pat, no doubt tired of my male posturing and hyperkinetic flirting, decided to show me something that will be forever stored in my hard drive.

"Wanna see the call of the wild?" she purred.

"Sure thing, Grouper. Wanna see the Polish python?"

She couldn't help but laugh, I am damn romantic when I want to be.

"I'm serious, you tool. You want to see this?"

Duly chastised, I softened. "Sure thing, kid. I'm always looking to learn new things, even if it is coming from a gym teacher which, by the way, is an oxymoron."

Patty produced one basketball, one lonely orange planet in the vast universe of the Moorzakunt gymnasium, and she started dribbling. Slowly, methodically, rhythmically.

Bam… Bam… Bam… Bam…

Sarcasm dripping, I inquired: "Am I missing something?"

"*Wait* for it."

Bam… Bam… Bam… Bam…

"Seriously Grouper, I've got better things to do with-"

"SShhh" and she pointed over my shoulder.

Bam… Bam… Bam… Bam…

I turned to look, and there, lurking around the doorway, were

3   Unless, of course, you just thought to yourself, "how did he know?" In which case, I'm saltier than a jumbo bag of kettle cooked potato chips.

two students.

"Anybody behind me yet?" she asked

As if on cue, the rear door to the gym, left open because it was Springtime, was immediately filled with the heads of two, then three, more inquisitive faces, drawn to the sound.

Bam… Bam… Bam… Bam…

Within minutes, every kid within earshot of the rhythm was milling around like moths around the proverbial flame asking, in a variety of ways "we gettin' a game up or what?"

Bam…Bam…Bam…STOP.

———◉———

Grouper palmed the ball, smiled her best smart-ass smile, and flipped her raven curls over her shooting hand shoulder and raised her eyebrows my way.

"Geez, I don't know guys, I was just dribbling a ball."

She dropped the ball and walked back into the gym office. I think it bounced once before somebody had it and sides were being drawn up for a game. I followed Patty the way a dog follows it's tail.

"Very impressive, Grouper. I could go on and on about the racial implications of such an experiment, or just inquire as to where those kids actually *belong* this period, but…"

"But such things do not *concern* me, Mister Step, as I am but a humble gym *instructor.*"

Her smile was the last thing I saw before she shut the office door in my face. I was left alone, enlightened, chastised, and horny as hell.

"Step! We need a ref! You good?"

"Sure, gimme a minute."

I could hear patty laughing inside the office.

Bitch.

Call of the Wild indeed.

The Finale: That dude is one hot cheerleader.

Jonathan Chrissy was, by his own admission, "whoop yo ass gay." That is to say, flaming and proud. Jonathan went to Moorzakunt Academy, a school that harbored the most violent, learning disabled, sexually confused bunch of miscreants ever to misinterpret the Pythagorean Theorum.

A 17-year-old black man in a skirt and padded bra in a school for thugs.

A barrel of nitro glycerin thrown into the merry-go-round.

The potential was limitless.

Before you concern yourself with Jon's well being, know this: I changed Jon's last name to that of my sister-in-law, Chrissy, for several reasons. One: Jon and Chrissy both changed their haircolor often. Two: Jonathan, like my wife's sister, was one tough little bitch.

Being neither homophobic nor threatened by Jon, I used to fuck with him on a regular basis, like I did everybody else. Jon understood this and, as a result, I never had a problem with him. Believe me when I tell you that put me in the minority.

━━━●●●━━━

"Jon, what the hell? That blouse doesn't go with that skirt, and wearing white before Labor Day? MAjor fashion fau pax, honey."

"You crazy, Step, and you know damn well this shit looks good on me."

"True dat, Jon. Why, if I didn't have several girlfriends that need my attention…"

"Don't tease me," John laughed, "you know I love me some big-ass white boys."

Now it was my turn to laugh. "That, young lady, is sexual harassment, now get your ass to class, princess, before I cry and file formal charges."

"Thanks, Step."

"Yeah, yeah, whatever."

Jon sashayed to class with all the grace and attitude of a Victoria's Secret runway model. The kid had balls, and I had to respect that. Not all of the young men of M.A. agreed with me.

Even now, I feel sorry for them.

You, my insightful reader, have guessed that there were a veritable plethora of fights at our humble home of learning. Most of those fights were sloppy, over quickly, and ended in a draw; largely because the participants were poorly conditioned, stupid, and male. Jonathan Chrissy was, for all intents and purposes, none of the above.

A fact learned far too late by his unfortunate adversaries.

"Get your faggot ass out the gym, bitch," directed Damon

"Yah," Antoine agreed, "dicks are for chicks!"

Many more hostile, homophobic, comments followed. John Wang, Shannon G, (gym teachers) and I waited patiently for the show to begin.

"Y'all finished?" inquired Jonathan, as cool as the other side of the gay pillow.

"Why, nigga? You gonna do a cheer or somethin'?"

Much laughter.

"You can't **beat** this nigga, though, can you?"

Much laughter stopped. John, Shan, and I adjusted our seats

and the wagering began in earnest. Having seen Jon throw down before, I took the "under" in time necessary for him to vanquish his foes.

"Watchyoo say bitch?" snarled Damon, doing his best *chest-out-arms-swinging-head- bobbing-I'ma-kick-your-ass* strut. You know the one. "We can do this right here."

"Oh, yes darlin'" Jon confirmed, sweet as pie. "we most certainly can."

"Minute and a half, tops." Johnny Wang, my esteemed colleague, wagered.

"Less." corrected Shannon.

"Way less." I confirmed.

———— ((●)) ————

The only reason the fight even *approached* a full minute was because Antoine tried to jump in and save Damon from what was, in retrospect, as savage a beating as could be administered in under 60 seconds. Antoine got his narrow ass kicked, too, not that he'd admit it.

(Antoine)"Let me go, mothafucka! They gonna think he won!"

(Me aka: mothafucka) "You're nose is bleeding, you've got a lump on your forehead, and I pulled you out from *under* him. News flash, he did win."

Antoine didn't like that. Nor did Damon, who was being dragged out by Wang and Shannon. Both young men proceeded to go on and on about what they were going to do to us if we didn't let them go, how they were gonna finish that little bitch, blah blah blah, UNTIL I got them in a secluded area.

It should be noted that I, like so many teachers, had to play the role in this particular scenario at least a hundred times throughout my teaching career. *Sing along if you know the words:*

Act I: Student *a* gets into fight with student *b*

Act II: Student *a* gets his ass properly served, which is fine with you because both *a* and *b* each deserves a beat down for a number of reasons.

Act III: You intervene, saving exhibit *a* from further embarrassment.

Act IV: You then become the recipient of student *a*'s misplaced shame and anxiety, as(s)he proceeds to curse you out for stopping the fight too early, causing them to lose, etc,

Act V: You contemplate feeding them back to student *b* so (s)he can finish the job.

Act VI: You defer, being the consummate professional that you are; that, and because everybody is watching at this point

Epilogue: (at least for me) Get *a, b*, and any other variables in a secluded area and remind them that they just got their asses kicked by an amateur, so they had best SHUT THEIR FUCKING MOUTHS before the *professional* started working on them.

Yeah, Yeah, I allowed fights to happen, I threatened students, I'm a bad person and a horrible teacher, I know. Horrible human being, disgrace to the profession, I've heard it all, and I couldn't care less; because the people who spew that junk don't get it, and they don't get it because they haven't lived it, so I don't give two shits what they think. I wrote this book for teachers and students and people who can handle reality.

Speaking of students, I still have a letter Antoine wrote me when he graduated, thanking me for everything I ever did for him, and how I inspired him to be a better person, so suck me sideways, haters.

But I digress.

Back to our "boy" Jonathan.

After disposing, with surgical precision, his antagonists, and asking the rest of the basketball boys if "if they wanted a piece of his sweet ass, too," and getting no takers, he straightened his v-neck cardigan, fixed his hair as best he could, and proceeded to continue jumping rope in the gym until I came back to claim him.

"Let's go, Jon." I directed, "grabbing him gently by the arm and escorting him out of the gym to the "time out" room, where he could calm down a bit more, fix himself up and, if he so chose, talk about his actions and their repercussions."

"GETcho hands off me!" Jon squealed, "you let me fight in the first place, DICKhead, and I'm gonna tell everybody that before I get in trouble. Bitch!"

It should be noted that I, like so many teachers, had to play the role in this particular scenario at least a hundred times throughout my teaching career.

Once again, if you know the words…

Scene I: You take a troubled kid into your confidence, try to work with him/her, and

Scene II: through an unspoken agreement with other teaches in a similar boat, try to help keep the kid out of trouble by intervening when (s)he acts up.

Scene III: You and said child develop a good relationship. The kids learns that not all adults are out to get him/her, and starts to develop healthy relationships that allow them to do better academically as well.

Scene IV: After sticking your neck out time and time again for the aforementioned kid, (s)he, after getting in trouble for something, throws you under the bus and disavows any friendship or that you've ever done anything to ever help them. It is, of course, *your* fault that they got in trouble.

Scene V: The kid eventually calms down, thinks back on all you have done for him, apologizes (usually with an emotionless "my bad," or something similar) and expects everything to be even stevens between you both.

Scene VI: You allow the bridge to remain unburned, knowing that the kid needs you if (s)he has any chance of surviving with their emotional stability intact.

Of course, I left out the always exciting scene when the parent, noticeably absent for months to years, shows up (in their one good suit, with their advocate and/or lawyer) and wants to ruin the life of the person who has done more for their kid then they have. I'm afraid I can't comment on this with any language that is even remotely acceptable on this, or any other, planet.

But I digress.

Jon eventually forgave me for the unspeakable crime of doing my job and was on to bigger and better things with a day or two. The little tussle with the boys in the gym had given him an idea. The basketball team didn't have any cheerleaders.

(insert voice of a shocked black woman here) Oh no he *didn't*!

(insert voice of fabulously handsome white author imitating the voice of a shocked black woman here) Oh, yes he *did*.

—————•((◦))•—————

"I wanna be a cheerleader," announced Jon, hands on his hips, resplendent in a pair of Capri pants and an Old Navy top.

"Great idea, Jon." Proclaimed coach Springsteen, barely able to control his shit-eating grin, "maybe you get some of your girlfriends to help. I'm sure the guys would love it." He had to turn back to his current task of feeding balls to the half of the team doing lay-up drills to keep from losing it.

I was not nearly as amused.

"2-4-6-8, we're behind schedule and running late! Now get the fuck out of my gym, princess, before I put my foot in your ass." (I only realize now what a poor choice of words that was.)

Jon, bless him, was unfazed. "Don't hate, Step – and you best remember what happened to the *last* boy done told me to get outta this gym."

I retorted "and you best remember that it's hard as hell to get blood stains out of cotton/polyester blends."

Jon just sucked his teeth, pranced out of the gym head held high, pissed only at the fact that I didn't acknowledge that his shirt was 100% cotton.

I approached my dear friend Andy Springsteen ready to use up my daily supply of question marks and exclamation points:

"Great idea Jon?!?! I'm sure the guys would LOVE it?!?!" I pleaded "Have you lost you're fucking mind?!?!"

"I don't know why you get so mad," Andy counseled , "you know as well as I do that this is gonna be freakin' hilLARious if it actually goes down. Can you imagine the looks on the faces of the next team we play if the cheerleading squad from *The Longest Yard* shows up?"

I thought it over.

"Hmmm, the next game is here, against Valley Night School, in a week and a half…"

"And their coach is the one that called us a joke last time," Andy reminded me, "because we (quote marks in the air with his fingers) *didn't take the game seriously.*"

"Fair enough," I surrendered, "this could be tragically ironic at best."

Jon poked his head in the gym door

"Get to class!" I roared, still mad that Andy had bested me yet again.

"I'm *GO*in', he ressured me, "but I just wanted to let y'all know that me and the crew will be puttin' it down at the next game, word is bond, it's gonna be bangin'! We gonna work it, work it..." and he exited down the hall pumping his fists and his hips to the rhythm of "work it."

I glared sideways at Andy, fully aware that this had the potential to be one of those stories that would eventually make it "into the book."

———— ((●)) ————

At least I wasn't wrong about that.

Don't ask me where they got the uniforms.

Yet here they were, positively radiant in their matching red, white and blue cheerleader costumes, complete with high quality pom-poms and bad quality weaves.

I, along with Andy and a dozen basketball players were, in a word, speechless.

For a moment.

———— ((●)) ————

Author's note: Sorry for the interruption, but this was too serendipitous not to mention. Got the old iPod blaring while I'm writing here, and **Dude Looks Like A Lady** by Aerosmith just came on in the shuffle mode. This must be a sign from God, or Steve Jobs, that this chapter is a keeper.

⸻ ◆ ⸻

"Jesus, it looks like the girl from the *"Oh Mickey You're So Fine"* video got raped by an ugly

black transvestite and had a litter of puppies."

My observation broke the uncomfortable ice, and many laughs and subsequent observations followed, to the point where we had to regain control just to get through warm-ups. Of course, any semblance of control we had was promptly shot to shit when the Valley Night squad emerged from the bathroom/locker room and were promptly greeted with the first rehearsed cheer of the afternoon. Went somethin' like this:

"Listen up y'all cause we hear to tell ya
ya uniforms is played out and your skin is ashy as hell, yeah
we hot, you not, and in case you forgot
we gonna take your ass and work it, work it, work it..."

Thank god Mr. Long intervened, because I thought Andy, my buddy Donnie Jagger (called in for crowd control), and I were going to asphyxiate. We were hanging off of one another laughing until tears came out of our eyes. Then next cheer, shouted in tandem just before the opening tip, started with

"Jump ball bitches, you don't want none of this
You old as dirt and slow as piss..."

Once again, Don, Andrew, and I (and the team) were howling with delight.

Mr. Long threatened to have the whole cheerleading squad removed, so they toned it down a notch, and the game finally got underway. Our guys, who were more familiar with the freak show, weren't distracted in the least. The intrepid young men of Valley Night Alternative School were not so fortunate, and every time one of them got caught looking at the "girls" bad things ensued, from lewd poses at them to easy lay-ups for us. By the half, we were up by a ton, and our opposition was still gloriously unaware that about 40% of our cheerleading squad had their own definition of a back door pass. Never was this more evident than when, in a run to the water fountain, the V.N.A.S. power forward grabbed our two guard, Chris Rosales, pointed to Jonathan Chrissy, and asked if Chris could help him "get those digits, yo."

Chris came back to our bench with a smile like somebody broke the Peyote Pinata and he was standing underneath it.

"Fuck you laughin' at," asked Adam, "we ain't up by that much, we need to…"

"Number 12 wants gay Jon's phone number" Chris interrupted.

Know that silence right before the grenade goes off? Me neither, but I'm guessing that it's what you would call a "pregnant pause" before the explosion.

It took them another millisecond to process what Chris just said, then BOOM.

Much laughter and a slew of simultaneous comments quickly simmered into a group decision to let this power forward flirtation carry on before playing cupid between these two young men that clearly had a lot in common. After all, they both loved dribbling balls. (4)

I'll tell you how fucking immature *I* am. I don't remember a damn thing about the third quarter except that number 12 kept shooting to impress Jonathan, missing all but one shot, a miracle three pointer that left him plenty of time to pose, hand in the air,

4   I know, I know…horrible. Bad teacher, horrible coach, I just couldn't resist. I'm laughing my ass off just writing it. I am going straight to hell. Sorry, mom.

WHY ARE ALL THE GOOD TEACHERS CRAZY?

flexing his muscles and staring down his favorite cheerleader. His teammates were pissed at him, his coaches were furious, his team was now in an insurmountable hole, and he was doing all of this for a pom-pom girl with a surprise under her skirt.

I do fucking *love* it when a plan comes together.

"Andrew, just in case I die in a car crash on the way home, thank you for talking me into this fiasco. I haven't laughed this hard in a long time."

"It's about to get better bud," Donnie nudged me, "check it out."

Sure enough, number 12 was on his way to the water fountain, conveniently stopping by Jonathan to "get his smooth on." His coaches were visibly disgusted, and his teammates were shaking their heads even as they admired the she-male scenery. When Jon batted his eyes, laughed like a schoolgirl, and blushingly gave our misguided protagonist the directions to the nearest unlocked bathroom, (intel courtesy of one of my better snitches,) Don and I looked at each other, daring the other one to intervene. Donnie broke the silence.

"Bud, (laughter) I'm gonna stop them, but (choking laughter) not until (suppressed laughter) that young man finds out that his bike (keeping it together) his bike has (ready to explode now) has a **kickstand!**"(uproarious laughter.)

———•◉•———

We never did play the fourth quarter. Number 12 must have swung for the fences during his rapid rendezvous with Jonathan Chrissy because he quickly discovered that something in that tiny bathroom was harder than Chinese arithmetic, and it wasn't the tile floor.

You can probably picture the chaos that erupted so I won't ruin your version with too many details. Suffice it to say, loverboy freaked, called Jon a faggot, Jon reciprocated by starting to beat the shit out of him, the fight spilled into the hallway, where loverboy's teammates were ready to jump on Jon until they realized what happened and then began to fall upon themselves in hysterics, prompting Jon to pop one of them, prompting the Valley night squad to rush Jon, prompting the cheerleaders to enter the fray, skirts and all, with the chain reaction engulfing our guys until the front hallway at Moorzakunt Academy looked like a gay, black version of the final fight scene from *Enter The Dragon*.

Ain't love grand?

Well, our basketball odyssey was temporarily suspended.

No surprise there.

<hr />

Jon finally lost a fight to, in the mother of all ironies, Jessie Satriani – one of only three real girls in the entire school. As much estrogen as Jon harbored, Jessie equaled him in testosterone. It was, by all accounts, one of the top ten fights of all time. I only caught the last thirty seconds as I was called from the front of my class to come assist with the break up, but the condition of both participants left little doubt as to who won this particular battle of the sexes.

"That little bitch fight like a man," spat Jon, through a bloody, swollen lip

I had to agree, given that Jess was walking out of room, flanked by Marc and Greg from the behavior management team, looking like she just stepped off the bus. Had it not been for the slight tear in her Pittsburgh Steelers jersey, I would have never guessed she was even in a scuffle. Couldn't say the same for Mr. Chrissy who, in addition to the aforementioned fat lip, was sporting a mouse over one of his eyes, several scratches, and a devastated little two-piece ensemble from Aeropostale. I couldn't help but ask.

"What happened *this* time Jon? She *breathe* the wrong way? Look in your direction?"

Jon huffed, then responded, as was his nature when calm, in perfectly annunciated English

"Noooo. She was speaking about my little incident at the game last week, and I told her

she needed to mind her damn business."

"I see, and Jess didn't like that."

"She said that she would make me her business, and she did. Baby girl whooped my ass,

and I'm man enough to admit it."

I couldn't resist: "Man enough, you say?"

"Fuck you step," but Jon couldn't help but smile as we entered the nurse's office.

⸺◆⸺

As I strolled back to class, I ran into Jessie, who was being taken to the principal's office. I knew that, given how much trouble she had caused in just her first month at Moorzakunt, she was destined to be a "Stepchild" in the very near future. Marc and Greg, who knew as well that she would be mine soon enough, stopped so I could talk to her.

"You know you're going to be put in my class, don't you Satriani?"

She expressed no problem with that: "Yeah, I was kind hopin' that would happen."

"Really? You *do* know that I don't tolerate stupid shit like this in my class?"

"Yeah."

"And you *do* know that my methods of preventing such dumb shit are, how shall put this?"

"Physical."

"I was think more along the lines of *effective*, but I guess that works."

"I'm cool with that. I just want to learn, and I heard you're class is the best."

Marc and Greg laughed, at least she knew how to play the game.

"Yeah well," I responded, "opinions vary. So I can expect no further bullshit between you and Jonathan Chrissy?"

"Who?"

"The young man that want to be a young lady that you just fought."

"Oh, him. Yeah, sure."

As she was being led down the hall, she shot back to me: "He don't fight too good, but I'll tell you what — that dude is one hot cheerleader."

Thanks Jess, there's a chapter title in there somewhere.

Bobby Chopper: the guy who handcuffed me in my underwear comes to my rescue.

Two things you absolutely need to know going into this chapter.

One, for those of you that skipped ahead to this chapter because of the title thinking you're gonna get some kind of weird insight into my sex life, you couldn't be more wrong. In fact, I waited this long because I wanted to build up our relationship before sharing some personal stuff with you.

Now, don't you feel guilty for betraying the trust I had in you? Go back if you want, but the bond is broken; know that I weep silently for what might have been.

Two, I had leave out several details of the original "cops and robbers" story here for various, and soon to be obvious, reasons (NONE of which involve actual crimes on my part, so chill out.) Maybe if you meet me somewhere and we get to talking and there's enough Patron' and good music…but for now, you get just enough of how Bob Chopper and I *first* met to set up the titanic irony of our *second* meeting.

So there I was, handcuffed to a couch, in my underwear

surrounded by angry, bleeding police officers...

Juuuuust kidding, a little background *first.*

———◆———

I was upstairs in an apartment I rented during my later years in college. (Very nice place, eternal thanks to the local businessman Tom Flanagan for recommending me as a tenant, as the owners didn't want to rent such a nice place to any "young whipper snappers.")

Shame that the door was about to be battering rammed by a bunch of vice officers that were responding to misinformation.

More of a shame that my sister was downstairs waiting for me.

Super-sized shame that I was in the process of getting ready for a family wedding.

———◆———

Seems that the folks at 2643 Wurmistaken Street were conducting a little pharmaceutical operation that involved neither co-pay nor prescription.

Problem: the humanoids that issued the warrants for the search and seizure of said operation were products of the Philadelphia public school system.

More of a problem: I resided at *2436* Wurmistaken Street.

Titanic problem: lack of proofreading and lack of pants were about to collide.

———◆———

I was almost done dressing.

Key word: almost. 6'3", 260 lbs, with long black hair, in a white dress shirt, tighty-whiteys, black dress socks, and a watch. I looked like a fucking Chippendale on a first name basis with Pizza Hut.

I heard the door explode and a very short, quickly muffled scream come from my sister. A few seconds later there were several men in plain clothes barreling up my stairs. Some things, you just know, are not going to end well.

The first cop-that-I-didn't-know-was-a-cop ran into a beautiful right cross coming downhill from my position at the top of the stairs. What happened next was a blur, but it ended in four out of seven vice officers in various degrees of damage, and a chunky Chippendale paying the price.

So there I was, handcuffed to a couch, in my underwear, surrounded by angry, bleeding police officers:

Humiliated because my sister was forced to sit next to me.
Infuriated because (she told me) one of the men put his hand on her mouth and threatened her after they knocked down my door, and
Completely clueless as to why they were there.

"Please tell me why you're doing this to me" I pleaded, still really overwhelmed by he whole situation. I was being ignored, my things were being trashed, and a bunch of angry, arrogant police officers were making comments about my sister and I. My anxiety soon gave way to rage, and it was building fast.

———————————

"One more time, please tell me…"
"We heard ya" interrupted a bearded guy in his forties who was

clearly the boss of the operation, " don't act stupid. Or maybe you *are* stupid."

"That's my Master's thesis your guys are throwing around, and I've actually *read* all of those books they're throwing on the floor, now can you tell my sister and I...

"Notice something," he interrupted me again, talking to the black cop next to him, "you and me didn't get touched when she was scratching up the guys, I wonder why? Maybe because she didn't want to fight people that could see the punches coming"

———⏺———

He interrupted me twice, insulted my sister, handcuffed me to the sofa with no pants on, and called me "she", all while trashing my very neat and clean apartment with no explanation. Now he was curious as to why he and the other officer never got touched during the initial assault. So I locked eyes with him, smiled, and offered my solution.

"Or maybe," I hissed, "because the nigger and the faggot were *too far in the back* for me to get to them." (1)

Well that certainly got their attention.

Let's wrap up "this was your life" and get back to the teaching stuff – the cops didn't find anything (well, duh.) The door was replaced and paid for by the city of Philadelphia. Molly and I had to use the old "car broke down" excuse for why we missed the wedding. (Sorry Tim and Trac, now you know,) and Bob Chopper and I left each other with the clear message that we would meet again and when we did, it would be Optimus Prime and Megatron to the death.

1   Yes, I said nigger and faggot. No, I don't apologize. They're just *words*, and I'm *allowed* to use them when I see fit. *So are you* – freedom of speech and all that. I'm neither racist nor homophobic, what I am is honest. I was justifiably pissed off and I was trying to get a reaction. I did. End of discussion.

Fast-forward to orientation at Moorzakunt Academy September 6, 19somethingorother, almost a decade after the "whoops, wrong house" debacle, and we are being introduced to the new director of discipline. Guess who? I'll give you three guesses.

Wow, You got it on the first one.

My entire teaching style, my position of autonomy, and my reputation were now at the mercy of a man whose spine I had threatened to pull out like the Predator. Maybe he wouldn't recognize me, or my name, it *had* been over a decade, after all.

Yeah, maybe penguins would fly out of my ass and make me a spinach salad, too.

<hr />

I retired to my room and stayed incognito for the rest of the day. The next day the kids arrived and, after the usual first day drama, I was going over the usual rules and regulations with my class. Things were going pretty smoothly, as 12 out of my 14 students were guys I had before and the other two were moving "up" from other classes so they already knew about me, and my methods. All eyes turned to the open door when Bob Chopper knocked and gave me the universal look for "sorry to interrupt."

"Sorry to interrupt, but I just wanted to introduce myself," as he extended his hand, "Bob Chopper. Call me Bob." He smiled.

I shook his hand firmly, "nice to meet you…Bob. Just about everybody calls me…"

"Step. I know," he said. I already got the scoop. Way I hear it, you and your guys run things around here, so I'm just gonna stay outta your way, let you do what you do and, hopefully, we can work together to make this place safe for everyone."

He smiled, an authentic smile, no hidden bullshit that I could discern.

"Sorry for taking you away from your lesson, we'll talk more when you get the chance. Have a good day, guys, you got a great teacher here."

Penguin spinach salad, anyone?

My first chance to gauge whether or not Bob recognized me came fairly quickly, in the form of not so little Alexio Earnest. Earnest was one of those kids, you know the type – thinks he's a gangster but he's just a slightly overweight bully who terrorizes people that won't fight back and kisses the ass of "real" gang members so he feels, and thus tells you (every chance he gets,) that he's "connected."

Alexio got strike one pushing a female teacher up against the wall and threatening her for having the audacity to ask him to sit down. He did this with the door open while I was walking by. I intervened and he pushed me, telling me "I didn't know who the fuck he was and…"

Steee-rike twoooo.

After I dumped his big ass unceremoniously over the nearest desk. I asked him, again, to apologize to the young lady and clean up his mess. Unbeknownst to me at this point, Jaron Jackson, (a young man I loved dearly but with whom I had a turbulent father-son sort of thing going on) happened to be coming in from sneaking a smoke outside and witnessed the following portion of our dialogue:

Posturing pussy: "You done fucked up now, jese'"

Bored teacher: "Whatever. Apologize. Now. Before I dump your fat ass again."

Wanna be gangsta: (flashing some sort of gesture that, I guess, was supposed to be a gang sign, but I sure as hell didn't recognize it) "I'm loco, bitch, you don't know me!"

Unimpressed enforcer: "Uh huh, and you don't know me, either."

Miguided Mexican: "I know *this* much, I know you got them car seats in the back of your truck, and when you…"

Suddenly very serious teacher: "You want to stop talking, *right* now. *Trust* me on this."

Asshole not taking the hint: "I'ma slash your tires, kill you and ya kids when…"

At that moment, the look on my face and my body posture must have been pretty intense because asshole Alexio stopped talking and started moving backwards quickly, it was only the hand of the aforementioned Jarren Jackson that saved his ass.

"Step, come on," he grabbed my arm, "we got to get to class."

———— ((●)) ————

I was so stunned to see him that I actually listened and went back to class. Once the rest of the guys came back from gym, we resumed our lessons and, just prior to the lunch bell, I got ready to give the old "check around your desks, pick up any loose papers, etc. etc." speech, when I realized that ALL of my guys were sitting, hands folded like they were in fucking Catechism class, in an immaculate room. *This* was not going to fly without comment from yours truly, because I saw what was coming from a mile away.

"I appreciate the sentiment, guys, but don't do it."

They tried to feign innocence, "Do what? Whatchoo talkin' about, Step?"

"Seriously, don't do what you're going to do."

At that moment, Jarren Jackson, borderline illiterate 15 year-old black child, dropped some knowledge on my ignorant ass – and dropped it hard.

"Don't tell us not to." He virtually spat at me. "How you gonna tell us not to? That boy threatened your kids. Your *kids.*"

He hung that last word out there just a bit to let it sink in.

"You always tell us we just like your kids, and you do all this shit for us, and now you gonna tell us not to fuck this nigga up for talkin' that shit. FUCK that. You can't do what you wanna do, so we gonna do it, because it's *right.*"

The rest of my "step" children nodded like Jesus had just given the Sermon on the Mount.

I did the only thing I could do. I shut the fuck up and dismissed my guys to their 15-minute lunch break, whereupon they invited their "buddy" Alexio Earnest behind the building to catch a smoke.

He caught something all right.

Fast forward ten minutes, and all of my guys are back in my room, noticeably lunch-less, sweating and, in some cases, picking leaves from, and brushing dirt off, their clothes. All of them had shit-eating grins on their faces - until Mr. Chopper came in the room.

"Hey, ahhh…Step," he stumbled, looking around the room at my sweaty instruments of righteous cruelty, "there was an… *incident*…involving Earnest, behind the building?"

The fact that he posed it like a question emboldened me a bit, as did Jarren's well-practiced poker face. Let the games begin:

WHY ARE ALL THE GOOD TEACHERS CRAZY?

"Who did you say was involved?"

"Earnest, Alexio Earnest. Big kid, real asshole, tried to assault Ms. Mendoza earlier today."

"Oh, yeah, *that* asshole, I stopped him."

"I know."

(Uncomfortable few seconds of silence. Ah, the moment of truth!)

"I don't know anything about any other *incident*. My guys were here with me for the last 20 minutes or so, eating their lunches."

Bob smiled, an authentic smile, no hidden agenda that I could discern.

"That's what I thought. Alexio's grandmother is on the phone asking *whaat kinda aschool we arunnin' here where kieedz get apaid to keek her beeutyful baby's ass and nobody know notting about it?!*"

"And you said?"

He smiled, a very knowing smile this time. "I told her that she was absolutely correct and that she should look into enrolling him in another institution." He looked around at the wolf pack, who were still uncertain whether they were off the hook or not.

"Thank you for your time, Mr. Step; and thank *you* boys, enjoy your lunch."

The minute the door shut Jarren spoke up. "Whicha you niggas got paid?"

The laughter and crossfire of shared recollections of the *incident* gave me a few moments to absorb at least two certainties. One, my guys had a primitive, but nonetheless touching, way of showing they loved me. Secondly, but by no means less important, it appeared that Bob Chopper and I were – for now- fighting on the same side.

The wolf pack and I, under the aegis of Bob Chopper, enacted many incidents, shenanigans, "funny stuff" and moments of questionable character. The school was, on the whole, as well behaved as it ever was by a long shot. Bob and I developed a friendship based on mutual respect, a healthy dose of reality, a few shots of debauchery, and a sprinkle of professional tension.

Eventually, as you might have guessed, I need to know, for certain, how *much* tension existed between us. The opportunity presented itself in the form of a golfing invitation. Bob invited me, my father-in-law, the recently "replaced" Mr. Long, and a few of the guys we taught with, to a golf outing at a club where he "knew the proprietors from back in the day."

(Translation: I knew these guys back when I was a cop but I can't tell you that because I don't want to blow my cover in case you forgot me and our past encounter.)

I figured – public place, everybody suitably lubricated via free alcohol, me appropriately humbled from playing shitty golf… perfect place to re-introduce myself to the guy that handcuffed me in my underwear and called me "she." But first, *on the Friday before* the weekend of the golf outing, another situation that forced Bob to not only step up to the line for me, but put his ass on it as well.

We had recently changed principals and principles at Moorzakunt Academy. We changed principals when Mr. Long was asked to step down (translation: had his back stabbed by a woman, with good intentions but little patience, named June Latrodectus,) We changed principles when the powers that controlled such decisions listened to the aforementioned Judas, er, woman, when she built her case against the man who had run M.A efficiently when there were 200+ students and less than 35 staff. (When June was unceremoniously and ironically dumped two years later in the month of June, the enrollment/staff ration was at a deplorable 90:50)

Aaaanyway, Madame Latrodectus had, as I mentioned earlier, good intentions.

Problem? No fucking clue whatsoever how to *implement* them.

Know anybody like that?

Tons of suggestions, none of which are rooted I reality?

I'll bet you do.

I'll bet you just said their name out loud to yourself.

Well, that was our new HBIC (2), and she didn't like my way of doing things. Go figure.

I was summoned to Latrodectus' posh new lair, er, office during activities on Friday afternoon. I told my guys to chill, play the Playstation I bought for the class, or just hang out in my room 'till I got back.

"Damn, Step," observed one Charles Crusha, " you get called to the principal's office all the time. I think you're badder than us!"

"*Worse* than us is the proper expression, Chuck; and yes, I am bad company; but that's why y'all love me so much," and I spun, pointed at the class, and moon-walked (poorly) out the door. Laughter at my pathetic dance skills followed me down the hall.

I was deeply wounded.

I began my death march to Juneville entertained by the notion that I *never* got called to the principal's office from first grade to junior year of high school, but I was setting a NASCAR-like pace since then.

I must be what they call a late bloomer.

———⸭⟨◉⟩⸭———

When I got to the newly decorated principal's office, Junie was waiting for me at the head of her ***fuck you I'm in charge and this***

---

2   Head bitch in charge.

table proves it table, along with Bob Chopper, the head psychologist, Sharon Brofy (a good all around person, clearly out of place here) and Anne, the lawyer from central administration who looked like the product of intimate involvement between Winston Churchill and a bulldog.

I scanned the table for friendly glances and got four looks that gave me the impression that we were at the World Series of Poker. Hmmm…gonna have to go "all in" early to find out if I had any allies at the Thanksgiving table from Hell.

> NOTE: Teachers, when walking into any meeting that looks like the Spanish Inquisition, be honest with yourself, know what you have done and what you deserve to have done **to you**. Accept accountability for your actions, even if it means severe punitive action; but don't allow yourself to be anybody's scapegoat or whipping post. I also recommend launching a pre-emptive strike, although perhaps not with the lack of subtlety I exhibited in this particular instance:

"Wow, this looks important." I observed, with practiced aloofness.

"Oh, it is, Mr. StepAnowski." chirped June, with a voice like a chilled shot of tequila, the perfect balanced of menace and iciness.

"Not important enough to send someone to cover those thirteen unattended SED kids in my room though, is it…*boss?*"

Fuck it, if we're gonna dance – let's dance.
I'll lead.

Bitch.

Sharon demurely and professionally covered her smile, Bob shook his head in disgust (of me?), Anne looked like a Winston Churchill bulldog that just swallowed a bad oyster, and June's cheeks took on that rose' blush that women usually get when I…

But I digress.

SCORECARD:

Sharon – on my side but not enough to stick out her neck for me.

Anne - wants me dead and ground into hamburger so she can devour me with an energetic flapping of her jowls.

June – high octane pissed off but too smart and too cool to show it.

Bob – wild card. Was all his back slappin' bullshit a set up or was he going to go "all in" with me?

I was read the riot act of my transgressions, usurpations, faux pas, and acts unbecoming a teacher of children with special needs. By the time June was finished, I was amazed at how painfully appropriate her last name was. I felt like I was being devoured until the wild card showed his hand (Sorry, gettin' outta hand with the cards metaphor, aren't I?)

Fuck it; my book, my extended metaphor.

Bob stood up, closed his file [all my bad shit on paper,] and looked Ms. Latrodectus in the eye with the steely glance of the lone gambler throwing down the card that would take down the pot that would change his life.

APOLOGY: Sorry, that was fucking terrible metaphoring, but I'm laughing my ass off at the sheer cheesiness of

it. That's what happens when you anecdote at 3 in the morning. Don't type on sleep deprivation, and don't drink and drive, and don't go in the water for an hour after you've eaten! Sorry…now where was I?

Right, Bob stood up and said, calm as could be, "If Step goes, I go."

Holy shit.

———————

That woke me up, and threw water on Joy's "Step piñata" party. You see, Madame June Latrodectus looovvvveed Robert Chopper, and all that he stood for. (She also loved the fact that he looked like a poor man's Chuck Norris – sorry Bob, you know that shit is true!) So when Bobby "lord o' discipline" Chopper gave his five minute treatise on how I was doing more real teaching in my class than the whole rest of the school combined, and how I was helping control the number of discipline problems and, well, I simply can't continue for fear of getting choked up…

At the time, however, I was thinking "Holy sheepshit! You *GO* B-Dawg!! In your faaaaace, you joyless twat, and fuuuuuck you too, you bulldog looking bitch!"

———————

I kept this all inside, of course. I was sitting, hands folded, like a properly chastised and then forgiven child; but in my head I was partying like it was 1999.

The meeting ended abruptly and not at all in the way that the Black Widow and Winston the bulldog wanted. I, gentle reader, wanted to hug someone. Since Moorzakunt Academy isn't filled with huggable people, and the ones that *do* want to hug you usually want to hump your leg as well, I did the next best thing:

"Hey Bob. Thanks, man. Really. That took a lot of stones, and I will not forget that. I am relentless in my loyalty to my friends and you, sir, are one of them."

"No problem, Step" he said shaking my hand firmly, solidifying a friendship that remains strong to this day.

I started to walk away, ready to start the weekend, when I heard from behind me,

"Besides, I saw what you did to four of my officers in your underwear, and I couldn't take any chances of getting you mad with your pants *on*."

I turned, stunned by the suddenness of the revelation, and got a look at, and a listen to that heartfelt laugh that never fails to cheer me up. Bob shot out his hand and shook mine with an intense sense of relief that exploded from both of us.

"JE-sus Christ! I'm glad that's over with!" he bellowed, laughing that "gotcha" laugh, and tripping over his own words explaining why he had kept our "special relationship" shrouded in shadow.

"When I first saw the name on the roster I thought, no freakin' way it's the same kid. Then I saw you walking into orientation and I thought, holy shit, it *is* him, and he's gotten bigger *and* meaner-looking. Then I find out you pretty much run the worst kids on campus and I'm thinking - what the fuck do I do if he holds a grudge? Then I get to know you, see how great you are with the kids, and how you fight all the bullshit here like that freakin' meeting we just came from, and I'm thinking, maybe he doesn't recognize me, or maybe he does and all is forgiven."

I listened intently, then I called upon my best acting skills. Blowing myself up like a cobra, muscles tensed, I fixed him with the most evil glare I could summon, and clenched my fists 'till my knuckles went white, and snarled:

"You handcuffed me. In my underwear. You taunted me. Laughed at me. Not so motherFUCKing funny is it now, detective?"

"Now, Step…" he countered, under control, "that was cops and robbers, I was just doing my job. You know that."

I couldn't keep up the method acting for one more second so I let him off the hook

"Yeah, well, I had to re-write several pages of that Master's thesis so you're buying the first beer tomorrow."

He burst into that contagious laugh of his again.

"You big bastard, you got me! JE-sus Christ my heart can't take that anymore. First beer, you got it."

"And I want a Mulligan on the front 9 *and* the back nine."

"You can have one on every freakin' hole far as I'm concerned. Thanks, Step"

No Bob, thank *you*.

For being a stand up guy, then and every day since.

Some Righteous Reality from the
Desk of Mr. Step

"I've seen these children, with their boredom,
and their vacant stares
God help us all, if we're to blame for
their unanswered prayers."

-Billy Joel (No Man's Land)

Acrimonious Acronyms

L D, CCI, ED, ADHD are now SLD, RCC, EBD, and, believe it or not, ADHD. If you are blissfully unaware of WTF that means, suffice it to say our special ed. student population is FUBAR because of this acronymic scrabble.

Specific Learning Disabilities, Residential Care Centers, Emotional Behavioral Disabilities, and Attention Deficit Hyperactivity Disorders aside, we have over-diagnosed our kids, slapping labels on them at a young age; labels that continually change (see a very small sample above,) resulting in a generation of kids that are becoming self-fulfilling prophecies of emotional and academic instability. In short, they're Fucked Up Beyond All Recognition.

I don't even think some of the acronyms my kids were carrying even exist now. (I don't teach special ed. exclusively anymore, so I'm a bit "out of the loop.") For example, when I taught at Ye Olde Moorzakunt Academy, most of my little cherubs were [as per the vernacular of the 80s] SED, which meant severely emotionally disturbed, a good percentage of them "suffered from" ADD (attention deficit disorder) and ODD (oppositional defiant disorder.) There were more, but you get the point. Some of my best kids had more letters after their names than the surgeons that worked with my wife at the hospital! Speaking of my lovely wife, she happened to be glancing over my shoulder one day when I was looking over IEPs (another acronym, don't get me started on those) and other volumes of paperwork related to my kids.(1) As her eyes surveyed the information, she stood back, flabbergasted, and asked

"This kid is SED, ODD, and ADHD and he's taking (medicine A) and (medicine B)

Do you know what this kid would be like if he didn't take his meds?!?!

I did my best not to erupt.

"Geez, I don't know, hon. Imagine if he, and the rest of the kids in our school, all with similar emotional and pharmaceutical situations, didn't take their meds and didn't have parents that care and went to a school that was lax with discipline because of the revolving door of teachers. Imagine what would happen then. Maybe, just maybe, it would TURN INTO THE FUCKING ZOO THAT I TALK ABOUT EVERY NIGHT AT DINNER, MAYBE *THAT* WOULD HAPPEN!?"

My animated sarcasm was not well received.

Later that night, as I dined alone and slept in a little bed wedged between my infant daughter Samantha and her stuffed bear, I contemplated how this alphabet soup of ever-changing license plate diagnoses was symptomatic of the larger problem with education in our beloved United States – we're so busy NAMING everything so it can be measured, then CHANGING those names so as not to offend anyone, that we're failing in one tiny, insignificant area...

We

Are

Not

---

1   as most people in the education biz know, the average "special needs" student has more paperwork associated with them than Ossama Bin Laden has in the CIA offices.

Fixing
The
Fucking
Problem.

Wait! That's too complicated (and far too real!) So let me come up with an acronym – something that'll look good on a banner or a T-shirt, something flashy that sounds good but accomplishes absolutely nothing, or maybe something that tricks people into thinking it's beneficial when it really compounds them problem.

I've got it!

Ready? You'll love this, ***No Child Left Behind!*** Good huh? I think we can…What?

Oh, damn.

———— ‹‹‹››› ————

How about this then – the problem with our educational system, and one of the main reasons why we're mass-producing morons, is because the people making the rules have a **L**ack of **A**wareness (due to their) **Z**en-like **Y**earning for us to stop giving **F**s to these **U**nderachieving, **C**onfrontational, **K**id**S**

Now if I could just come up with an acronym.

If you think of one, let me know.

———— ‹‹‹››› ————

In the meantime, here's another fun fact from your uncle Step. You can take things that you, personally, need to learn more about and turn them into lessons! I gathered some information on the aforementioned army of assaulting acronyms and got busy learning and teaching simultaneously.

>**NOTE: There ain't nothing wrong with getting paid to learn, providing you're educating at the same time.**

>**CAVEAT: Doing your homework for grad. school while your class does busywork doesn't count.**

"Okay," I began, "ODD stands for oppositional defiant disorder."

"Yeah, that shit's on my paperwork, Step" admitted one Joshua Kates, "what's it mean?"

"Well," I answered, "according to the experts, that means you often lose your temper, argue with adults, actively defy or refuse to comply with adults' requests or rules, deliberately annoy people, are often touchy or easily annoyed by others, and you're usually angry, resentful, spiteful or vindictive.

"True dat." Responded Josh. "But yo, Step, I don't mean to be disrespectful but..."

"Yes?"

"That kinda sounds like *you*."

"Hmmmm...I think you're right." I freely confessed. "Hey! Maybe that's why I relate to you guys so well, maybe I'm fucked up too! In fact, if I'm OCD and ODD, that explains why I want to strangle the shit out of you when you mess up my bulletin board!"

Much laughter and no small amount of agreement followed.

"Right, right, settle down. Now, LD stands for learning disability."

"It says that on my check!" shrieked Peter Patrick

"Really? Well according to this..." and we spent the entire afternoon learning about each other, while I earned a minor degree in special education terminology. During certain times, I would let the guys read to me, fully aware that they were "teaching" me stuff I didn't know. They felt important, realized I was (gasp) NOT omnipotent, and everybody came away more aware of how they were perceived. Funny thing, as honest as all of us were about our bullshit, we discovered, in a little room with 12 special ed. kids and a mediocre teacher, what legions of experts seem to have missed.

—————»((•))«—————

The label drawer is empty but the tool box hasn't been touched.

That's why I start the year, every year, with the same speech. I fire out every potentially offensive term I can come up with. Mick, Kike, Nigger, Spic, Chink, Faggot, Pollack, Cripple, Retard, etc. then I mix in the terms that the school uses to "rank" kids. All schools have 'em — we use Foundations, Explorations, College Prep, and GT (Gifted and Talented,) but every school has their own euphemisms for the smart and the stupid - then I throw in some other potentially limiting labels: Democrat, Republican, Crip, Blood, Jock, Bird, Nerd, etc. etc.

You get the picture.

Usually, this shocks the kids into silence long enough for me to deliver the "why would you let anybody limit you by hanging a title on you?" speech. After that, they're usually ready to explode when I close with my "don't educate yourself to make me happy, don't even do it just to pass some test, do it to *prove those motherfuckers wrong!*" rallying cry.

You'd be surprised how misplaced teenage angst and aggression can be re-channeled into academic achievement.

Alas, I've rambled on too long. Sorry, I was diagnosed with SIS (self important syndrome) as a young lad, and it manifested itself in RAT (rambling asshole tendency) when I hit high school, culminating in my life long struggle with DOM (diarrhea of the mouth.)

So you see, it's not really my fault.

The 10 ½ Commandments of Teaching.

I.

Thou shalt come to grips with the fact that 90% of what you say is boring/stupid/useless/etc. to your audience; hence, you will present massive amounts of information, only to be blatantly ignored by a population unwilling to accept that they are playing into the hands of a society that perpetuates their ignorance so as to make them easier to deceive and control.

II.

Thou shalt learn, at some point, to rejoice and remain inspired in the few students that take accountability, work hard, and care, rather than beat thyself up over the overwhelming tide of lazy, misguided underachievers.

Speakingeth of the lazy and misguided, when you feel compelled to strangle a kid...

III.

Thou shalt call home. Once you find who the kid is living with *this week,* at a number that isn't disconnected or incorrect, speaking with the legal guardian for more than a few minutes may result in your having sympathy for the child, because:

IV

Ignorant, lazy, racist, stupid apples often cometh from ignorant, lazy, racist, stupid apple trees.

V

Thou shalt become friends with the secretaries. The ladies behind the desk run the school. (learn how they like their coffee, buy flowers, remember birthdays, write poems on you printing requests, include them in your book) P.S. – Janet Rosenberg, Joyce, Rivera, Ms. Collins, Anne Brown, love you ladies! XOXO –Step

VI

Thou shalt purchase a good, dependable, all-in-one printer/scanner/copier and invest heavily in spare ink. This can saveth your ass when the copier is down (or if you failed to obey commandment V)

VII

Thou shalt accept the **algebraic certainty of parent-teacher conferences**, which sayeth the following:

For every 10 parents that show up:

- 8 will be parents of the "A" students that just need to be reminded that they're doing a good job. (They are, and you should be glad to tell them that. Ask them for advice; the involved parent is becoming an endangered species.)

- 1 will be the parent of a kid who might be struggling, even disrespectful, but he/she is dealing with the same behavior at home and wants to work with you on securing the kid's future. (Take your time with this one, and stay in touch with them, they need the help and their support will prove invaluable later.)
- 1 will be one of those apple trees from commandment IV, and they will blame you for everything from their child's lack of reading skills to the price of gas. (Smile, be professional, and contemplate their immolation over a beer later. Remember, nature is a living thing, and all living things have to shit out wasteful items from time to time.)

VIII

Thou shalt not be a phony. Be yourself, folks, flaws and all. Teenagers, despite being COLOSSALLY clueless in many ways, can smell insincerity like sharks smell blood in the water, and they will feed on you in much the same way of you try to bullshit them. Every year I get a ton of letters and cards from students thanking me for "being real" with them, and you will too if you're honest. Be the same person in front of the room as you are in the parking lot.

IX

Thou shalt learn, and re-learn, and <u>internalize</u>, the material you plan to teach. You must be able to translate said material into digestible bites than you can then relate to stuff that your class is actually interested in.

How the hell am I supposed to know what these kids like? Glad you asked…

X

Thou shalt KNOW THY ENEMY. (If that means watching The Hills, reading Twilight, listening to Lil' Wayne, or knowing why the Dominicans in your school are at war with the Puerto Ricans, do it.) Ask questions. Actually **listen** to the answers. Believe me, students remember The Faust story better when you teach it through The Little Mermaid or Ghost Rider. This is NOT succumbing to your students or "dumbing down," this is teaching – learn to love it. While we're on that subject…

X I/II

Thou shalt love your job. It can be love/hate, like any good relationship, but if you don't love the kids, you'll suck at this job, and we've got too many shitty teachers already.

Why tenure is bullshit

Tenure - (n.) commonly refers to life tenure in a job; specifically to a senior academic's contractual right not to have their position terminated without just cause. Synonyms: bullshit, nonsense, horse pucky, aegis of the weak.

Translation — after x amount of years, teacher y becomes tenured; thus, nearly impossible to fire despite doing a shitty job for z amount of years.

Translation (minus) algebra - there are a lot of teachers collecting paychecks and doing next to nothing to earn them. Complacent, ignorant, and [often] more ignorant than the students they're supposed to be teaching, they hide behind the archaic concept that somehow, because they're TEACHERS [insert choirs of angels here], they can't be fired without evidence akin to a handwritten note from Almighty God.

I read in Newsweek about Chancellor *Michelle Rhee,* who leads D.C. Public Schools, offering up to $130,000 a year for teachers that are willing to go on "probation" and sign away ONE YEAR of tenure.

A hundred and thirty GRAND?!?!?

Ms. Rhee, if you're listening, I'll sign a LIFETIME no tenure contract IN BLOOD for the chance to earn $130,000 doing what I already do; which is to say, bust my ass and pay money out of pocket for materials to remain relevant and vigilant as a teacher.

If you're with me... good on ya, mate!

If you think I'm crazy, and you hold onto your tenure like a heroin addict holds onto his methadone... you are teacher *y*, and you're diluting our profession.

Addendum: shortly after I wrote this, my dear friend and English teacher without parallel (true), Mr. Barret (fiction) put the note on the following page in my mailbox (true.) After 4 years at my present position [they didn't count the first year as I was listed as a "long term sub"(true)] I was on the cusp of achieving that lofty status that I had so eagerly anticipated (fiction) – tenure. As usual, Mr. Barret's wit speaks with more eloquence than I could ever hope to on this particular subject matter. God bless him, he'll be right in Hell beside me. (unfortunately, true.)

—————⊙—————

Hey Step,

Well, you've done it. You have finished your initial (official) three years at _____ *[No, your fifteen years in Hellville, PA, do NOT count!] and can now assimilate into life as a tenured teacher. This is undoubtedly an achievement and most vitally a perk! I know all too well how vociferously (devil head) (1) you've coveted tenure; I've seen the saliva drip from the corner of your mouth when thinking of the new life awaiting you. Now your time has come, brother.*

1   allusion to *KING DORK*, a book by Frank Portman that deserves you attention.

———((❍))———

You will no doubt want to start enjoying this new station immediately. I expect you'll want to start by reducing the stress in your day. You'll likely make some big changes, and perhaps I can help. First, forget all those hours you put into making precise and helpful comments on student's papers! Who needs THAT bullshit wasting all their time? No, the Elite Aligned Tenured Indolent Teachers chapter of _____ , or EAT IT for short (you'll get your membership card and parking space soon) don't bother themselves with triviality. Now, when grading papers and assignments, you can be content to just leave simple, vague comments, no more then one per paper, and try to make it a three word phrase, near the top, at the most. No more of the constant work you've put into improving rubrics or bleeding over the research papers with red ink. Feel free to randomly select an arbitrary numeric grade from the top of your head, without any justification or explanation; **you've earned the right!** *Did the whiny students complete three full years and one day teaching here, or was it you? ALL YOU MY MAN.*

Your lessons will also be a source of relief. Rather than planning interesting, time consuming, creative lessons based around actual students' needs, just copy about 150,000 word searches and take a nap. Hell, most students would much rather complete mindless busy work — it will help them prepare for the rest of their lives! If you feel that nagging sense that you're not giving them enough, switch up your lessons by assigning silent reading, questions from the text, and a reproducible test from the teacher's edition. Take it slow, though, Mr. tenured Teacher, you don't want to put yourself out there for nothing! THEY CAN'T TOUCH YOU NOW! That's right, your shit OFFICIALLY doesn't stink!

The award of tenure doesn't just pertain to classroom teaching, it in fact encompasses your entire day at _____Your duty period? Please. As long as the kids aren't stabbing each other too badly, feel free to show up when you want, if at all, and when you do come just ignore the kids and enjoy your period in the kitchen with a steaming cup of coffee to wake you up from your slumber. No need to break up fights in the hall or chastise students with electronic devices. Just travel in your own beautifully tenured world, secure in your salary and self-righteousness. Imagine sandy beaches full of Brazilian bikini models, or just have a little nip from the bottle. Kids will see fights and injustice all though their lives, and it is just not the tenured teacher's job to fabricate an unrealistic safe environment. You answer only to yourself, and your only concern is having a good day and passing the time from 7:19 to 2:10. Come to think of it, why not show up halfway through second period?

Disrespectful students? Disillusioned parents? Writing and reading skills? Misinformed and misguided pupils? Not your problem. No, you've **done** *your job. Your three year sentence is up and now it's time to delve into what teaching is really about: plodding through shit covered halls, accomplishing nothing, babysitting for 9 months with summers off. Sure, you might want to mention the state tests to your 11th grade students so that they know it exists, but your three years of exemplary scores more than make up for the rest of your teaching career. Career is such a dirty word, in fact, let's just call it your teaching diversion.*

———=((●))=———

I am sure that you'll be given all of this information in a more organized version at the next Tenured Teacher's meeting, along with your "kiss my tenured ass" t-shirt and a beach chair for behind your desk - which should be unoccupied by papers and teacher supplies for the foreseeable future. I simply wanted to give you some suggestions and my congratulations. So next year, if you happen to wake up during an inclusion class to the snores of students gleefully going nowhere, stop by my room for a high five and a high ball. I'll be as unproductive without guilt as you will.

Congrats!
Barrett

———◦《◉》◦———

Damn you, Mr. Barret, for your rakish wit and deep insight into the profession.

Despite being some 15 years my junior, he has already established himself as one of the young alpha wolves that will ultimately my place at the head of our pack – the underground group of teachers that are as serious about our jobs as we are irreverent to everything else.

Yeah, folks, it isn't easy out here in the forest of Academia, but there are those wolves, both young and old, out there in search of something deeper, more meaningful than the next contract negotiation or the achievement of tenure.

Money ain't everything, and tenure is bullshit.

If however, you're one of those sheep that needs tenure to sleep at night, re-read that letter, and check for your resemblance in the mirror.

See yourself?

Too b-a-a-a-d for you, sheepie.

The wolves know where you live.

The Mission Statement you wish your school had.

(Sing to the tune of Bad Company's Rock N' Roll Fantasy)

"It's all part, of my
Teach and Learn Fantasyyyyy."

Teachers of the world! Imagine a chain of alternate schools where you could teach what you wanted, the way you wanted, free from impractical standards and bullshit.

Imagine Darth Vader-like autonomy to discipline the little bastards that get out of line. You could do what you KNOW would work without jumping through bureaucratic hoops. I think my next book will be a fantasy novel dedicated to teachers and all the shit we wish we could do without restrictions. (1) I visualize Harry Potter-ish lines of parents lined up to pay us top dollar to do what we do for pittance now– raise their children.

When I mentioned this to Joseph Ferrante, fellow English teacher, master of the Great Gatsby, proud husband, father and bathroom renovator supreme, he (predictably) threw water on the flame of my creativity by pointing out the fact that I would have to get licensure, fill out tons of paperwork, write a mission statement...

---

1   ...actually I *know* it will be. Already working on it. Pre-order a dozen now!

"Whoa," I threatened, "you know how I feel about that word."

"Yeah," he chuckled, in that insidious voice of his, "but I thought maybe I could inspire another one of your mad scientist creations."

Hmmmmm.....

Let's pretend that I started a chain of alternative schools

Let's pretend, while were at it, that I gave them a cool little acronym that properly hides my sinister intent (cough, cough.... NCLB cough cough...)

Finally, let's pretend that I was forced to explain my motivation and the grand scope of my intentions in a (gagging noise) MISSION STATEMENT.

Hmmmmm......

January 21, 20andsomethinginthefuture

When I decided to create a school where responsible, educated adults could teach teenagers to become responsible, educated adults, I had a vision of what said school should entail. Of course, this being America, home of the free land of the bureaucracy, I was asked to compile a mission statement.

Can I tell you something? The words "mission statement" make me throw up a little in my mouth. A mission statement is an idealistic wish list written by out of touch people who hope for the best in the face of a veritable tsunami of evidence that disaster is as fucking evident as the U.S. dollar becoming worthless in the world economy. However, this education "thing" is, sadly, a business; so when the men in black show up and request your mission statement, ya gotta play ball.

This is a synopsis of the mission statement that I was forced to submit to the president (who was busy printing money), the secretary of education (who was busy misappropriating it), and about a thousand other people (who were busy trying to look busy), resulting in what I'm sure was the loss of a small portion of our national forest land in paper.

As you may have guessed, I'm paraphrasing here:

We, the highly dedicated instruments of righteous cruelty that will staff the T.E.A.M. (Trust in our Extreme Alternative Methodology) school will employ, as our cool but misleading acronym suggests, extreme (that is to say, outside the tapioca pudding realm of the status quo) methods to fix the broken foundation of our current educational system. Specifically, we will embrace, in Statue of Liberty fashion, the tired, poor, hungry, stupid, ignorant, arrogant, hyperactive, disenfranchised...oh, for Christ's sake, we'll take 'em all!

We will embrace all of the miniature versions of the bigger versions who were coddled (and therefore failed) by an educational system that protected their precious feeling right into a state of borderline functional retardation. We, at T.E.A.M., will teach you to read, write, and think in a manner that might not always be politically correct, but will always be practical and insightful. We will, in addition, "modify" your behavior in such ways that are necessary to ensure that you conduct yourself, always, in a way that will show, and earn, respect.

In short, we will do the job that your parents should have done, and your parents will pay us dearly for it. In the event that the aforementioned guardians can't afford us (and they probably can't because they didn't pay attention in school when they were there,) they can apply to the state for financial aid, and they will gladly receive it from a government who [almost too late] realized that a nation of fucking morons leads to a shitty economy and a high crime rate which, in turn, lead to everyone working for the

Japanese in a matter of a few years. Thassa no joke, gaijin.

The curriculum at the T.E.A.M. school will be a dynamic, ever-evolving manifestation of the needs of our student population. We will teach what needs to be taught and, once it is learned, move on to the next area of immediate need. All killer, no filler. We will not waste time following an outdated curriculum to the letter, and the lesson plans of our teachers will be replaced by constant observation and assistance from our administrators, (who will be fired the minute that they forget that they, too, once worked IN a classroom.) Students will be engaged, supported, and empathized with so that they might reach their true individual potentials; provided, of course, that they comply with the most basic standards of mutual respect.

If they don't...

The renowned author and lecturer Alfie Kohn, eloquently observed: "students need virtually zero extrinsic motivation in order to become the robots that our educational system has urged us to produce." This from a text entitled Punished by Rewards. We, at T.E.A.M., will take the opposite approach, we will reward by punishing. Simply put, we will beat you into submission because we know what's good for you. If you knew what was good for you, you're half-assed guardians wouldn't be paying us to do their jobs, and you would be getting paid to teach here instead of getting reimbursed to be bussed here. Clear? Good.

The chain of command at the T.E.A.M. school will be a dicktatorship with I, Frank Stepnowski, serving as the dick. (remember, paraphrasing here) I love you all, and I truly want the best for you. Every student that graduates from my school will be a citizen that I would be proud to welcome into my home with my family, and I will back that promise up.

— 321 —

Less talk, more action.
Less paperwork, more teaching.
Less enablement, more empowerment.
Education as it should be, as it once was, with liberty and justice for all.

Any takers?

Any teachers or administrators out there who would work for a little less money but more autonomy and room for creativity?

Any creative minds out there that would go into (or *back* into) education if the expectations were realistic, the discipline was consistent, and the pay was commensurate with your effort?

Wow...that's a lot of you.

The Race Card

Hey students! Ever heard of the race card? You have, well… Don't play it.

Ever.

There are racists in the teaching profession, as in every other profession, but they are so nearly non-existent as to not even warrant mention; suffice it to say, nobody goes into this business with the intention of using their platform to keep anyone else down. Those people go into politics.

Besides, you aren't failing because the teacher hates you because you're black, or white, or tan or purple, you're failing because you aren't doing the work necessary to pass the class.

Stop looking for excuses.

Grow up.

Learn accountability instead of weakening yourself hiding behind a fictional shield you run behind when anything goes wrong.

I've had professors who tried to make me feel guilty for *being* white, and I've had parents accuse me of failing their kids *because* they were black. I've had Hispanic parents give me standing ovations, and white parents try to get me fired, and I've had gay students ask me to be the moderator of their club in the same year I was accused of being homophobic by one disgruntled student that happened to be homosexual.

I treat them all the same folks, and opinions are like assholes, everybody's got one.

I'll leave it to one of my students to have the final word on this one. Osiris Brown, after finding out he was suspended this past January, yelled down the hall (in front of the principal and several other administrators)

"Hey Step, I'ma be out for a while, what am I gonna miss next week?"

"Martin Luther King Day, Barack Obama's inauguration, and my birthday!" I yelled.

"That's three bad niggas right there!" Osiris laughed

I thought my principal was going to choke on his coffee

"You're damn right," I shot back, "but only one of 'em is going to help you pass English this year."

Osiris laughed, handing me his make-up work sheet, "

True dat, Step. True dat."

Hey teachers and educational staff! Ever heard of the race card? You have, well...

Don't play it.

Ever.

You're going to encounter racists in your classroom, but you're students are products of their environments, and they can be taught to break free of the shackles of ignorance; suffice it to say, the way you act (not what you say) will be instrumental in providing them with a role model for compassion and tolerance.

You're probably going to encounter racists at least a few times among your administration, too. Unfortunately, empathy and cultural awareness are not required to be a scholastic supervisor, principal, etc. However, 95% of the administrators are good people

— 324 —

caught between Scylla and Charybdis (1), having to satisfy parents, staff, students, school boards, insane politicians (cough…cough… No Child Left Behind…cough) and *their* supervisors, often at the same time.

Besides, you aren't being reprimanded because your supervisor hates you, or because you're yellow, or beige, or red or teal, you're being reprimanded because you fucked up.

Stop looking for excuses.

Grow up.

Learn accountability instead of weakening yourself hiding behind a fictional shield you run behind when anything goes wrong.

Hey YOU! Ever heard of the race card? You have, well…

Don't play it.

Ever.

There are racists in the world.

Deal with it.

But don't deal with it by perpetuating racism the other way, against "the other guy", the "other group," whatever.

Familiar with the expression "divide and conquer?"

If you are, then you know what I'm getting at. If you aren't, it's pretty easy to understand (in fact, any of *my* students could explain it to you,) the more we fight amongst ourselves, black vs.white, Mexican vs. Puerto Rican, gay vs, straight, *Crip vs.Blood, Democrat vs.Republican,* (2) Fox News vs. CNN, I could go on and on…the easier it is for the 10% of the people that control 90% of the money in this country to manipulate, divide, and keep *all* of us

1 Monsters of Greek mythology, scourge of sailors, located so near to each other as to represent an inescapable threat – if you pass one the other gets you. The original "between a rock and a hard place."

2 interesting that two of the biggest gangs in the United States have the same color scheme, and same disregard for one another, as the two biggest political parties, ain't it?)

from questioning, learning, and THINKING for ourselves.

As I'm writing this, I'm listening to Bill Maher talk about how America is a dumb country. While I don't like Maher, I understand what he means. We just witnessed a presidential election that exposed how many people in this country have absolutely no idea what the person we voted for (McCain or Obama) represented beyond the color of his skin, and that's why, for as long as I can remember, we've been getting fucked by those at the top of the food chain. We are not a dumb country, we are an ignorant country, and the first step to overcoming that is to stop worrying about *them* and start thinking as *us*.

Before I go, let me launch a preemptive strike on those non-white, non-heterosexual, non-whatever the hell you see me as, people who will claim "that's easy for you to say."

No. No it's not, actually. It very, very, very hard for me to say "don't play the race card," because I've had to teach for two plus decades and I *practice what I preach*. Go ahead, dig as deep as you can, you won't find ONE instance of me taking the easy way out, and you had *better* have your shit together if you want to challenge me.

"...and you yourself shall be pierced with a sword."

- "...and you yourself shall be pierced with a sword."

(Luke 2:34)

Hey guys and gals,

First, thanks for reading this far into my book; I still can't believe anyone other then my immediate family and friends bought this thing. I hope you've had a few laughs so far and, just maybe, seen yourself somewhere in all this craziness. That having been said I can't, in good conscience, go any further without being serious for just a minute.

I can hear you from here, "why would he take a perfectly good, absolutely hilarious, future best seller that will make him independently wealthy and ruin it with depressing reality?"

(OK maybe that's not *exactly* what you said;) nonetheless, I said in the beginning that I wrote this book for teachers, so down the dark road of truth I must venture for a minute.

If you're a good teacher, you will have your heart broken.

There is no escaping this. Just as being a parent means having your heart walk around outside your body in the form of your children, so to does being a teacher mean that you have voluntarily opened your heart to an army of young people, some of whom, *many* of whom will abuse that privilege by stepping on it.

There is a silver lining here, in cliché form, surely you've heard the old chestnut that "you only hurt the ones you love?" It's true. Experienced teachers know it; new teachers would do well to remember it. Our audience is, by virtue of their age, emotionally unstable, hyperanxious, and impulsive. They will, on occasion, manifest their love of you by lashing out at you. You'll be blamed for everything from their failing Algebra to the Kennedy assassination, and you'll be guilty of none of it. This is not to say you won't suffer – quite a bit in fact – from the mere accusations that you are anything but caring and diligent.

Stay strong. Continue to fight the good fight. You are an awesome person doing one of the few truly honorable jobs left in this world. I'll leave it to a pair of friends that are infinitely smarter than me to have the last words here.

———— ((◉)) ————

A dear friend of mind who I've since lost touch with, Rochelle Walcott, once told me (when I asked her how she grew up so well adjusted) that she knew she was loved. "If your kids always know that you love them, everything else will fall into place." Thank you, Chelle', wherever you are, it's worked like a charm, both at home and in the classroom.

A young man I admire very much, Mr. P. Hardjello, expanded on the previous theme in classroom context. He said "when you're right, you do what you want." This may sound a bit arrogant, but it isn't. In a world of politicians, administrators, supervisors, and other teachers just trying to keep their jobs, and parents, guardians, and lawyers trying to blame you for the shortcomings of every kid on the planet despite the fact that you've done more to improve them morally and academically than anyone, you must be true to yourself and allow your love of the kids to be your one and only guide.

You're going to be hurt. You're going to doubt yourself. You're going to question why you ever chose to be a teacher. But guess what?

I know why you *became* a teacher, why you *stay* a teacher when more money and more recognition are a few résumés away…

SShhhhhh…

Ready?

You don't teach 'cause you <u>want</u> to, you teach because you <u>have</u> to.

I know, it's a curse, right? But there's a thin line between genius and insanity. Walk the line, cross it if you have to, but go forward confidently.

And know that you are never

ever

alone.

A letter to the good kid.

Hey teachers, we all love templates, right? Basic frameworks that we can tweak and personalize to suit our own needs. The problem is, there are no templates for the REALLY important stuff. With that in mind, I present you with a variation on a letter I've written more times than I care to count to the kid in the class that really does care about getting an education, often when surrounded by other students that make this near impossible. Reproduce, modify, and enjoy at your leisure.

Dear_____

I appreciate you making me aware of what's going on in class while I'm teaching, but I feel that you should be aware of something:

I know that the kid over there is texting under his desk, and I know that it isn't the first time. I also know that the guy behind you cheats on his quizzes. Kind of makes you wonder how he's still failing, doesn't it?

The little group over in the back row that talks when I'm talking? Don't worry about 'em — I'll shut them up if they start disturbing your learning, but they don't bother me.

Trust me, I see everything and I hear almost everything, The fact that I don't react or respond doesn't mean that I'm not aware, it just means that I don't care.

I have learned to put my effort into making sure that you get an education instead of wasting my time and energy on the people that don't want to hear what I'm saying.

So if you can't understand why I don't say anything when they don't turn in homework at all, yet I criticize you for not being as neat as you could be on yours...understand this:

The highest compliment I can pay you is to treat you as I would my own children, and I don't give my own children any breaks. You may not want to hear this, but I am hard on you because I love you.

...and I love the fact that the texter, the cheater, and the talkers will be working for you someday.

Teaching is like digging a hole in the sand.

If you're like me, you get a good book, you read it in one sitting if you can, sitting up all night knowing you can't go to sleep until you finish it, then hate yourself for not prolonging the awesomeness.

That has absolutely nothing to do with the insipid excuse for a book you're holding right now. However, I figured you probably need an excuse to grab an iced tea, make a quick trip to the bathroom, maybe check the scores on Sportscenter, so here's a quick observation to contemplate while you're losing to your kids at Wii golf, blending a protein shake or reading *Newsweek* on the potty. Read, absorb, discuss among yourselves if you see fit, and I'll see you in a little while.

An observational simile on teaching made on the beach in Wildwood, N.J.

Today I sat on the beach watching my son Mason dig a hole in the sand. No big deal, right? Kids do it all the time. Every June the beach shovel and bucket business is booming, and thousands of kids descend on the sand, digging more diligently than any federal employee, content to have produced a big honkin' hole that will disappear moments after the high tide rushes in, much to the squealing delight of the other kids. Watching him, helping him, and seeing others compliment him on this seemingly colossal waste of time made me realize something:

Teaching is like digging a hole in the sand. (1)

You bust your butt to create something memorable, despite being given inadequate tools and (very often) little long-term support, only to have other people question your methods and, occasionally, mess with your work when you turn your back. After an arduous, backbreaking effort, you have a few moments to admire your effort and criticize yourself for all the things you should have done before you're forced to let it go. Very shortly, all signs of your hard work will have either completely disappeared, or they'll be noticed only by others when you're not around to enjoy the adulation of the mob.

Occasionally, you'll get a bunch of help. You and your comrades will defy beach tradition and you'll work together to create a crater worthy of the "oohs" and "aahs" of passing ice-cream covered toddlers and sunburned hotties. As with your other monumental efforts, your hole will be a memory within moments after you've packed up your materials and enjoyed a post-dig lemonade. However, the hole isn't the part you'll remember. You and your co-workers will learn from the experience, and the cooperation and the fun of building the most awesomest hole ever *together* will be the stuff of many an amusing anecdote told over the hoisting of many more lemonades.

The sad part?

The hole ALWAYS becomes the property of someone or something once you're done, and you may never know how much fun some little dude or dudette had using your hole, or how meaningful it was to a wayward posse of sand crabs, etc.

---

1   That's a *simile*, students. I'm comparing two unlike things using the words "like" or "as." If I would have said: "teaching is swimming against the current with no lifeguards watching, that would be a *metaphor*. There <u>will</u> be a quiz later!

Bottom line, you will not be the one to witness the penultimate fruits of your labors.

The funny part?

You'll break out your sandy shovels,
sit out in the sun, smile
and dig again tomorrow.

You crazy bastards.
No wonder I love teachers.

"Increscunt anime, virescit volnere virtus."

NOTE: You've worked hard enough reading through this trivial, below-average tripe I call my first novel. Therefore, I took the liberty of outlining this chapter for you, so as to ensure that you don't miss the important points, all of which are a variation on the THEME that _good teachers are driven by a sickness that is often misunderstood by those outside the profession._

Never let it be said I wasn't helpful.

I asked myself many times during the writing and editing of this book, "what story should I close with?" What anecdote, after all, is the quintessential "closer?"

Then it hit me.

This started as a funny book, a collection of crazy, maybe funny, surely controversial stories that I was asked to tell again and again, usually by the people that lived them with me.

But a funny thing happened on the way to the publishers. I noticed, as I re-read my offensive little opus, an insidious little THEME had infected my book. Like a computer virus, a reoccurring idea worked its way into the fabric of my funny stuff, giving it an edge that was never there during my happy hour re-tellings. A message, or MOTIF, if you will, started to make itself heard above the laughter, cheers and jeers of my proofreaders…

I love teachers.

———— ((◉)) ————

The good ones, the ones just starting and the ones who've been at it longer than I've been alive. The ones that came before me and those that have yet to hear the call of the wild. The ones that struggle and the ones that make it look easy. Teachers, the crazy, underpaid, under appreciated, lot of them, I think they're awesome. Check out the YouTube video *What Teachers Make* by Taylor Mali for a beautifully angry expression of why I think teaching is such a righteous calling <u>This is a profession that will never earn as much as doctors, lawyers, baseball players, or politicians,but it will be the one that *creates* them.</u>

I'm proud to be a teacher, and I've never been afraid to announce that in any sort of mixed company. I think it takes a certain breed of person, with a certain as-yet-undiagnosed strain of insanity to do this job well – hence the title of my little book. That having been said, my final story came to me in the present day, and it provides a fitting end to this labor of love for my brothers and sisters in the profession.

Unfortunately, my inspiration came in the form of a *really* shitty week, and it happened just as I was wrapping up the writing portion of the book.

———— ((◉)) ————

Why did I ever come home from the shore?
On Sunday, July 19, I was slurping oysters on the half shell with

my sister Molly and knocking back root beers with my youngest son, my brother-in-law and my dad, the other three "Franks" in the family. Life was good. My sister and her family, my parents, and my wife's extended family had all converged on our shore house in North Wildwood, New Jersey. It was my sister's birthday weekend and everyone, young and old, were enjoying warm breezes off the ocean, cold drinks from the cooler, and hot steaks off the grill. Mixed in among the flavors of the weekend was the subtle taste of redemption and renewal, as past hostilities and lingering tensions were put to rest, buried forever under the sandcastles our children (and our parents' children) built on the beach; I'm sure a lot of those previously hard feelings aimed at me were well deserved, as sometimes, unfortunately, one's dedication to *other* people's children isolates you and desensitizes you to those that are most important to you.

As the sounds of Reel Big Fish blared from the speakers, I clinked my bottle against my brother-in-law's

"Two best things about teaching?"

"July and August," he laughed, having heard that one about a million times.

The truth was, neither one of us had "summer's off." We had six kids between us, and he had football camp, conditioning work, and professional development. I (until the year before) managed a seasonal business that devoured most of my "down time." The point is, everybody thinks being a teacher is great because "you get summer's off." *That,* my friends, is horseshit. Most teachers I know work harder in the summer than the 12 month employees that envy them so much.

⏤◉⏤

Everybody had a great time, and my wife performed the inhuman task of ensuring that everyone's plates were full, drinks were fresh, and smiles were omnipresent. I cleaned up, with help from the congregation, and everybody chilled, exchanging stories and laughs until the wee hours. To the untrained eye, my wife and I looked like the happiest couple on God's green Earth.

But everybody went home on Monday, and we were left with the kids and ourselves.

...and the 90% of the iceberg that was floating menacingly beneath the surface.

Loooong story short (most of you could probably fill in the blanks anyhow) my wife and I have been busting our asses to improve ourselves professionally – she's a nurse practitioner read: doctor minus the license to cut people open - in between conceiving and raising four children. She has to keep increasing her certifications to stay viable. In my case, <u>when you're a teacher, you are (by choice and by law) a student for life.</u> Of course, Dawn is as dedicated to her patients as I am to my students (maybe my next book will be *Why Are All the Good Nurses Crazy and why don't they bring their bedside manner home with them?*) Of course, her work hours are longer than mine and, for years, we haven't enjoyed dinner, a movie, miniature golf, or sex without her Blackberry going off.

Thank god she doesn't answer it during miniature golf.

O.K. Step, you're saying, what the hell does this have to do with the theme of your book?

Well, if your job involves influencing the lives of hundreds of individuals, you almost always [inadvertently] surrender so many of your own hopes/dreams that you grow resentful; and, very often, you [misguidedly] blame your significant other for the fact that you are, for lack of a better word, unfulfilled.

Ouch. Fucking truth hurts doesn't it? Admit it, Oprah, you broke a lot of hearts on your way to being the queen of altruism. (1)

So, to recap, great weekend down the shore. We're back home, it's Monday night, and the kids are in bed. Dawn and I have had the usual storm clouds brewing, due in large part to the facts that I'm trying to get a book written and she has just finished a project that monopolized almost all of her time of late. Dawn's already at maximum stress level, believing that between her job and PhD studies, she's neglecting her family – a fact that I, selfishly, agreed with wholeheartedly, and I told her that.

I know, I know…what the hell was I thinking?

Divorce came up, as did the severing of one of my more precious body parts. To add to the fun, Dawn woke me up (on the couch) the next morning with the soothing strains of *"my goddamned computer is frozen and this goddamned project is due at 5:00 today because my goddamned instructor made us re-write it!"* (2)

Guess we're still married.

So I get on her computer, and it is infected with a capital "I", so I rig up my laptop to her printer, get it working in safe mode, and help her proofread the next few renditions of her project, as her %$#@! instructor seemed to have missed that day when you're taught not to be vague in your instructions but specific in your

---

1   Sorry, couldn't resist. It's always been a dream of mine to be chastised by the big O.

2   My wife is actually a very sweet woman, and she usually eschews both profanity and anti-religious verbiage; but hey, I have that effect on women.

corrections. <u>Even in the midst of the chaos, I couldn't help but think "what if this isn't fixed by September, how am I going to put together worksheets and articles for my classes?"</u> Needless to say, every revision of her project further exacerbates the tension between me and the wifey, as she felt more and more guilty for the time she's spending on work and I felt more and more selfish for mentioning it.

Anybody been there? Raise your hand.

Holy shit, seems I'm not alone in being alone.

So, to recap again, wife and I are at war (sort of,) her computer is fried…

Oh, and I've got an appointment tomorrow to see if I've got skin cancer.

During her birthday bash down the shore, my little sister Molly told me, in between stories about her daughter Sophie and her son Lukas, that she was diagnosed with melanoma and that her doctor said her siblings should be checked immediately.

Thanks, Mol, can't wait to get out in the sun again tomorrow.

My *other* sister, (technically sister-in-law but awesome enough to count as a real sister) Chrissy, overheard this and generously offered to give me a dermatologist appointment that she waited three months to get. Thanks, sis, you rock harder than a Metallica concert in a phone booth.

I won't bother you with the details of the Wednesday appointment, but it involved getting my ass chewed out by a 4-foot tall Asian woman and having three pieces cut out of me to be sent to the lab for evaluation. Lovely. My first thought was, "no matter what happens, this fucking cancer shit can't stop me because I'm going to be alive to walk my daughter down the aisle someday." My second thought, *right behind it*, was "I've got to remember to warn my students about the dangers of sun damage." I'll repeat that, as it may be important to my theme, <u>I may have had skin cancer and I was thinking about how I could use that to educate my students.</u>

I had my examination in the offices where Dawn works, so she came down to meet me after it had ended.

"Interesting week."

"That's one way of lookin' at it," I laughed. "Spent three hours debugging a computer on Monday, four hours under a tattoo needle last night, and I just got reprimanded and carved by an angry Asian. I can't wait to wake up tomorrow and see what happens."

I thought I was being funny.

Key word: thought.

I'm going to do something I rarely do here. I'm going to keep something private. Usually, I'm a *leave-it-all-on-the-field / heart-on-my-sleeve* kinda guy, but what happened the day after the skin cancer appointment was so excruciating that I'm going to forego recounting it here. The only thing that I will mention, (and this makes me certifiable in 48 of the 50 states,) is that

<u>I actually thought, as I lay in bed that evening, "who is going to teach my kids in September if I'm not around?</u>

———)(●)(———

Folks, I love ya, but it's actually bumming me out just recounting the *tsunami* of *tshit* that happened on that week in July, and I know (unless you're a high school student) that you've already fully absorbed the point I've been hammering you with. Therefore, I'll fast forward through the remaining events of the week, driving home my main point in dramatic, albeit honest, form. Seat belts fastened? Good.

AfterasurpisebirthdayforherdadthatDawnhadtoworkonalldayFridayshereceivedyet anotherrequestforrevisionofherproject,makingherborderlinesuicidal.SoIofferedto

takeheroutandcheerherup,unfortunately,my13yearolddaughter(beinga13yearoldgirl)

madeitworsebybeingselfishandhormonal,soIyelledatherandnowshehatesme

Ohwellgotacallfromapublishersaying''welikeyou'rebookideabutrightnow

wer'ebackedupblahblahfuckyouI'llpublishitmyselfMymarriageisrecovering

nicelybutofcoursetensionsremainforthereasonsIstatedearlierthanksforasking

andIhaven'theardfromtheskincancerdoctoryetsoIdrovebackdowntheshorewith

myboyshopingtoescapeanymoredramaandgetbacktoworkingontheisbookwhen

wewalkedinthedoorweweremetwiththesightoftheroofhavingcrackedandleaked

inseveralspotsafterarainstorm!

I laughed.
The boys looked at me like I was crazy.
Of course I am, didn't you read the title of the book?

Now it's review time. Go back and re-read the underlined parts that you outlined so proficiently. I'll go to the potty while you re-read.

————◦《◉》◦————

Sorry about the wait. It was quiet, I started reading a magazine, you know how it goes.

So what have we learned?

1. Good teachers often get so absorbed with doing everything they can for their students that they occasionally neglect those close to them, and almost always put them selves last on the priority ladder, and

2. the aforementioned dedication often leads to misplaced aggression directed at those who are often their biggest supporters, but

3. the people that love teachers forgive them because they know that their hearts are always in the right place, as evidence by the fact that

4. teachers think of teaching their students even during the most chaotic moments of their lives a fact that almost always goes unnoticed and unappreciated by those particular students.

WHICH IS WHY I WROTE THIS BOOK!!! If you're married to, dating, love, employing, or being taught by, a teacher – give them some slack! They're killing themselves to make the world a better place at the expense of their own sanity and happiness.

P.S. The title of this chapter comes from Friedrich Nietzsche, and it means (roughly translated) "the spirit grows, strength is restored through wounding." So take heart, my friends, all that stress and heartache is developing character and making you stronger and more resilient.

Famous Last Words

I will never understand why people come to me for teaching advice.

I'm a "work in progress" (at best) as a husband, father, and friend; but, as a *teacher*, I have a list of tragic flaws that, if written on toilet paper, could clean up all the shit that's weighing down our educational system. Alas, you misguided lot keep asking me questions, so I keep giving you answers. That having been established, I'm going to close the book by answering the question I am asked most often by fledgling teachers (and parents, come to think of it.) Goes like this:

"What is the one thing I need to do to get the kids to listen to me?"

Wow. No pressure there.

Couldn't I just balance the budget or initiate world peace, instead?

All kidding aside, I'm going to trick you the way I trick my students and all advice seekers. I'm going to tell you what you already know, *and then* convince you that I taught you something profound.

Crap. There goes my secret. Oh, well...Ready? This is going to be like a vaccination shot: it's going to be brief, it's going to hurt, but it's good for you. Goes like this:

THEY (kids today) are overwhelmed by a never-ending wave of

crap that they have to process, which they then have to prioritize, remembering the important stuff, internalizing the *really* important stuff, and letting go of the stuff they don't think they need. Unlike you and I, they're not financially independent, don't have a clear sense of identity, and they're scared shitless that they might be wasting time in a world that people are telling them is going to end in 2012.

YOU (teachers and parents of today) are overwhelmed with rules, regulations, and expectations that change as fast as you can satisfy them. Teachers know that the standardized tests that may impact our job security are bullshit and that scores and levels of performance are manufactured, modified, and just flat out changed to satisfy an educational system that doesn't want to admit just how far behind we are on the global scale. (Parents, teachers, you think I'm kidding? Ask yourself a question: If we had a uniform testing policy that accurately assessed the progress of every student, in every classroom, in every school, in every state, in every country, world-wide, and compared their current rate of achievement, where would your kids place?

Scared of the answer, are you? You should be.

Combine what THEY think with what WE know and you create an infinite combination of reasons why these kids don't want to listen to you.

So how, you ask again, *do I get these kids to listen to me?*

Simple, really: **Convince** your kids that you love them, and that what you are telling them is important. **Explain** why it is important and **prove** to them that you believe in what you're teaching by **practicing what you preach.**

Of course, if you don't love them (for reasons beyond my comprehension), don't believe what you're telling them is important (because you didn't really put any time into knowing your kids or

your material,) and you can't live by example (because you're a
hypocrite who expects kids to "do as you say but not as you do,")
then

  you

  are

  screwed,

  and so are your kids, and so is our country.

  "But," cry the righteous voices of the revolution (teachers and
parents included,) " I **do** love my kids, and I **want** to teach them
things that are important, and I'm not above **explaining** why, and
I'm **willing** to practice what I preach. I just don't know how to do
all that without driving myself crazy!"

  I know, folks, I really do. So this is me, putting my hand on your
shoulder, smiling warmly and knowingly at you, now I'm helping
you close the book – come on, you can do it – and pointing at the
front cover.

  Feel better?

  I hope so, folks, I really do.

Preview: Oh no! He's writing another one?!?

Hey everybody! First of all, thank you for reading my book. For all those people that will yell at me that "this book should have been written years ago!" I apologize. Gimmee a break, people! I was raising three young children, teaching or coaching thousands more, and developing new schemes to get my wife to pay for additions to my already titanic iTunes account. But there is good news! (maybe)

Now that I've got the hang of this "writing for publication" business, I have a new book on the horizon! This one is going to be much more fictional – so the gloves are *really* off this time.

The basic premise is that I open an "extreme alternative" school of the future, where teachers and administrators can do all of those things we always (in hushed tones in the teacher's lounge and slurred words at happy hours) wished we could do. My goal is to provide a catharsis for all of my brothers and sisters fighting the good fight every day in the hallways and classrooms of the world. Because you're awesome and I love you, here's a little taste of things to come…

The Absentee Parent Act of 2012
December 5, 2020

I'll be honest. I voted for John McCain in the 2008 election. I thought the media manufactured infidel war hero would do a better

347

job of pretending to run the country the then the as-yet untested walking race card rock star.

That having been said, when President Obama passed the Absentee Parent Act during the last year of his first term, I not only voted for him for his second term, I sent an Email offering to mow his lawn and trim the hedges, maybe do some nice topiary in the shape of a triumphant donkey, or a bipartisan elephant, or Bill O'Reilly. *That* would've jolted the Commander in Chief awake every morning. Truth is, I love O'Reilly – his reaction to my TEAM approach to scholastic reform was enthusiastic to say the least. I even said I was willing to go on his Fox News T.V. show provided Megan Kelley did the interview.

I'd let her grill me like a Memorial Day hot dog.

Frankfurter fantasies aside, when president B.H.B dropped the metaphorical bomb that essentially launched my first "alternative methodology" school, he locked up my vote for president for life, (which is what he really wanted, anyway.)

When the president passes the A.P.A of 2012; hereafter jokingly referred to in teachers' lounges as the "Obama gonna hamma baby mamma" bill, people started scrambling for educational placements that would do what schools had always done – raise their kids for them.

Only this time, they actually got involved in the scholastic process because they faced the very real possibility of going to jail if they didn't.

The Absentee Parent Act was a 1,073 page document that said, and I'm paraphrasing here, " *every 'baby daddy' and welfare mom out there who are ignoring their kids, or using them purely to cash an SSI check, had better get their collective asses in gear and start actually raising their children (preferably better than they, themselves, were raised) or they will receive a free course in responsibility via the state penitentiary, where they will learn to schedule classes on the value of proper parenting in between a full schedule of senseless violence and anal violation."* Lest those six figure income parenting conglomerates think *they* were beyond the law, the A.P.A stated: (again, I'm paraphrasing,) *"you self-righteous cocksuckers that think your gross annual income gives you the right to let your arrogant little offspring raise themselves are horribly misguided, and you had better start working princess and the prick into your iPhone calendars, because if Brittany and Hunter continue to throw away perfectly good educations in your absence, they'll be visiting your bloody white collars in the land of rape and honey.*

There's more, but I think you get the point. The law was put into effect on September 6, 2012 amid much fanfare and, as you might expect, nobody changed their behavior in the slightest way.

Until October 6, 2012; hereafter referred to in hushed tones in mini vans and supermarket lines as "the day Big Brother stopped watching and started shitting on the fan."

We had pulled an old TV into the classroom, and one of my students rigged the antenna with McGyver-like initiative. Soon, students and staff alike sat riveted while we watched scene after scene of parents being taken into custody for ignoring their parental duties. There was a plethora of screaming, crying, attempted bribing, and at least one televised episode of pant-shitting.

I think I spoke for all of the teachers when I finally shouted "Holy sheep shit Batman!

This is the greatest day in the history of education!" I would have said more, but the moment that forever changed my life intervened, in the form of one woman who was televised being dragged from her Hummer hybrid with 26" rims. As the camera closed in on her frantic eyes, streaked black with tears and L'oreal eye shadow, she screamed loudly and clearly into the TV:

"They want me to raise my kids, but what the fuck do I know

349

about how to raise these little bastards?!? You can't trust the churches, they're full of pedophiles, the military doesn't want them because they can't even read, and THE SCHOOL SYSTEM CAN'T CONTROL THESE KIDS, LET ALONE TEACH THEM, so what the hell is a parent like me supposed to...

Click

The TV went off, and the light bulb over my head went on.

"You're doing that smile again, Step," noticed Kenny.

"You're not thinking about what I think you're thinking about?" demanded Mr. Kauffman

"What the fuck happened to the TV?" wondered Adrian.

The rest of the commentary from room 3 was lost to me, as I was having an epiphany.

"The schools — *the way they are now* - can't control these kids, let alone teach them." I thought. "So what the hell are parents — *desperate parents* - supposed to do?" I thought.

"What the fuck is up with the TV?" moaned Adrian

I snapped out of my daydream of world domination and into action. I promptly walked down the hall, around the corner, and into Mr. Hossler's office.

"I quit"

Mr. Hossler muted the TV he had been watching and turned to me, his hands folded to conceal a wry smile dancing upon his lips.

"Somehow," he responded, "I knew you would."

"I totally dig this job, I've spent the best years of my life here, and you were totally cool to give me my first teaching gig, but…"

"But you have something you need to do," he finished for me.

"Yes"

"Somehow," he smiled, "I knew you would."

I turned to leave, filled with the original ideas that would soon manifest themselves in the very first TEAM (Trust in Extreme Alternative Methodology) school, when Mr. Hossler fired his

parting shot:

"Hey Step?"

"Yes, sir?"

"For all of us…go ***all the way***, or don't fucking bother."

"Yes, sir."

To be continued

Acknowledgements

I was one of those kids that always read the "special thanks to…" sections at the back of the lyrics section of albums, tapes, and CDs. I would be rocking out to KISS, Iron Maiden and Judas Priest (much to the chagrin of my dad) and reading about all the people that inspired the awesomeness that was fueling my adolescent fire. Now that I've got your attention, I've got a boat load of stuff that inspired me that I'd like to make you aware of. The following nouns were instrumental in the completion of this here novel.

Supportive People:

I could fill two books with just he names of the people that kept my reckless ass on task and out of trouble, but (since this book is about my experiences teaching) I'm just going to focus on the people in charge that could have stuck it *to* me but stuck *by* me instead:

The Old Guard: The late *Joe Kopp*, for tolerating an insufferable kid and turning him into something vaguely resembling a teacher. *Bob Long*, for taking a chance on me, and for knowing exactly when to take off the leash and when to reel me in. *John Hom*, for being the glue that holds as all together. *Linda Gallagher*, for hiding me when the angry mobs showed up with torches and pitchforks, then kicking my ass after they left. **_Stanley Stein_**, for having my back, and trusting that I wouldn't abuse the autonomy you afforded me. **_Carolyn Cabello_**, for keeping me plugged in and turned on.

The New Guard: **_Diane Joyce,_** good teachers can't teach without support and guidance, and D.J. is the best supervisor in the world, period. **_Tamara Schmidt,_** another academic goddess, her support has made my job easier than it ever should be.

Special thanks to **_David Kawula, James Ney,_** and **_Gina Horiates_**, three of my all time favorite students, for providing me with a title for this book, **_Pete Nardello_** for his proofreading prowess, and **_Jason Secoda_**, for challenging me to get this thing done – sorry, Jay, now you have to read a book that's really long and has many big words.

Nice Places:

The gym. As any teacher will tell you, coffee and methamphetamines can only do so much, so staying in shape is imperative to keeping the triumvirate of strong mind, body and soul intact.

My "street cred" with my students seems to go up exponentially when they find out I am "heavily inked;" so many thanks to the righteous guys at **_Tattoo Odyssey_** in Philadelphia.

Funny Things
The music and videos of **_Reel Big Fish_**, a band that should be a hell of a lot more famous than they are. I listened to several thousand hours of RBF during the process of this book.

The books of **_Christopher Moore_**. Playboy magazine once said, "If there's a funnier writer in America than Christopher Moore, let him step up." and that was my motivation for a while, until I realized that Moore is funnier in his sleep than I am on my best day. Read one of his books, then prepare to read them all.

The humor of **Craig Ferguson**. Intelligent and irreverent, a cocktail that intoxicates me every time. Any teacher will tell you, sleep time is more valuable than gold; giving up sleep to watch this guy is worth it.

Finally (and most importantly) The family unit:

Dawn. My greatest friend and fiercest adversary, every time I talked to teenage girls about how a real woman should conduct herself, you were the person I envisioned. Like so many other things in my life, without you this book doesn't happen.

Samantha, Mason, and *Frankie.* No father has ever been blessed with a more perfect combination of compassion, intellect and independence in his children. Everything I do revolves around making this world a better place for you. That having been said, I can't wait until you're trying to write papers with deadlines for college so I can make an unholy racket and ask you to drive me somewhere every ten minutes.

My late son *Cain.* I am trying so very hard. I hope you're proud of me.

About the voice

Step is a product of the educational system he thinks is in the toilet, and that alone proves him right. He reads Playboy for the articles and Food Network magazine for the pictures. He likes his in-laws, loves his country, exercises regularly, and reads for *enjoyment*. His still says "please," and "thank you."

Clearly, he belongs locked away somewhere.

Until they catch him, you can send him your compliments, criticisms, gratuitous sexual advances, or death threats by contacting him on *MySpace*; but beware, his daughter Samantha screens his messages, and she simply does not tolerate nasty things being said about her dad.

CPSIA information can be obtained at www.ICGtesting.com
Printed in the USA
BVOW08s0542280515

402152BV00009B/121/P

9 781432 748296